Mental Toughness

MENTAL
TOUGHNESS

A CHAMPION'S STATE OF MIND

Karl Kuehl
John Kuehl
Casey Tefertiller

With a Foreword by Tony La Russa

IVAN R. DEE
CHICAGO

MENTAL TOUGHNESS. Copyright © 2005 by Karl Kuehl, John Kuehl, and Casey Tefertiller. All rights reserved, including the right to reproduce this book or portions thereof in any form. For information, address: Ivan R. Dee, Publisher, 1332 North Halsted Street, Chicago 60622. Manufactured in the United States of America and printed on acid-free paper.

www.ivanrdee.com

The paperback edition of this book carries the ISBN 1-56663-723-6.

PHOTO CREDITS: pages xiii, 13, 65, 91, 115, 147, 195, 245, 248: Michael Zagaris; pages 5, 89: National Baseball Hall of Fame Library; page 56: Arizona Diamondbacks; page 62: Karl Kuehl; page 79: Cincinnati Reds; page 112: AP Photo / Evan Vucci; page 169: Milwaukee Brewers; pages 176–177: John Kuehl; page 183: John Kuehl, Robert Rogers; page 264: New York Yankees.

Library of Congress Cataloging-in-Publication Data:
Kuehl, Karl, 1937–
    Mental toughness : a champion's state of mind / Karl Kuehl, John Kuehl, Casey Tefertiller.
        p. cm.
    Includes bibliographical references (p.) and index.
    Includes index.
    ISBN 1-56663-617-5 (alk. paper)
    1. Sports—Psychological aspects. 2. Athletes—Conduct of life. I. Kuehl, John, 1967– II. Tefertiller, Casey, 1952– III. Title.

GV706.4.K82 2005
796'.01—dc22

2004058266

To Norma Kuehl and the late Ruby Tefertiller,

who demonstrated the ultimate in mental toughness

in their battles with cancer during

the years spent preparing this book

Acknowledgments

The authors wish to thank the many professional and college coaches, players, and managers who were interviewed and helped in the preparation of this book. Their names appear thoughout the book itself. We are also grateful to many others who contributed to this project:

Special appreciation to Dave McKay whose interest and encouragement initiated this project.

Sandy Alderson, who as general manager of the Oakland A's embraced the importance of the mental game, and Harvey Dorfman, who helped elevate the concepts to prominence throughout baseball.

Walt Lockwood, Larry Wilson, Jim Kondrick, Mel Didier, Bob Mattick, the late Jim Baumer, Steve Boras, Keith Lieppman, Dr. Ron Smith of the University of Washington, Dr. Gary L. Roberts of Abraham Baldwin College.

Dave Hudgens, Ron Hopkins, Billy Beane, Ted Polakowski, Nasusel Cabrera, Raymond Abreu, Ron Plaza, John Farrell, Mark Shapiro, Dominic Johnson, Jason Cooper, Derek Shelton, Rich Harden, Bob Boone, Gene Mauch, Bob Watson, Merv Rettenmund, Dr. Dan Landers of Arizona State University, Tony Gwynn, Gary Carter, the late Willie Stargell, the late Dick Bogard, Eric Kubota, Tony La Russa, Ron Fairly, Grady Fuson, Juan Marichal, Walt Jocketty, Ray Karesky.

The A's media relations staff of Debbie Gallas, Jim Young, and Mike Selleck; Maria Jacinto and Karen Sweeney of the Giants; Charlie Manuel, Eric Wedge, Dave Duncan, Rick Peterson, Dr. Charlie Maher, John Couture, Tim Tolman, John Goryl, Tim Belcher, Dave Miller, Randy Phillips, Bob Geren, Orv Franchuk, Rod Carew, Rich Gossage, Peter Gahan, Larry Hisle, Tony Olivo, Ted Simmons, Ron Vaughn, Greg Sparks, Wes Stock, Darren Lewis, Clint Myers, Dan McDermott, Chris Pittaro, Ron Vaughan, Steve Lubratich, Bob Milano, Alan Regier, John Hughes, John Kazanas, Rodney Davis, Lou Medina, Mack Newton, Fred Stanley, Dave Garcia, the late Larry Martin, Steve Ellis, Jeff Morey, Curt Young, Ron Romanick, Cyn Poweleit, Pam Potter, Brad Newcomb, Max Roberts, Carina Roter, Joe Marvin, Carol Tefertiller, Larry Knuth, Bianca La Russa, Mel Bowen, and former Santa Cruz High baseball coach Bill Dodge, who taught mental toughness to generations of players.

Michael Zagaris, Robert Rogers and Bill Burdick for photo assistance. Agent Gerry McCauley, Ivan Dee, Hilary Meyer, Johanna Russ.

John Kuehl adds special thanks to his wife, Beth, who endured the many hours spent on this book; his sons Ethan and Trevor; and his sisters Kara and Stefani.

Contents

Preface

Nobody, but nobody, gave Mike Bordick much of a chance to play in the major leagues. Not even Mike Bordick—at least when his career began.

Bordick attracted virtually no attention at the University of Maine, passing through the 1986 draft without even having his named called. He could catch and throw, but he lacked speed and offensive skills and had a poorly conditioned body burdened with a bubble butt. Then came his break. The A's could not sign their top shortstop draft pick and desperately sought someone, anyone, to fill the hole for their club at short-season Medford, Oregon. Scouting director Dick Bogard and scout J. P. Ricciardi had seen the undrafted shortstop from Maine who could catch and throw, and signed him to a contract.

Bordick did well enough in short season to get an invitation to spring training the next year, and was assigned to Class A Modesto mostly because the A's needed another infielder there. But Bordick had not yet taken baseball seriously, had not committed himself to the sport. The A's required that their players participate in a mandatory weight-lifting program, which the twenty-one-year-old Bordick assiduously avoided. While others began building their bodies, Bordick remained a bubble butt with a sense of humor.

One day midway through the season, A's Director of Player Development Karl Kuehl came through the clubhouse, took one look at Bordick, and asked the obvious question: had he been lifting? Bordick laughed and made a loud, joking comment, mocking the weight-training regimen. Kuehl's temper flared.

"If you don't want to get with the program, you can pack and leave now," Kuehl growled. "I don't even want you to come back tomorrow. You have some ability. You can catch and throw. You get a jump on the ball and have an idea how to play. You can bunt and make contact. If you work and get stronger so that you can drive the ball better, and work and improve your running some, you have a chance to play in the major leagues. But if you don't work at it, I don't want you around."

Bordick sat pondering his situation. A couple of hours later he came to the manager's office and said he would begin weight-lifting. He wanted to stay.

"That was the first time anybody ever said I had a shot in this game," Bordick said of the face-off in Modesto. "It made me sit down and think. It changed my whole approach to the game, and my life."

So Bordick made the transition from all fun and games to a gamer. He made his own fun by working just a little harder than those around him, and by approaching every day with a level of mental intensity that could rarely be matched. Bordick may not have been the most naturally gifted player on the field, but he found a way to succeed. During his first major league spring training in 1990, he found a glimmer of light. With the big leaguers locked out by the owners, the camps were made up of minor leaguers getting a chance to show off. When the lockout ended, Bordick literally refused to leave. After being assigned back to minor league camp, Bordick began a regimen of working with the minor leaguers in the morning, then returning unsolicited to the major league games in the afternoon to fill in for

Mike Bordick made the transition from fun
and games to gamer.

the last couple of innings. His work ethic, drive, and ability
made such an impression that the A's found him impossible to
ignore. By the end of the season, he was even on the World Series roster, appearing in three games against the Cincinnati
Reds. Through the decade of the 1990s, Bordick emerged as
one of the premier shortstops in baseball, using his limited tools
to every advantage and continuing to develop and grow.

This is the stuff of mental toughness. It is not about what gifts
we may be granted, physically or intellectually; it is about what

we do with them. There is nothing more common in baseball, or in the world around us, than squandered talent. Mental toughness is the art of taking control of your life, taking charge of the dynamics that surround you. No one can ever fully or realistically control the elements of luck, fate, and fortune, but all individuals have the ability to take charge of their lives and prepare themselves to face the most difficult challenges. They can all place themselves in a position to succeed.

This book is about baseball—and this book is about more than baseball. Obviously not everyone has the natural gifts to play in the major leagues. But everyone does have natural gifts that can lead him or her to success and achievement in one arena or another, and to a life of fulfillment. The same concepts that make for mental toughness on the diamond make for mental toughness in school, in business, and in life. The recognition of how attitudes affect our lives will carry over from the ballpark to the workplace. Understanding how to focus and concentrate makes not just for better ballplayers but for better students and business leaders.

A basic precept of mental toughness is the concept of self-determinism: that people can improve themselves and make the decisions that will carry them to achievement. The authors believe that people have the will and strength to overcome the burdens they carry with them. This book is designed to help them understand that.

Karl Kuehl has served as a minor league manager, major league manager of the Montreal Expos, director of player development for the Oakland A's and Toronto Blue Jays, and in 2002 joined the Cleveland Indians as a Special Adviser for Baseball Operations. In his five decades in baseball he has won a reputation as a leading authority on the mental game. Through his years of learning and study he has developed concepts that help players get the most from their ability. John Kuehl spent fifteen years in professional baseball as a scout and minor league manager and player. He carries on his father's work.

Many major league players contributed to this book by allowing some of their personal stories to be told, to help illustrate the decisions players face. Their names appear throughout the pages of this book, and we acknowledge with gratitude their contributions.

A note on pronouns, which get a lot of writers into trouble these days. Our preponderant use of "he"—rather than "she" or "he and she"—throughout this book is not intended to ignore or disrespect women athletes; it's simply the easiest way to present our ideas without making the sentences cumbersome. The principles we describe are just as applicable to women as to men.

Foreword
by Tony La Russa

In June 1986 an opportunity arose that any manager in baseball would have jumped through whatever hoops necessary to secure. The Oakland A's, with outstanding ownership, general manager and front-office staff, scouting, and player development personnel, were seeking to fill their field manager vacancy.

When I became their choice, the title of baseball's luckiest man belonged to me. In addition to all these organizational assets, the A's also had a strong core of talented players at the major league level, and a wealth of future stars in their minor league system.

In fact the 1986 team featured Jose Canseco, who became the American League Rookie of the Year. Canseco was the first of three consecutive Rookie of the Year recipients produced by the A's farm system. Mark McGwire won the award in 1987, and Walt Weiss secured the honor in 1988. The system also developed such winning players as Terry Steinbach, Tony Phillips, and Mike Gallego, to name just a few.

All those pluses translated into a lot of wins and a contending team. The mix of experienced veterans and talented young stars produced championship teams. As I watched and enjoyed the performances of our young players, I wondered what the minor league system was doing so well to develop these talents.

My questioning led directly to the A's general manager, Sandy Alderson, and the director of minor league operations, Karl Kuehl. I was able to observe firsthand how deeply and completely they approached the challenge of developing young talent into productive players.

Their approach was a mix of traditional and innovative methods. They were implemented throughout the A's system by quality baseball men such as Keith Lieppman, Harvey Dorfman, Brad Fischer, and many others. The core of the A's approach is the subject of this book. Mental toughness was somehow connected to every aspect of their development program.

Every player who signs a professional contract has a level of talent that is special enough to create a chance to play major league baseball. But the percentage of signed players who actually reach the majors is relatively small. Sometimes the explanation for failing is an injury or a circumstance that could not be overcome. In most cases, though, having mental toughness defines those players who make it—and a lack of it dooms the ones who don't.

Dedicating a book to the subject sends a clear message of its importance to anyone who is trying to become a winner. Recognizing the problem, or its importance, is only the first step. To be really effective, the first step must be followed by the specific means to solve the problem or settle the issue in your favor.

For example, as a coach you identify that a hitter is hitting too many balls in the air. You fail, however, to help him correct the problem with specific recommendations. In this instance you have done the easy part but not the most important.

One of the strengths of this book is that the subject of mental toughness is presented in detail with each element explained completely. It provides you with the what, why, and how of mental toughness. If you decide to improve your "toughness," then the "how," or elements, are keys to achievement.

When I recall examples of success from my career, mental toughness is always a critical factor. Whether it's a player or team, it is always essential. Mental toughness was the difference for Mark McGwire's record-breaking 1998; for Mike Bordick developing into a star; for Carlton Fisk becoming a Hall of Famer; for Harold Baines collecting almost 3,000 hits; for Dave Stewart earning four straight 20-win seasons; for Albert Pujols becoming baseball's first player to hit 30 or more home runs, have a batting average of .300, and drive in 100 or more runs in his first four major league seasons; for the 1983 Chicago White Sox to win the city's first baseball championship since 1959; for the 1989 A's to become world champions; and for the 2002 Cardinals to overcome the deaths of Jack Buck and Darryl Kile to come within three wins of the World Series.

A lot of mental toughness examples are presented here, because a lot of your future depends on understanding this concept. It's a talent you can acquire. Start by reading this book.

Mental Toughness

1

MENTAL TOUGHNESS: A WAY OF LIFE

In the racially torn America of the 1940s, the idea of bringing African Americans to major league baseball seemed abhorrent to some players and fans alike. But with a growing social undercurrent that opportunity should be open to all races, Brooklyn Dodgers general manager Branch Rickey set out on a noble experiment: to begin the integration of baseball by bringing a black player to the Dodgers. What Rickey understood completely was that the man who broke the color barrier would need intestinal fortitude and tenacity almost beyond realistic measure. Rickey knew that fighting back physically against generations of inbred racial attitudes would serve only to intensify tensions and probably turn the noble experiment into an ignoble flop. For this mighty role, he made the surprising choice of Jackie Robinson, a man who had made a life of fighting back, both in college at UCLA and during his World War II stint in the army. When Rickey made the offer to Robinson in August 1945, he said:

"We can't fight our way through this, Robinson. We've got no army. There's virtually nobody on our side. No owners, no umpires, very few newspapermen. And I'm afraid that many fans will be hostile. We'll be in a tough position. We can win only if we can convince the world that I'm doing this because you're a great ballplayer and a fine gentleman."

Rickey detailed the troubles he expected Robinson and the Dodgers to face, from taunting fans to slashing spikes, all of which Robinson would have to endure without reprisal. Robinson looked at the general manager and asked, "Mr. Rickey, are you looking for a Negro who is afraid to fight back?"

"Robinson, I'm looking for a ballplayer with guts enough not to fight back," Rickey told him.

Jackie Robinson broke the color barrier during the 1947 season with restraint and resolve. Early in the season the Dodgers hosted Philadelphia. Alabama-born Ben Chapman managed the Phillies and instructed his players to heap abuse on Robinson in order to shake him and throw him off his game. The Phillies yelled at him to go back to the jungle, hurled racial epithets, and slung hate. Bench jockeying was a norm for baseball of that era, but this level of abuse exceeded any standard.

"I have to admit this day of all the unpleasant days in my life brought me nearer to cracking up than I ever had been," Robinson wrote a quarter-century later. "For one wild and rage-crazed minute I thought, 'To hell with Mr. Rickey's noble experiment. It's clear it won't succeed. I have made every effort to work hard, to get myself into shape. My best is not good enough for them.' I thought what a glorious, cleansing thing it would be to let go. To hell with the image of the patient black freak I was supposed to create. I could throw down my bat, stride over to that Phillies dugout, grab one of those white SOBs and smash his teeth with

Jackie Robinson, chosen by Branch Rickey to break the color barrier in major league baseball, did it with restraint and resolve.

my despised black fist. Then I could walk away from it all. I'd never become a sports star. But my son could tell his son someday what his daddy could have been if he hadn't been too much a man."

Instead Jackie Robinson showed restraint. He seethed under the surface but never let an emotion show on his face or in his body language. In the eighth inning against Philadelphia he singled, stole second, and scored the winning run. Robinson won the game, and he won the day—not with his fist, but with his mind.

This is mental toughness. It is the mind-set to meet a challenge and overcome the obstacles that stand in the way of success. It is the inner strength that creates resolve and dedication, the courage to fight back from failure. It is the understanding that achievement rarely comes without enormous hardships along the way, and that the mentally tough are those who can work their way through the ordeals and persevere to success. It means keeping your head when others around you are losing theirs, and it means having the courage to speak up at the right time—or stay silent, as in the case of Jackie Robinson. The goal for mental toughness is a conscious decision a person makes in order to increase his or her opportunities for success.

Baseball is a game, a lifestyle, in which mental toughness is particularly necessary. It is a sport in which the mental elements are as demanding as the physical; where talent and mind-set combine to create achievement. Enormously talented athletes wash out because of a lack of desire or a breakdown of mental toughness. Far less talented players find their way to the major leagues for long and successful careers because of their mental strength. Of Jackie Robinson's teammate, Eddie Stanky, Rickey said, "He can't hit, he can't field, he can't throw. All he can do is beat you." In baseball, many less talented players reach higher levels of achievement than their more talented brethren. This happens in high schools, colleges, and on to the professional levels. It is almost always because of the formidable combination of desire, perseverance, and attitude that makes up mental toughness.

When professional scouts or instructors refer to "makeup," they mean mental toughness. It's a collection of values, attitudes, and emotions, a blend of the flexibility to make adjustments with the stubborn perseverance to overcome obstacles. Players who are mentally tough know how to control their emotions to perform in clutch situations; they can stay calm when breaks go against them; they avoid becoming intimidated; they don't give in by changing plans, losing sight of goals, or taking the easy way out; they do the work to grow tough physically as well as mentally; they push themselves to become their best, even working through exhaustion; they are disciplined and avoid easy distractions; they bounce back from disappointments and adversity; they are prepared and know how to prepare; they do not make excuses, particularly to themselves; they overcome fear. Mental toughness requires a state of alertness that allows the player to react quickly to changing situations while remaining intensely focused. It is a combination of self control and discipline that allows quick, intelligent decisions at the most intense moments. Everyone feels fear; the mentally tough learn to execute despite fear.

Mental toughness and physical toughness are very different. Bulging muscles and brawn are no measure of the person within. Confusing the two is a mistake that athletes often make.

The vast majority of people bound through life almost adrift, reacting with emotions and feelings rather than reasoning out the consequences of their actions or their best course for success and achievement. When something goes wrong around them, they fail to evaluate the reasons; instead they make excuses, rationalize, and blame others. Mental toughness would enable them to take control of their own destiny and get the most out of their ability. It will not always work; there are no perfect solutions to every problem. But it is, simply, the most effective approach to virtually all arenas of competition. Mental toughness is a quality that has been exhibited by virtually all leading athletes, by military leaders from Hannibal to Colin Powell, and by exemplary titans of business.

Baseball is different from most other sports in that it is a team game filled with individual challenges. In football, all players must work together to make an offensive play click, and other defenders can make up for a missed tackle. But in base-ball the batter stands alone in the box, and there is no second chance if the outfielder fails to catch that drive in the gap. Yet teams must work together to score runs or turn double plays. Within the game itself are subplots and dramas. A pitcher may try to gain an advantage over the hitters by using intimidating body language, such as the fabled "death stare" of Dave Stewart, his almost bloodthirsty gaze of defiance toward every hitter. Pedro Martinez pitches inside with force, and he never allows a hit batsman to affect his concentration. Martinez gains an advantage because no one enjoys being bludgeoned by a ninety-five-mile-per-hour fastball. A subtle psychological drama unfolds on nearly every play, since every event is a failure or success for one side or the other. If a hitter has a bad at-bat, or has a hit stolen by a great play, he must learn to put the failure behind him immediately and not allow it to affect his defense. Baseball demands dealing with failure—the best hitters fail 70 percent of the time.

Without mental toughness, failure eats at the soul, erodes confidence, and can snowball into disaster. Although the basic concepts of the mental game in baseball have been part of the sport almost since its inception, it has received growing emphasis in the last dozen years. Athletes and coaches have begun to recognize that talent alone does not translate into success. Many college coaches emphasize a player's mental skills in recruiting, choosing players with a strong work ethic and great competitiveness over players who may be more talented but less motivated. Major league teams ask their scouting staffs to grade personal attributes—such as dedication, aptitude, and maturity—along with a player's physical tools. This allows teams to better understand the person as well as the player. A few teams even perform personality tests on prospective draftees to get a better handle on a player's mental makeup.

Everyone who has participated in sports has a mental game at some level of refinement. In baseball the mental game is critical because of the idle time involved in the game, which allows the mind to wander. What is the player thinking about between pitches, at moments of inaction? Is his mind on the game, considering the next set of possibilities? Or has his mind drifted to his date after the game? TV analyst Bob Costas wrote in his book *Fair Ball*, "In any sport, the anticipation of what *might* happen is almost as important as what actually happens." Confidence, concentration, attitudes, and an approach to learning are all elements of the mental game. Mental toughness brings these elements together and allows an athlete to perform to the best of his or her ability.

But mental toughness is a skill, not a talent or a gift of nature. It is learned and developed. The individual must determine whether to choose a path of honing his or her mind toward a course of strength, power, and preparedness. It is a personal choice to take control of one's abilities and strive for success. Mental toughness is a process of using your mind to gain the most from your abilities. It is, very often, the difference between being a talented person and being a successful one.

2

ATTITUDES: THE MENTAL EDGE

From the day Mark McGwire signed with the Oakland A's, he had a stubborn streak. Success came easily in college, then in the minors and the majors. He launched forty-nine home runs during 1987, a record for rookies. Arguing with success becomes impossible, even if all the right pieces are not quite in place. From the beginning, McGwire could hit breaking balls and crush fastballs on the outside part of the plate, where he could extend his long arms. But those fastballs to the inside part of the plate gave him trouble, so he just took them and waited for the pitch he could handle. A's hitting coach Merv Rettenmund knew this was the making of a problem down the line, that eventually major league pitchers would spot the weakness and dive-bomb the slugger with fastballs on his hands. McGwire refused to worry. When A's coaches tried to pull McGwire into a video session to analyze his swing, McGwire asked the same question: "Was it a good swing or a bad swing?" If the coaches wanted him to watch the bad swings, he refused. He had no interest in changing; he wanted to reinforce the positives.

McGwire's plan worked fairly well through the minor leagues and during his first three seasons in the majors, then pitchers caught on. Word got around that McGwire had a weakness on the inside part of the plate, and it soon became the only diet they would feed him. Staunchly, McGwire waited for a pitch he could hit. Rarely would that pitch arrive. He finished the 1991 season at .201, with 22 homers and 75 RBIs in 154 games, career lows in all directions for the 28-year-old. The game had fallen apart for a burgeoning superstar. He lost confidence in his swing, and in himself. McGwire decided to return to his roots. The next season he headed to the A's base in Arizona two months early for spring training, to renew the hitting drills he had learned in the minors, with the instructors who had helped him on his path.

"What do you think of my swing?" he asked them. It was fine. The instructors watched him work in the cages and saw no clear mechanical problems. How were the pitchers getting him out? they asked. "Inside," was his one-word response. By watching tapes, the instructors realized that as his career had progressed, McGwire had continually moved closer to the plate, making it impossible for him to handle the inside pitch. The unnoticed shift surprised even McGwire.

"It must have happened unconsciously," he told the instructors.

In 1988, his second season, McGwire had been beaned in successive games, and word circulated through the American League that the slugger had grown afraid of being hit. McGwire's instinctual reaction had been just the opposite. "In my mind I was thinking, 'They are not going to run me out of this league.' Then I moved closer to the plate. I didn't even think about it at the time. And I guess every time I got knocked down after that, I moved closer until there was no room in the box."

When the problem was diagnosed, the A's instructor told him, "Mark, you have two choices. You either have to back off the plate or, if you want to stay where you are, you'll have to get inside the ball."

So McGwire faced a conscious decision. After years of trusting his ability, he would have to make the adjustments he had long resisted in order to compete again. That meant learning a shorter, quicker stroke so that he could get the fat part of the bat on inside pitches. He looked to the instructors and said, "Let's do it." After years of resistance, McGwire made the adjustment in about five minutes. He recognized that the alteration made his hands quicker and actually increased both his power and his ability to handle the inside pitch. He kept working through spring training and into the season to master the quicker stroke, and wound up with an outstanding year, hitting .268 with 42 homers and 104 RBIs. This would only be a portent of what was to come. Seven years later the baseball world would stand still, transfixed by McGwire's sweet shortened swing and watch as he shattered the most hallowed of baseball records by hitting 70 home runs during the summer of 1998, then following with 65 the next year.

After the record-setting season, McGwire shook his head and said, "Man, I wish I'd known what I know now when I was a younger player."

What McGwire learned is a lesson just about everyone learns on the course to achievement: attitude breeds success. Before McGwire could make the mechanical adjustments necessary to carry him to the next level of stardom, he had to make the mental adjustments that would allow him to get there.

The right attitudes make it possible to take the mental edge. This can be the edge over an opponent, or the advantage over a difficult situation. When the game seems to go in the dumper, it is attitude that often makes the difference between a situation

Mark McGwire made the adjustment to hit
the inside pitch.

that spirals into disaster or a player who picks himself up to take
the edge. Rather than give up or remain rigid, Mark McGwire
decided to take the mental edge and move forward.

Attitudes dictate who we are as individuals, both on and off
the field. They direct how we approach our sports, our profes-
sions, our lives. They make up our personality; they create our
identity. Attitudes control how we act—how we interpret information and how we respond to it. Interpretations of life experiences and what we accept as truth form our attitudes. A good
baseball definition of attitude would be: the thoughts, beliefs,

opinions, feelings, or intentions with which you approach your tasks and goals. More than anything else, attitudes will determine what you achieve, how you feel, and how happy and satisfied you are with your life. Attitudes are the power behind great accomplishments. When used to advantage, attitudes change lives for the better. These familiar statements are thrown out by coaches and motivators from many different directions. It takes an exceptional person to improve his attitude and make the adjustments that lead to achievement.

With everything in baseball, and in life, individuals have a choice of different attitudes. At times a certain "good" attitude may not be the best attitude for a particular situation. Sometimes circumstances change, demanding an attitude adjustment. McGwire's attitude worked until the circumstances changed. The challenge becomes discovering the attitude and combination of attitudes that works.

As simple and obvious as Mark McGwire's small adjustment may have seemed, it demanded a change in mind-set before he could make the alteration that would redefine his career. He had to recognize the problem, then seek a solution. The ability to adjust and improve is a direct result of attitude. All improvement is a result of change. To gain a new and improved result requires a new approach, whether mental or physical. A change in attitude precedes a change in behavior. To successfully make a mechanical adjustment, first must come the attitude adjustment; a player must think, "I want to change." McGwire had to decide consciously to regain the mental edge over his problem.

When Roger Craig took over as manager of the bedraggled San Francisco Giants late in 1985, the players grumbled endlessly about the miserable playing conditions at frigid Candlestick Park. Craig almost immediately convinced his team to use the inclement conditions to their advantage: visiting teams would have difficulty adjusting to the icy winds and blowing dust, so his players could make the most of their situation. Within two seasons the Giants were in the playoffs and a franchise had been turned around, partly by what seemed to be a simple change in attitude.

This is not brain science but common sense. It has been evolving since baseball became a professional sport. Back in about 1909, the left-handed-hitting outfielder Josh Devore could not stay in the box against lefty pitchers for fear of being hit. Finally an exasperated manager John McGraw ordered Devore to allow himself to be hit by a soft-throwing southpaw or he would be fined the mighty sum of ten dollars. Devore took the lump, then began staying in and actually getting hits against even the toughest lefties. Attitudes and mind-sets, conscious and unconscious, must be altered to deliver improvement. Winning attitudes are rarely a natural gift—they are learned and honed, developed through the maturation process. Mark McGwire had the natural talent to succeed; his attitudes made him into a superstar.

An attitude can give you the mental edge. It can be the edge over an opponent or a situation. In every player's career there will be games under miserable conditions—battling bug infestations in Cleveland, trying to hit with the wind coming off the lake in Chicago, or wilting in the humidity during an American Legion game. From high school to the pros, attitude provides the edge that allows a player to give just a little more, to work just a little harder, and to take an advantage for himself.

Here are a few simple guides for learning to take that mental edge.

Emphasize positive experiences. Mentally reliving success helps build confidence that success can be repeated. Remember achievements and use them to create a framework of self-confidence. "I know I can do it because I've done it before." If you have not had success in certain situations before, it can be difficult to have a positive attitude. But through visualization you can create positive expectations.

Commit to the attitude. Only by making a serious and sincere determination to believe in an attitude can it be effective. Attitudes are not about lip service; they demand dedication. If a hitter has a poor strike zone, he cannot solve the problem simply by saying he wants to change. He must dedicate himself to making the change.

Visualize positive expectations. Sometimes a player needs to stop, shut his eyes, and see himself getting a hit off a tough pitch or pitcher; or a pitcher needs to see himself making a well-executed pitch. The more realistic the visualization, the more impact it will have. By seeing yourself succeed in your mind, you are reinforcing a winning attitude.

Use self-talk to ingrain attitudes. The player speaks to himself with conviction and emotion until these attitudes become natural, ingrained in the subconscious mind. Understanding the situation and knowing yourself will dictate the right emotional level for the task, and that level can be controlled by the speed and intensity of self-talk. The player trying to calm his emotions should talk slowly and coolly; the player attempting to become more aggressive will speak to himself faster and with greater intensity. Pushing oneself requires loud, strong self-talk, emphatic and enthusiastic. Volume and intensity can increase energy levels. Talking aloud makes it easier to control thoughts.

Commitment and repetitious affirmations of attitude. As with everything in athletics, attitudes demand practice and regular rededication. A player must reestablish his goals and renew his reasons for providing such intense dedication. The more these thoughts are repeated, the more ingrained they become. Discussing this with a friend or teammate will help affirm the attitude and hold the player accountable.

POSITIVE ATTITUDES

In a world torn apart by war and rebuilt by valor, Americans spent the late 1940s singing, "Accentuate the positive, eliminate the negative, watch out for Mr. In-between." In 1952, Dr. Norman Vincent Peale published his landmark book, *The Power of Positive Thinking*, to a hungry audience seeking the path to achievement. The importance of a positive approach has long been preached and accepted, in churches and sales meetings. It is the root of enthusiasm, determination, and self-confidence. Succeeding comes first from believing that success is possible.

Despite this emphasis on positive thinking, most of us still fight negative attitudes every day. People with positive attitudes are often the exception, sometimes drawing criticism as insincere phonies or causing others to marvel at their blind optimism. "Keep smiling and the world will wonder what you are up to," is an oft-quoted adage. In his book *Life Is an Attitude*, Elwood Chapman writes, "Observations and hundreds of interviews dealing with the subject of attitudes for over forty years has convinced me that there is a subtle but consistent pressure that pushes a dark film over our perceptual fields. The movement has a tendency to cover up the positive and highlight the negative." Chapman calls this "negative drift," a phenomena that seems almost unavoidable for most people as they lapse into self-doubt and negative approaches. In baseball this takes form when a player takes a couple of bad swings in batting practice, then expects to have a poor game.

Why does this happen? Why is it so hard to maintain a positive approach on a consistent, daily level? Dr. Daniel Goleman suggests that we should view our brain actually as two brains: the rational brain and the emotional brain. Our rational brain is the problem solver; it reviews, often time and again, all our positive and negative experiences. It tries to figure out what went wrong, why it happened, and who or what is to blame. It also anticipates potential negatives and problems to help in preparation and in avoiding surprises.

The emotional brain, on the other hand, is irrational. It refuses to let negative thoughts fade away. Anger, frustration, fear, disappointment, and embarrassment overwhelm and override the rational mind, triggering negative thinking. It becomes a struggle to force negative thoughts from the mind and reclaim a positive attitude.

To overcome negative drift, anticipate the downslide and prepare the rational mind to take control of the thinking process. When an athlete catches himself drifting into negativity with a thought such as "I hope the ball isn't hit to me," he must immediately catch the attitude flaw and respond with conviction: "I want the ball, and I know I will make the play." To conquer negative drift, the achiever must anticipate the problem and force the rational mind to take control of the situation.

Negative thoughts are pessimistic, resulting in negative feelings and lowered expectations. All thinking that is not positive has a negative drift. For example, saying, "I hope I get a hit today" lacks determination, conviction, and enthusiasm. There is no confidence in "hope." Compare this to the positive attitude that exudes from the statement: "I know I am going to hit the ball hard." Often players can be beaten in their minds against certain pitchers, or pitchers against certain hitters. A couple of poor at-bats against a certain pitcher may lead a player to question his ability to hit the pitcher. This is a test of positive attitude; the player must come back with intensity and confidence despite past struggles.

Players who reach the post-season are often heard saying, "I'm just happy to be here." This can be viewed almost as a subconscious surrender—"I have already succeeded, so now I can accept losing." The same positive attitudes that led to earlier success must be maintained at all times. Dr. Karl Menninger wrote: "Attitudes are more important than fact." This is especially applicable in athletics, where confidence and approach often lead less-talented teams or athletes to victory. David can defeat Goliath by being smarter, better prepared, and believing that victory is possible.

The benefits of positive attitudes are:

• Enhanced optimism and positive expectation.

• High positive energy.

• Higher levels of confidence: you are likely to trust yourself, not thinking too much or giving too much effort.

• Better concentration.

• Better decisions: viewing possibilities instead of obstacles.

• Better learning.

• Greater determination and commitment, with a "can-do attitude" and a refusal to give up easily.

• Greater happiness and peace of mind.

• Enhanced perseverance.

• A greater willingness to accept challenges.

Here are some strategies for developing positive attitudes:

1. Establish a goal of being positive at all times. Make this a habit, and emphasize in your mind the importance of remaining positive.

2. Have attitude awareness: constantly understand your attitudes and motivations. Without attitude awareness, it's not possible to control attitudes. Attitudes that are not helping will continue, and undesirable new attitudes will fester on their own. Attitude awareness provides for the conscious reinforcement of beneficial attitudes and for the development of new improved attitudes.

3. When positive feelings lapse, *will* yourself into thinking and acting positively. It may feel forced and even phony, but it will stop negative drift and bring you back to the positive.

4. Use a positive distraction to overcome negative emotions. When you cannot drive the negative thoughts from your mind, divert yourself by doing something particularly enjoyable, such as going to the gym to work out anxieties, reading a book, playing a musical instrument, or seeing a movie—something that will divert your mind from the negative.

5. Stay away from people with negative attitudes. Negative attitudes are a virus that can be contagious. If a teammate cannot be persuaded to improve his attitude, don't be influenced by him.

6. Right yourself emotionally after a mistake, otherwise you will be more likely to make another mistake. Assuming confident body language becomes a conscious effort to think and feel positively and allows you to move past the mistake and refocus on the game.

7. Plan and control your attitudes. Attitudes control what you do and how you do it. When someone truthfully says, "I don't know why I did that," there is an unconscious, out-of-control attitude at work. Positive thinking is a choice of the rational mind, with the ability to convert negatives to positives and prevent negative drift.

Attitudes control performance and affect all parts of your life, including:

1. Feelings and emotions.
2. Energy and tension levels.
3. State of mind.
4. Interpretation of events around you.
5. Anticipation and expectation.
6. Judgment and evaluation.
7. Goals.
8. Determination of personal needs.

In baseball, attitudes affect:

1. Motivation in every phase of the game (including work, hustle, alertness).

2. Ability and eagerness to learn.
3. Work ethic and work habits.
4. Quality and amount of preparation.
5. Level of confidence.
6. Ability to concentrate.
7. Relationship with coaches, teammates, opponents, officials, family, and friends.
8. Degree of team spirit.
9. Results.

THE THREE TYPES OF BASEBALL ATTITUDES

Baseball attitudes can be broken down into three types: personal, situational, and approach. Personal attitudes concern character and core beliefs. Situational attitudes involve the situations in which we find ourselves—no two are ever quite the same. Approach attitudes define our intentions and how we plan to go about accomplishing them.

There is never just one attitude at work in baseball. Instead there is a combination of attitudes that guide and influence every aspect of a player's performance. This combination involves personal, situational, and approach attitudes and almost always includes more than one attitude from each category.

Personal attitudes. Personality is an important part of what shapes attitudes, and personal attitudes are really an extension of our core value system. They influence all our other attitudes and motivations. Baseball coaches and managers often discuss what a player "brings to the party." This means the core personality a player takes with him to the team, a game, or a situation: the tendency to be positive or negative—is he a worrier or a planner? Does he perform with enthusiasm, tenacity, and show a solid work ethic? Does he thrive in situations of adversity? Is he a team player or selfish?

When Whitey Herzog took over as manager of the St. Louis Cardinals in 1980, he found a cadre of players not to his liking. "I've never seen such a bunch of misfits," Herzog wrote in *White Rat: A Life in Baseball.* "Nobody would run out the ball. Nobody in the bullpen wanted the ball. We had guys on drugs— and another guy who sneaked off into the tunnel between innings so he could take a hit of vodka." When Herzog reported to owner Gussie Busch on the state of the team, he said, "You've got a bunch of prima donnas, overpaid SOBs who ain't ever going to win a goddamned thing. You've got a bunch of mean people, some sorry human beings. It's the first time I've ever been scared to walk through my own clubhouse. We've got drug problems, we've got ego problems, and we ain't ever going anywhere." So Herzog started a complete housecleaning, ridding himself of the players he considered trouble and replacing them with men of higher character. At the time, some of the moves were publicly interpreted as Herzog trying to find his type of player. In fact he was searching for men of quality who could win as a team.

Quality players know and live by the concepts of mental toughness: they do not shy away from clutch situations or shrink from pressure. They place the welfare of the team above their personal desires. They do what is necessary to achieve victory, whether it means learning to become a better bunter or hitting to the right side, giving up an at-bat to advance a runner.

The highest, mightiest, and best among us understand the combination of pride and respect. In an incident that occurred during the American Revolution, a work crew building a barrier could not lift the final log into place as the corporal stood by commanding them to heave it. A tall man walked up and helped the workers push the log the extra few inches to the top, then turned to the corporal to ask why he had failed to help. "But sir, I am a corporal." George Washington responded, "I am a general." Pedro Martinez, perhaps the finest pitcher of his era, stopped to help a woman on a cleanup crew in Seattle. Pride is not a trait built around showing disrespect for others; it is about enhancing the strength of your own character.

Another personal attitude of success is the desire to be a competitor. Surprising as it may seem, many top-level players shy from the desire to be "the man" when the game is on the line. One of the ingredients of becoming a clutch performer is the ability to muster mental toughness in the most tense situations. Yankees shortstop Derek Jeter says, "When I come to bat in a pivotal spot, I want people to say, 'Uh-oh, here he comes.'" Jeter wants that responsibility of being considered "the man." In 1941, Ted Williams told *Time* magazine, "Naw, there ain't no tension for me hitting in the clutch. I'd like to have the bases loaded every time I come up." In contrast, Raul Mondesi with the Dodgers in 1999 did not want the challenge of hitting in the cleanup spot, projecting an attitude of "I can't hit in the fourth spot." The result was, he didn't.

A winner projects these personal attitudes:

• I am a competitor: I love challenges.

• I love pressure. I love to be tested because that helps me improve. That's what it's all about, because I am a competitor.

• I want to be there when the game is on the line. I am not afraid to fail. I will learn from it, adjust, and go for it again.

• Tell me I cannot do something and I will find a way to do it.

Many players grow hypersensitive about how others view and judge them, and personal attitudes toward pleasing others and living up to the expectations of others can create problems. This issue can become a major distraction and a source of pressure. It's almost like looking over your shoulder to see who's watching, and assuring yourself that you *are* being watched—like the child yelling "watch me" to his parents. If a player catches himself expressing the following attitudes, it's an indication of poor confidence and an excessive concern about the opinions of others:

- Everybody is watching me. I don't want to let them down.
- They expect me to carry the load, and that's not fair.
- I don't want to embarrass myself in front of my friends.
- I signed a big contract, and now I'm expected to make the difference.

When a player becomes obsessed with these types of attitudes, it becomes impossible to prepare properly and focus on the job. A player has to be his own man and not worry about living up to the standards set by others. The player must focus on living up to his own standards rather than trying to please family and friends. Beneficial attitudes for achieving this focus include:

- I will not worry about the expectations and judgments of others.
- I will prepare and do what I need to do, the way I know I need to do it. Then I will look in the mirror and evaluate myself according to my standards of preparation, execution, and effort.
- With every worry and concern, I will determine whether I have control or not. Then I will not worry about things I cannot control or influence.

Situational attitudes. One element that keeps complicating baseball—and life—is that very rarely are two situations *exactly* the same. Some little nuance always complicates the situation. The last bases-loaded, one-out at-bat came against a breaking ball pitcher, while this one is against a guy with a big heater. Or, bases loaded with one out: the last time we turned a double play, but this time the runner at the plate is faster and we may not be able to turn two. Situational attitudes concern every different situation in which we find ourselves: one classroom versus another, driving to work, pitching in a meaningless game, playing when the game is on the line, taking instruction from a high school coach versus a former major leaguer, and many more. Despite these differences, there are basic situational attitudes that apply in all situations.

At the Oakland A's Instructional League camp, players are given an attitude of the day, so that each attitude can be taken individually, digested, and understood. What follows is a list of situational attitudes with which to approach and play baseball. An effective way to make these attitudes take hold is to follow the attitude-of-the-day plan, taking each attitude and firmly ingraining it in the mind before moving on, then going back later to reinforce each attitude.

• I hustle all the time, even when I am tired and it does not seem important or necessary.

• I will not worry about things I cannot control.

• I will be ready and focused on every pitch, because every pitch has the potential to be a turning point in the game. I do not take anything for granted; I do not want to be surprised or embarrassed.

• I am always alert, anticipating errors and mistakes by the other team. I always hustle so that I am in position to take advantage of mistakes.

• I am a winner, and winners do not give in or give up. If I am having a bad day, I will make an adjustment and find a way to finish strong. If we are losing by many runs, I will keep playing hard and trying to chip away and get back in the game.

• The score will not affect how I play. I do not care what the score is; I do what I am supposed to do to execute.

• I work hard and hustle all the time. I am in the game mentally. I do what is expected of me. These attitudes make me a winner.

• I have fun and enjoy the game. I love the challenge of being the best I can be.

• My challenge is to play the best I can and to improve as much as I can. I will not judge myself by comparing myself with others, whether I am better or worse.

• I know that winning is a result of playing the game properly.
• The statistics and even the score do not tell me if I won or lost. I give it everything I have.
• Although I might become frustrated or disappointed if something does not work to my advantage, I will get over it quickly and become ready for the next pitch or play.
• When something goes wrong, I do not make excuses or whine. I take responsibility and find a way to improve.

Approach attitudes. When major leaguers discuss their approach, they refer to their mechanics and strategy. Approach attitudes are a sort of guidance system for what a player intends to accomplish and how he will go about doing it. For example, a hitter recognizes the importance of being relaxed at the plate. How he goes about accomplishing this is his approach attitude. From self-talk and preparation, he relaxes himself before he steps into the box, then advances with his plan. Perhaps it will be to start early and easy with a short swing, then to hit a one-hop bullet through the infield. A pitcher's approach attitude may be to stay loose, stay back, and feel the ball come off his fingertips, hitting his target on the lower outside third of the plate.

Approach attitudes have to do with more than mechanics. As players advance, mechanics often become instinctive, and the approach attitudes concern the plan for the at-bat or a certain pitch. Players have approach attitudes for just about everything they do in a game. These can change from pitch to pitch as the job and the situation change.

APPROACH ATTITUDES FOR HITTERS

Hitters have approach attitudes for every at-bat. These include seeing the ball; determining the best point of contact for hitting the ball to the opposite field, up the middle, or pulling; bunting for a hit, sacrifice, or squeeze; hit and run; and establishing a strike zone. A positive approach attitude builds confidence; a negative attitude erodes the ability to succeed. If a hitter steps into the box thinking, "The pitcher won't challenge me, I won't get anything to hit," or "The ump is giving away the corners, I won't get a decent pitch," he is already at a disadvantage before he walks to the plate.

Even in the most difficult of situations—against a solid control pitcher or with a big-strike-zone umpire—a hitter needs to seize the mental advantage. Al Oliver, one of the great hitters of the 1970s with the Pirates, Rangers, and Giants, said he approached at-bats by thinking, "I know the pitch is going to be down the middle, and I am going to hit it right back through the pitcher. I am not guessing, I know. I can even feel it is going to happen, and if the pitch isn't there, I just take it." Mark McGwire stated it simply: "My job is to get a good pitch to hit and have a good swing at it."

In anything but a two-strike situation, the hitter takes the mental advantage with the attitude, "I know the pitcher is going to make a mistake. I am going to be nice and easy, keep my head down, and hit the ball where it is pitched."

Hitters often get themselves in trouble by changing their approach when they get ahead in the count, 2-0 or 3-0. They approach the swing with the attitude, "He's got to throw a strike. It will be down the middle, and I will hammer it." As a result, the hitter becomes too aggressive and chases anything close to the strike zone. Even if that good pitch comes, he does not hit it well.

The approach attitude should not change until the at-bat becomes a two-strike situation. With less than two strikes, a hitter should think:

• Anytime I am hitting with less than two strikes, my attitude and approach are the same, from the first pitch until there are two strikes against me.

• I am going to stay "within myself"—not too hard, not too soft—and get a pitch I can drive.

• I am in control. If the pitcher does not throw a pitch I can drive, I won't swing. I'll just give him another chance to make a mistake.

• I know I am going to get a good pitch to hit. I am going to have a nice swing at it. I will be under control and be able to stop my swing if I see it's a pitch I cannot drive.

A hitter may find himself in a hole with runners in scoring position because of unsatisfactory approach attitudes. If a hitter pressures himself by thinking, "I've got to drive in that run," or "I can't get behind in the count, so I have to be aggressive," or, worst of all, "I wish somebody else was in this spot and not me," he has already placed himself at a disadvantage by being overly aggressive or overly careful. Attitudes of this sort diminish the hitter's concentration. He is not ready to hit, he is ready only to fail.

Rather than dwelling on pressure, a hitter can be better prepared for the situation by using approach attitudes such as:

• I will be nice and easy, and I will get a pitch I can drive up the middle.

• I will forget about the runners and just be myself—see the ball, hit the ball.

• I know the pitcher doesn't want to give me anything to hit, but I know he will make a mistake and I will be right on it.

• The pressure is on the pitcher. My job is to be ready, see the ball, and have a good swing at it.

Approaches like these create the mental atmosphere for success. A hitter should always assume he will get a good pitch to hit, and that he will be swinging. A hitter does not see the pitch and decide to swing; rather, he expects to swing and may decide to stop if he does not get a good pitch to hit. This may seem like a fine distinction, but it is an important element of mental preparation for hitting: the hitter approaches each pitch with the expectation that it will be a pitch to hit, then he holds up his swing if it is not the right pitch to hit, or the wrong pitch for that situation.

TWO-STRIKE APPROACH ATTITUDES

When the count goes to two strikes, the approach and situation change. The wrong approach attitude places the hitter on the defensive and unready to take advantage of a pitcher's mistakes. If the hitter now thinks, "I just want to get a piece of the ball to stay alive," or "I have to protect the plate," or "I just want to put the ball in play," he is at a mental disadvantage to hit good pitches when they come.

In almost every major league game there will be a two-strike confrontation where a hitter fouls off a series of pitches before finally lining an important hit. Will Clark, one of the best two-strike hitters in recent baseball history, outlined his two-strike thinking this way: "I am a great two-strike hitter. The pitcher does not have an advantage, because he has to throw it over the plate. There is no way any pitch in the strike zone is getting past me." This will not always be true, of course, but this approach provides the mental edge that leads to making a good two-strike hitter. Mark McGwire said, "The pitcher has another chance to make a mistake, and I will be ready and have a good swing at it." A critical part of succeeding with two strikes is for the hitter to avoid beating himself mentally.

A single attitude, as good as it may be, will not make you a good two-strike hitter. Being a good hitter with two strikes takes a combination of attitudes, because the pitcher can throw different pitches in different locations, which calls for different responses by the hitter. Taking the mental edge means being prepared for whatever the pitcher throws.

The most overlooked but most important part of two-strike hitting is being ready for the mistake pitch—the "nothing ball" that fails to move or break and travels right down the middle of the plate—and hitting it solidly. The worst outcome of a two-strike count is to take a pitch right down the middle, letting the pitcher get away with a mistake that would have been crushed earlier in the at-bat. Before all else, a hitter must have a strong, dominating approach attitude that prepares him to hit mistakes.

When a pitcher makes a great pitch, such as a nasty splitter that nips the strike zone down and away, a hitter must be prepared to take less than his best swing while maintaining the determination to hit it for a line drive, even if he is completely fooled by the pitch. The hitter approaches with the attitude: "If he fools me and the pitch is in the strike zone, I will stay on the ball and hit a line drive. Even if I can't take a good swing, I can hit it foul." A hitter also needs to have a plan for the two-strike pitch that gets in on his hands. "Blocking the ball" refers to the half-swing, or check-swing, that an experienced hitter uses to fight off tough inside pitches on his hands. Because hitters are widely taught to look for pitches on the outside part of the plate with two strikes, in order to cover the width of the strike zone they are often susceptible to strikes on the inside corner, especially in on the hands. An effective approach attitude in this situation is: "If the pitch is in the strike zone and it ties me up, I will fight it off by blocking the ball foul, if that's what it takes. I will not surrender." Hitters who persist in taking a full swing when they are fooled or tied up by a pitch will swing and miss, striking out. Sometimes a hitter must give in and take less than his best swing to stay alive and give the pitcher another chance to make a mistake.

Many experienced, professional hitters have disciplined strike zones and do not chase bad pitches until they reach two strikes. Then they chase pitches they could never reach because they approach the situation with an attitude of "I will not allow the umpire to call me out on strikes. I would rather go down swinging than have the ump take the bat out of my hands." This is not an effective attitude for success. With two strikes, the hitter should expand the strike zone somewhat, but he must not swing at pitches that are clearly out of the zone and beyond his range of contact. When the umpire calls a third strike on a pitch out of the zone, the hitter has no control over that call. The hitter must accept the call and realize that even had he swung, he would have either hit the ball weakly or struck out. The hitter must control what he can control, and that means not giving away an at-bat by swinging at a bad pitch or taking a good strike. If the umpire makes a mistake, the hitter must assume the attitude, "That's just baseball. I refuse to let that get into my head and change my game."

In 1988 the American League MVP Jose Canseco hit .302 and became the first hitter ever to hit 40-plus home runs and steal 40-plus bases in the same season. Canseco had a two-strike stance that spread his legs so wide he did not stride toward the ball. The stance also lowered his head closer to the strike zone, which allowed him to better see the ball. He had so much success hitting with two strikes that he began using the stance in RBI situations, on the advice of Dave Parker. A good two-strike hitter makes physical adjustments that are a direct reflection of how his attitude changes with two strikes. The last major leaguer to hit over .400 was Ted Williams in 1941, and he raised his hands on the bat handle—commonly referred to as choking up—to gain better barrel accuracy with his swing. Barry Bonds, who set the single-season home run record in 2001, also chokes up on the bat handle. Physical adjustments are often necessary with two strikes in order to execute a plan successfully.

Following is an example of a combination of two-strike approach attitudes in proper sequence:

1. I am a great two-strike hitter. I can hit anything he throws. The pitcher is in trouble now, because this is when I am at my best.

2. I am not going to chase anything too low and slow.

3. I will take what he gives me. I will go with it and stay within myself.

4. If he fools me or makes a tough pitch in the zone, I am going to stay on it, hitting a little line drive or fighting it off. I will battle.

5. Above all else, a hitter must assume this attitude and see it in his mind as the truth: The pitcher is going to make a mistake. I will have a good swing, nice and easy, and hit it on the button.

The two-strike drama plays out again and again in every major league game. A sharp observer can read a hitter's attitude through a TV screen or even from the bleachers at Fenway Park. A good two-strike hitter—a Derek Jeter or an Albert Pujols—does not give in to the pitcher. He approaches the situation with a thought process that gives him the mental edge.

APPROACH ATTITUDES FOR BASERUNNERS

Baserunning tends to be underemphasized in many professional organizations and in the colleges. Sometimes speed is not the element that makes for a good baserunner; rather it is anticipation, canniness, and execution, all of which begin with proper approach attitudes. Hall of Fame catcher Johnny Bench, by no means a speed burner, was considered a top baserunner because he knew what was expected of him in all situations, he was always alert, and he could estimate when he could take the extra base. Despite his lack of speed, Bench became an asset on the basepaths because he learned to become a good baserunner. This begins with a player's approach attitude to running the bases. If a player begins by thinking, "I'm so slow that nobody expects me to run hard," or "I'll look for the coach and he'll tell me what to do," or "There is no need to run hard when I know I'm going to be out," the player is already putting himself in a hole. He could lose the ability to take the extra base. As with Johnny Bench, even slow runners can become assets on the bases by being alert and preparing to be aggressive when the opportunity arises.

Successful approach attitudes are aggressive and do not take for granted that the defense will execute the play:

• I am going to go as hard as I can out of the box and all the way through the bag.

• I am going hard to put pressure on the infielders. If they take too much time or their throw pulls the first baseman off the bag, even slightly, I will be safe.

• When I get a single, I will run hard to first and take as deep a turn as I can. I will look for the opportunity to take an extra base off the outfielders.

As he neared retirement, Hall of Fame third baseman George Brett said, "In my last at bat, I would like to hit a ground ball to the second baseman and run it out as hard as I can, because that is the way I have played the game; that is who I am. That is what I want people to remember." This is the essence of professionalism that makes for greatness: by never conceding an out on the bases, players such as Brett and Bench pick up an extra base or create errors by the opposition. This can be the difference in scoring a run, the difference in winning and losing a game.

How a player takes a lead off a base is a result of his attitude. Many players barely consider their leads or think, "I'll just do what I have to do, get far enough off so the coach won't criticize me." Instead, winning attitudes are: "I get every inch I can, because I know that can be the difference between being safe or out," and "After my lead I hold my ground, hoping and looking for a passed ball."

One of the great mistakes made by many players is to believe that baserunning is simply about speed. It cannot be overemphasized that success on the bases has much to do with approach and attitude. If a hitter approaches a simple ground ball with the thought that he will force the defender to make a perfect throw by hustling to first base, he is far more likely to force the error. The Mariners' Ichiro Suzuki places constant pressure on infield defenses by running out ground balls that appear to be obvious outs and turning even the slightest bobble into an error. If a hitter approaches his at-bat with the expectation of perfect defense, he will be giving away bases. If, instead, he uses an approach attitude such as: "I run hard, so if the infielder boots the ball or the outfielder plays it slowly, I will can take an extra base," the runner is taking the edge and preparing to succeed. Even the slow of foot can change a game with alert, aggressive, and impassioned baserunning. Every player, at every level, will find chances to change a game on the bases. The players who begin with an approach for success are most likely to succeed.

APPROACH ATTITUDES FOR RECEIVING SIGNS

"I never missed a sign in my entire career," Pete Rose said. "Players who don't get signs are not good team players: they are players who are playing for themselves, they are thinking about themselves instead of the team. My attitude was, 'I want to score a run, and if the manager is going to put a play on, I am not going to miss it.'" This attitude exemplified Rose's "Charlie Hustle" style of play and was a big part of his winning edge.

Signs are a part of baseball strategy. Missing a sign can result in an out or a blown opportunity. When a hitter or runner misses a sign on a hit-and-run, it means giving away outs. Successful teams execute well, and execution includes getting the signs straight. One of the elements that makes baseball such an intriguing game is that a less talented team that executes well can often be more successful than teams with greater talent.

Throughout professional baseball, players constantly miss signs. They miss because of lack of concentration, failure to remember the signs, or, often, because they take a poor approach to receiving signs—they unconsciously do not wish to bunt or slap the ball on the ground for a hit-and-run. Pete Rose's comment exemplifies the proper approach attitude for receiving signs: the player wants to get the sign right to help his team score runs. A player who is good at receiving signs will even learn to think as his manager thinks and know what his manager does in certain situations.

APPROACH ATTITUDES ON DEFENSE

Many players approach the game of baseball as if they are auditioning for the job of designated hitter: defense just whiles away the time between at-bats, or is a distraction from the real job of hitting. Much of a player's success on defense comes from concentration and anticipation. This is an area where desire to succeed becomes most visible, where hard work pays dividends. It is also a place where approach attitudes are critical. If a defender approaches a play with negative thoughts, it diminishes his aggressiveness and preparation. Such negative thoughts as "I hope he doesn't hit this ball to me" make the defender less likely to make the play.

An alert, dedicated defensive player approaches every pitch with the desire to make the play. Effective approach attitudes for playing defense include:

• I am aggressive. I will take charge, be loud, and use my voice to call plays.

• I will anticipate every possible play before every pitch.

• I will help my teammates, making sure they are ready for every pitch.

• I will have total concentration on every pitch and every batted ball.

• I will get a great jump on every pitch because that extra inch might be the difference in making the play. I will go after every ball that is hit my way.

• Hit the ball to me, I want it. I want to make this play.

• I will make a difference in the game with my defense.

• There are no easy plays. Every play has the potential to be tough until it is over, and I will maintain my concentration even when the play appears easy.

• I will be moving on every batted ball, even if it is on the other side of the field. When it isn't my play, my job is to back up the play.

• When I make an error, I will learn from it and get ready for the next pitch. I will never hang my head and let one error cause me to make more mistakes.

• I love to play defense and take runs away from the other team.

Defense cannot really be quantified by statistics, and it often seems to go unnoticed in newspaper reports. Yet it makes for successful teams. Hitting the cutoff man or backing up the play may not draw headlines, but they become a point of emphasis for the player seeking the winning edge.

APPROACH ATTITUDES FOR PITCHERS

Nearly every pitcher with a fastball that can break a windowpane decides that he can overpower hitters. At some point that attitude almost always changes. So much of pitching happens inside the head; it is the chess game of sport, where various art forms flourish. A Greg Maddux gets his outs by changing speeds and sinking and cutting the ball; a Randy Johnson thrives on power and control. A pitcher must know himself and how he can find a way to succeed. He must have confidence in his ability and show that confidence on the mound. This all begins with attitude.

Attitude will determine whether the pitcher has a positive approach or a negative approach. Whether a pitcher thinks about it or not, he will have an attitude toward each of his individual pitches. If he believes in his curveball, he will throw it with conviction; if he believes in his change-up, he will be more likely to execute the pitch. Pitchers' attitudes affect how they approach fielding drills, backing up plays, conditioning, and taking signs from the catcher. If a pitcher believes these are important, he will devote more attention to being where he is supposed be on every play and spend the extra hours learning to field his position. A pitcher also encourages or discourages the fielders around him by the attitude he takes toward them.

Pitchers often approach a situation with the attitude, "I just want to throw a strike." This is a flat-out poor approach that does not get the job done. When Michael Jordan shoots a basketball, he is not simply aiming for the backboard. The idea is always to throw a quality pitch in the right location. In all situations, the pitcher's goal should be to hit the target. Just trying to throw a strike is what leads to mistake pitches—the hitter's feast. Proper approach attitudes include:

- Just me and the glove.
- I am going to reach out and put the ball in the glove.

- I am going to hit the catcher's mitt.
- I am going to hit the outside corner.

One of the plagues that often leaves pitchers behind in the minors, instead of advancing to the top, is the inability to overcome problems. For a starter, a first-inning struggle can mean giving up and simply believing he does not have his good pitches on that day. He surrenders the game. Top major leaguers learn to try to pitch past trouble, and this starts with attitude. Hall of Famer Gaylord Perry said, "There were a lot of games I pitched in that I didn't have it in the first or second inning, but I didn't get down. I told myself, 'It's coming. I am getting better, I am getting in the groove.' Most of those days I did get in the groove and keep our team close. We came from behind and won a lot of those games. Without those wins, I would never have gotten close to the magic 300-win circle." A pitcher must learn not to give up on himself even when his curve does not work or his fastball lacks the normal pop. This happens to every pitcher, and the best of them learn to find a way to get outs. Success starts with attitude.

Many pitchers also fall into trouble when they get a big lead. They alter their pitching style and forget about their off-speed pitches. Rather than thinking about getting outs, they think, "I don't want to walk anyone," or "I am going to just throw fastballs and let them hit the ball." This can cause a pitcher to lose his groove. If he needs to throw a breaking ball, he may not be able to find it. Tom Seaver said, "No matter what the score is, I pitch like it is a 1-0 game." Perry said, "I don't care what the score is, I just keep pitching. Even if I have a big lead, I am not going to 'lay it in there.' I don't want to give them a chance to get back in the game, and I don't want to build their confidence where they think they can hit me."

When the game is on the line, the normal thought process for a pitcher is to try to reach back and get a little extra on the fastball or break the curve a little more sharply. Most major lea-guers agree this does not work. The pitcher's challenge in key situations is control: self control and control of the pitch. A pitcher can develop an attitude that puts him in control of his emotions, concentration, delivery and control of the ball, and ef-fort level (staying within himself). Effort and concentration must be there at all times.

Thriving in intense situations is the product of effective atti-tudes. Many pitchers approach the clutch with attitudes such as, "If I don't get this hitter out, we lose," or "I've *got* to make a good pitch." These are negative attitudes that cause tension and serve only to apply pressure. Other pitchers approach with more positive thoughts, such as, "I'm going to be aggressive and chal-lenge this guy," or "If I get this guy out, I will win the game," or simply "I'm going to get this guy out." These are positive atti-tudes, but they are incomplete since there is no plan for success. The winning, positive approach attitudes for clutch pitching are:

• I am going to be aggressive and challenge this hitter. Now, it's just me and the glove.

• The game is on the line. My challenge is to be myself and do what I can do. I am going to forget about the batter and hit my targets.

• This pitch will decide the game. I am excited and nervous, but that's okay. This is where I want to be. This is fun time. I am going to stay loose and focused. I am going to throw the ball how and where I want.

• I will make sure that my delivery and release point are right. I will hit my spot.

Some pitchers try to combine too many attitudes as they de-liver the ball. At the time of release, the mental process should be clean, with one dominant thought. This can be, "Hit the glove" or "Be aggressive," but it must be a clear, dominating at-titude. Preparation for the pitch requires a number of attitudes, but at the time of delivery there must be one clear, focused, prevailing attitude so that the mind will be clear of confusion. Attitudes will grow and evolve as a pitcher matures. This is much of what is meant by the baseball term "learning how to pitch." Just about every young pitcher loves to show off his arm and blast fastball after fastball, but that is usually a ticket to failure in the pros. Greg Maddux made the big change in his career after watching Dodger star Fernando Valenzuela keep hitters off balance. Maddux recognized that hitters have trouble reading the speed of the ball, and changing speeds is an effective way to collect outs. His attitude toward pitching changed when he watched Valenzuela, and Maddux made success his highest value.

Pitching is very much a matter of mind-set. One of the most common statements among big leaguers is that someone has grown from being a thrower to a pitcher. This all begins with attitude—the attitude that a pitcher wants to make the adjustments that lead to consistent success at a higher level.

For a pitcher, hitter, or fielder, thriving in the clutch begins with attitude. It is the mind-set of succeeding in these situations that leads to coming through with the big hit or the big pitch that can make the difference between winning and losing. Mental toughness is a process of learning to shrug off pressure and enjoy the situation; of taking that mental edge rather than giving it away. The players who succeed in the clutch are nearly always the players who learn to love being in clutch situations. Noted clutch hitter Joe Carter once said, "It's not the pressure of the competition but the pleasure of the competition." Clutch performers learn to love the role.

CONFLICTING ATTITUDES

The benefits of positive attitude should be abundantly clear by now. Few defeatists survive in the major leagues, and virtually all successful players embrace some sort of positive attitude, whether consciously or not. It is a distinct advantage to enter situations with confidence and preparation, rather than to blunder mindlessly into challenges. But then comes the rub: what happens when attitudes conflict? What happens when an emotional attitude gets in the way of a rational attitude? What happens when two positive attitudes seem to contradict each other? This is where the whole concept grows complicated and emotions often take over, creating stress, doubt, and indecision. This is where a player of exceptional attitude will find a way to make a situation work to his advantage by determining the right attitude for the moment.

When an emotional attitude conflicts with a positive attitude. The conflict can come both on and off the field, in the clubhouse and in private life. This happens when emotions and desires get in the way of dedication to a proper attitude. For an attitude to be effective, it must command the player's dedication.

In baseball, every pitch or play requires a new commitment of attitudes. Both pitcher and hitter must approach every pitch with confidence and the expectation of success. Consistency is often the difference between major league careers and lingering in the minors; a primary reason for not establishing consistency is the inability to focus with an effective attitude on every play. A pitcher needs confidence in every pitch that he throws in order to make the results effective; a batter must believe in his ability to hit in any situation or count.

For example, a pitcher can take pride in his fastball and approach games with the attitude that he can throw it past any hitter. This is confidence and belief, generally a positive approach. Then comes the situation where it is clear that the fastball is not the best weapon. Rather, a change-up or a breaking ball would keep the hitter off balance or alter his sight line. The pitcher has a good off-speed pitch, and he knows it's the right pitch for the situation. But, subconsciously, he is so proud of that heater that his real desire is to throw the fastball. The result often becomes a no-win situation: the hitter is sitting on a fastball and crushes it, or the pitcher lacks resolve and throws a hittable breaking ball. To achieve and achieve consistently, a pitcher must believe in the pitches he throws, approaching them with determination rather than halfheartedly flinging something to the plate. Lack of *mental* resolve too often results in the inability to give full *physical* effort. Or as former Cy Young Award winner Frank Viola said, "When you doubt your pitch selection, you don't have anything. You end up throwing the 'other' pitch, and you don't give it your all because you're not really committed to it."

The same types of conflicts occur for the hitter. Many hitters take great pride in their ability to hit the fastball, so much so that even when they know the pitcher is going to throw an off-speed pitch, they still have fastball in the back of their mind. The hitter thinks, "I know he is going to throw an off-speed pitch. I will wait on it and hit it up the middle or to the opposite field." In doing this, he is taking the best attitude for the situation. But in the back of his mind he thinks, "If he tries to trick me and throw a fastball by me, I will be ready for it." The usual result of these conflicting attitudes is that the hitter is not fully committed to either pitch. No matter which pitch the pitcher throws, the hitter is just a little off.

Of course, a player must first master the fundamental skills. It does little good to have confidence in your breaking ball if all it does is hang in the hitter's eyes. Assuming the tools exist, the next step is mental commitment to each task: making the decision that throwing or hitting a certain pitch will be approached with complete determination and without being hindered by conflicting attitudes. A pitcher may step back from the rubber, slow down his thoughts, and recommit to his plan. Three-time Cy Young Award winner Randy Johnson said, "In the [2001]

NLCS, I took my time a little bit more between pitches, and I felt that it helped. At times I felt I wanted to throw the ball a little bit harder, and I found in certain cases that it would make my location be off, so I took my time between pitches and concentrated on location, more so than velocity." Johnson resolved his conflict by recognizing his need to choose location over velocity, then committing to his choice.

Hitters can do the same thing. Tune in any major league game on television and watch hitters step out of the box between pitches. After getting any signs from the third-base coach, they will talk to themselves as they look at their bat or out toward the field. The good hitters are recommitting to their plan. If a bunt play is on, they may think to themselves, "I am going to get a pitch over the plate and lay down a perfect bunt inside the first base line." The conflict for the hitter comes when he does not want to bunt but wants to hit; thus his approach lacks the necessary dedication to execute a quality bunt. It is essential that the player convince himself to be fully dedicated to each pitch or plan, removing the conflicting attitude from his mind. This is a mental challenge. It often makes the difference between a major league career and a lingering life in the minors.

This conflict of attitudes can take another form and pose moral issues. Like it or not, a part of professional baseball is the demand—in rare instances—to throw at a batter in order to protect teammates. Late in the 2001 major league season, left-handed pitcher Mike Hampton of the Rockies hit Diamondback Randy Johnson in the back. After the game, Hampton said something had to be done because Johnson had hit their best player, Larry Walker, in consecutive games and had hit a number of their hitters over the course of the season. In this day and age, most major league managers agree that a pitcher should throw only at the selected hitter's waist or buttocks, the site likely to do the least damage. Some managers will say from the shoulders down. On very rare occasions a manager may still order chin music. This is where a moral conflict can arise for the pitcher who is ordered to throw at a batter's head. Most pitchers on the professional level accept the responsibility to provide protection, and throwing at an opponent's rear is sometimes a necessary request. But throwing at an opponent's head is dangerous and life-threatening, something many pitchers at every level consider immoral. If a coach or a manager places one of the team members in the position of moral conflict, the coach or manager is simply wrong. This is more than a conflict of emotions, it is a conflict of morality. Moral conflicts dig deep at the core of a human being and can harm the relationship between the coach or manager and the team member. A player should never be placed in a position of fighting his own morality.

Attitudes may conflict off the field as well. One particularly hot 1991 August day in Arlington, Texas, Oakland catcher Terry Steinbach dragged coach Rene Lacheman and teammate Jaime Quirk to the ballpark for early work. Steinbach's footwork and throws had grown sloppy the previous few days, and he needed a work session to bring them back to form. After two and a half hours of sweating in the Texas sun, Steinbach's footwork came together, and he was again throwing on target to second base instead of bouncing throws short of the bag. It would have been much easier to wait for a more comfortable climate to correct the footwork problems, but Steinbach decided to make the adjustments immediately. He faced the attitudinal conflict of needing the work versus waiting for a more conducive climate than sizzling Arlington. Steinbach chose getting the work. In a sport where success is often dictated by the attention to detail in mechanics, practices and pre-game workouts are important in keeping a player's skills sharp.

The conflict comes when forces tear a player in different directions. If a player recognizes that he needs extra work time to conquer a mechanical problem, or needs more time in the gym for strength training, or even simply needs private time to focus and mentally prepare—but he is torn by other obligations, it creates a problem. During the 2001 season, Sean Casey of the Cincinnati Reds had a time conflict when playing at home, and it affected his game performance. Casey was hitting for a significantly higher batting average on the road than he was at home, partly because of the many family and business obligations he had when he was in Cincinnati. He was trying to spend time with his wife, who was pregnant. He was also doing community service appearances, and when he got to the park he felt a responsibility to satisfy all the fans' requests for autographs and conversation. These were all things he enjoyed doing and wanted to do regularly. Late in the second half of the season, however, he realized he had stretched his time too thin and had rushed through his game preparation. On the road he had more time to prepare mentally and physically for games, and he performed better and more consistently. For the college or high school player, this sort of conflict may have to do with homework or studying for a test versus going to the weight room or giving 100 percent focus at practice. Even a girlfriend can cause a player to be torn between obligations and emotions if she is asking him to spend more time with her instead of always playing baseball.

This is where a player must establish priorities in his mind. The player must evaluate the conflict between demands and choose his course. This does not necessarily mean that baseball always comes first. Family and personal obligations may demand priority from time to time. Studying for a test should also be given priority when conflicts arise. There may be compromises, too, where competing obligations are all squeezed into shortened time periods. But the key is to understand the importance of each situation and give full dedication and focus to each task in its proper time. Sacrifices may need to be made in order to stay focused on the prioritized task. Attempting to accomplish something with a mind clouded by other thoughts usually leads to a substandard performance. Sean Casey's game performance was compromised when he let other obligations and responsibilities interfere with the time he normally set aside for game preparation. Casey found he could manage his conflicts by setting priorities during the course of the day, leaving himself time to adequately prepare for that day's game. Establishing a list of priorities is the key to managing conflicts; giving your mind time to think about what you are doing without feeling guilty or distracted is essential for "quality time." Priorities may also change as circumstances change.

Attitudes that work together are based on giving priority to the values that are most important at a certain time. Some attitudes must have a higher priority and greater value, otherwise the player runs into constant conflict between attitudes, which leads to confusion.

Conflicting positive attitudes. Perhaps the single most difficult challenge for any player to overcome is when *positive* attitudes conflict. It is fairly easy to recognize that an attitude of "I will learn something new today in practice" is more effective than "I can't wait for batting practice, when I can stand in the outfield and tell my friends about my date last night." It is not so easy when two positive attitudes run on a collision course. This requires dedication to an attitude, a decision, and sometimes a little creativity. Sacrifices may also need to be made.

One situation is commonplace for minor league players who begin advancing through a team's player development system. A new player to professional ball often carries the attitude that he will outwork the competition and stay focused on his game plan. He also enters pro ball with the attitude, "I will fit in and be a good teammate." This often works well through Rookie ball and Class A levels, only to run into conflict at the more advanced levels. The hard worker often finds himself in a situation where more experienced teammates tell him to tone down his style a bit because he is making the rest of the team look bad with his relentless work ethic and hustle. The player then faces the conflict between "I will outwork the competition" and "I will fit in and be a good teammate."

This situation has existed for generations in professional baseball, and different players have found different solutions. The conflict of attitudes arises from veteran players who have stopped hustling because of their inability to make a major league team. Two players in particular found their own ways to deal with this conflict: Pete Rose ignored the pressure to conform; Roger Clemens came up with a creative solution.

When the Cincinnati Reds signed Pete Rose in 1961, the organization made a regular habit of signing young Cincinnati-area players to fill its minor league rosters. Rose was signed not because he was an attractive prospect but because he was from the area. When he arrived at spring training in Tampa, Florida, he had one above-average tool—his speed—plus an abundance of enthusiasm and determination. His arm strength was barely average, his defensive skills were unimpressive, and he lacked power. But Rose was always among the first to work out in the morning and the last to stop at night. When his assigned team was not scheduled to be doing anything, he would mix with another team and find some way to get extra work. Rose had been assigned to Karl Kuehl's Class D Geneva, New York, team for spring training, but one day Kuehl went over to the Triple A contest after his game ended and found Rose playing in the game. One game was not enough for Rose, so after his workouts ended he would dash over to the Triple A game and tell the veterans, "If you've had enough for today, I'd love to finish the game for you." When a veteran chose to opt out, Rose would take over for the late innings. No other young player had the nerve to make such an outlandish request, and it paid off for Rose—he got noticed and kept moving through the system.

Rose thus ignored the tacit demands to conform, and he advanced by not being afraid to be different. He chose extra work and spending time with more advanced players over team bonding. This takes some degree of courage, since he did make himself stand out from the crowd with his work ethic and relentless hustle.

Roger Clemens approached the demand to conform in a different way. At the ballpark he did all the normal work with his teammates, but he performed extra workout sessions earlier, before his teammates arrived, or away from the ballpark altogether. Clemens followed an intense physical regimen to build his body to supreme strength and prepare mentally, but he chose to do so in private rather than draw attention to himself.

This is how two legitimate star players dealt with the problem of conflicting positive attitudes. They both valued their work ethic and stuck to their attitude to outwork their competition; but Rose chose to sacrifice fitting in with some of the veteran minor league players, and Clemens found a way to get his work in without showing anybody up.

Conflicting positive attitudes can occur in many different ways. Many young players struggle with the positive attitude that they want to pull the ball and drive it for power, but they are being told and learn to believe that they should hit the ball to all fields. They are torn in their desires, and this can lead to lost swings, wasted at-bats, and even slumps. Players must learn to choose an attitude and fully commit to it.

Finding resolution. The first step in resolving conflicts is to recognize that something is wrong. Sometimes the only indication of internal conflict may be a sense of uneasiness when the player steps on the rubber or into the batter's box, or the realization that there is no clear plan of what he wants to accomplish. It may be a sense of doubt or defeat. A player must make a conscious effort to dig out those conflicting attitudes from within his mind. Otherwise he will continue to react poorly and make the wrong decisions.

It is important that the player be aware of his attitude for the situation. Some attitudes are unconscious—the feelings are there, but they haven't yet been identified or labeled—so it is imperative that a player make himself aware of his thoughts and emotions. Unconscious feelings can be powerful and leave a player perplexed as to why he did or did not do something. For example, a minor league pitcher recently acknowledged his fear about pitching inside, because he might hit the batter and put him on base. As a result, he was unable to locate his pitches inside effectively, and he got hit. Because the fear was unconscious, he was always left wondering what went wrong or why he felt so uneasy about pitching inside. Not until he identified the underlying attitude was he able to conquer the inside part of the plate.

Prioritizing attitudes is also essential in choosing the best approach. Clemens and Rose valued their work ethic most, and they adapted a strategy for it. A player must answer for himself what he values most and which attitude will make him better. Sometimes there are no perfect or easy solutions: a player must simply accept that there will be a price to pay, now and in the future. What it comes down to is this: When you select the attitude you want to focus on, approach it with dedication and resolve. You will find that without conflicting attitudes cluttering your thoughts, you will feel more confident in your actions. If you feel you are getting unsatisfactory results with your chosen attitude, you should adopt a new one. The best attitude in the world may be ineffective for a given situation, and a player must be flexible enough to change. An attitude of "I will play hard all the time" may get in the way of a hitter who is overswinging and needs a little more finesse.

These positive contradictions also occur with game approaches. One of the hardest is for a hitter who faces conflicting theories: "Be selective and wait to get your pitch" versus "Be aggressive and don't give away at-bats." Both attitudes are effective, and it is possible for an experienced hitter to become "selectively aggressive." But for many professional and amateur hitters, these two theories contradict and confuse when put together. Being selective encourages a hitter to be patient and wait for a mistake pitch over the middle of the plate. Being aggressive helps a hitter get his swing going so he can meet the ball out front and drive it, instead of getting jammed. The problem arises when a hitter who is being selective waits to start his swing until he reads the pitch—but the aggressive mentality tells him to get his swing going. Players confused between the two approaches either take good pitches to hit, or swing at poor pitches. Players even comment that they freeze up and don't know what to do. The solution is to make a choice between the attitudes in order to gain better focus and confidence at the plate. Evaluate the situation—the pitcher may dictate whether the hitter wants to be more selective or more aggressive. This is an important point: a player should select the times when it is acceptable to alter his attitude, and find the attitude that is best for the situation.

Conflicting positive attitudes are one of the greatest challenges in making attitudes an effective tool in building success in any arena. The difficulty must be approached with consideration, decisiveness, and sometimes creativity. A player must determine which attitude works best for the given situation, and then proceed with confidence in the attitude selected.

ATTITUDE DEVELOPMENT

An attitude for success must be developed and honed, brought to maturation and constantly affirmed. It is not a natural gift to be born with such an attitude; it is a skill that becomes what in baseball is called a "tool." Attitudes for success become the most important element a player takes to practice and into a game. Attitudes either help or hurt a player; there is no middle ground. In baseball, as in life, one of the key aspects of maturity is taking responsibility for actions and attitudes. People can't control the fortune or misfortune that surrounds them; they *can* control their attitudes and put themselves in a position to achieve when the opportunity arises.

The first step in asserting a positive attitude is to recognize the attitudes that you now bring to the game. A player must understand his motivations and desires in order to improve his outlook. At times you have to dig deep to get to the attitudes that are lying just beneath the surface of your conscious thoughts, in the back of your mind. The fear of looking bad or foolish usually hides inside and plays a big factor in why some players fight making adjustments. Following is a series of questions that can help you understand the evolution of your attitudes and perceptions. By sitting down and writing out the answers, you can gain a better understanding of your own attitudes.

1. How strong is my desire to be the best I can be? What price am I willing to pay? Can I work harder and put more into it? Do I want to work harder?

2. Why am I playing? What do I want to achieve by participating? Am I challenged to be the best performer I can be, or am I just trying to be better than those around me? Am I playing just to be with friends or to please or gain recognition from parents or family members?

3. Can I be a better learner? Do I have an open mind, and can I open my eyes to new opportunities to learn? Am I willing to try new things?

4. Am I treating my coaches, teammates, friends, umpires, and opponents with the same respect I'd expect from them?

5. Am I capable of following instructions? Am I doing what is expected of me?

6. Can I have better poise and self-control? Do I recognize times when a lack of poise has damaged my performance?

7. Can I be a better competitor? Am I fighting myself as well as my opponent, or am I competing with myself to do the best I can?

8. How do I want others to see me? What can I do to make it happen?

9. What are my attitudes toward all phases of the game? If I am a pitcher, do I fail to cover first base or back up plays at times? If I am a catcher, do I avoid practicing blocking balls in the dirt? If I am a position player, do I work as hard on baserunning as on hitting? If I am a hitter, what are my attitudes about being selective? Am I ignoring some of the less glamorous aspects of the game? Am I willing to give the extra effort to improve all parts of my game?

10. Am I intimidated in certain situations? Or am I the intimidator?

11. Do I ever catch myself thinking about not wanting to look bad?

After identifying where and what you want to improve, examine the attitudes concerning each by asking yourself the following questions:

1. How did I develop my current attitude? Most attitudes develop unconsciously. Many of our attitudes come when we rationalize by giving reasons and making excuses. Numerous attitudes piggyback off expectations, both our own and others. Attitudes can develop from our imaginations, from imitating the behavior of others, and from people telling us what they think our attitude should be.

2. Is a certain attitude helping or hurting me?

3. Is it in conflict with my other attitudes?
4. Which attitudes need improvement?

After determining which attitudes need adjustment, experiment with different mental approaches. Trying new attitudes to find what delivers success is just as important as experimenting with new physical techniques and mechanics to see what works best in a swing or pitching delivery. People are different and have different motivations and desires. They must find the best attitudes to give them the mental edge.

ATTITUDES AND THE INDIVIDUAL

Henry Ford, an innovator and the founder of the Ford Motor Company, said, "Think you can, think you can't. Either way, you'll be right."

Attitude is really that simple. A winning attitude helps a player succeed; a defeatist attitude nearly always leads to failure. A player who expects to fail usually reaches his expectations, no matter the talent level. A player who embraces a positive attitude can go as far as his ability will carry him—in some cases, well beyond. Effective attitudes become the mental edge in conquering adversity and making the adjustments necessary to compete. Attitude can be the difference between persevering to success and surrendering when something goes wrong.

"This game is more mental than physical," NFL great Paul Hornung said. "Every club is loaded with guys who have something physical or they wouldn't be here. It's the guys who are right mentally who come out on top."

The individual has to decide what attitude he wants to embrace, on the field, in the classroom, in business, and in life.

3

CHARACTER AND VALUES

Curt Schilling came to the major leagues adoring the good times and dedicated to enjoying the aura that surrounds being a big-league pitcher. Sporting an earring and long hair that he once dyed blue, Schilling sampled the pleasures of the majors with the Orioles, then the Astros. A twenty-four-year-old kid in a big man's body, he lived by his talent and loved the lifestyle, bothering little with those nasty distractions of preparation. "I was at a point in my career where I thought I could just show up and pitch every fifth day and everything would take care of itself. I didn't realize there was a lot more to this game off the field than on," Schilling says. After the 1991 season, he stopped by the weight room at the Astrodome, where Houston resident Roger Clemens happened to be working out.

"I was just kind of wandering around the weight room, at a bright, young age, and I was told Roger wanted a few minutes of my time," Schilling recalls. "About an hour and fifteen minutes later, with no butt left, I walked back to the other side of the weight room. I can't repeat a lot of what he said. It was one of those conversations your father has with you when you're going down the wrong path, and it saves your life if you're able to make a right turn."

Schilling sums up the chewing out with three axioms: "Respect your teammates, respect your team, respect the game." Clemens recalls telling Schilling he needed to approach the game with greater devotion. "I told him, 'If you're not, you're going to put your ten to twelve years in the game and just be wasting your time.' He had the body and the prototype to be a great power pitcher, but there's thousands of those stories of guys who waste it all," Clemens says.

Schilling took the little talk to heart. It was the turning point in a career that would lead him to become one of the top pitchers of his time, a dominant force on the Arizona Diamondbacks' 2001 world championship team and the co-MVP of the World Series, then excelling for Boston's 2004 World Series winner.

What happened to Schilling was a change in values. Blessed with enormous talent, he could have cruised through a routine career, collected a pension, and satisfied himself with mediocrity. Instead he changed his values and developed his character. "He's gone from being the least-prepared pitcher I'd ever met to the most prepared," said Bob Melvin, who caught Schilling with the Orioles when he first came up, then served as a Diamondbacks coach on their World Series team. Schilling arrived in the major leagues with poor values, then developed into both a better pitcher and a better person by changing his values. He became a major force in contributing to and helping organize fund-raisers for charities, and he has made an effort to give back to the community some of what he has acquired through his success.

Curt Schilling decided what was important to him. Every player faces this same decision process: choosing what is important,

A talk from Clemens was the turning point in Curt Schilling's career.

what takes priority. This is really what values are all about. Every player must make the decision: "What is important to me? What do I really care about?"

Achievement usually comes to those who are goal-oriented. The touch of destiny most likely falls on those who set goals, then make reaching those goals the priority in their lives. Goals fall into two categories: destination goals, such as "I want to be a major league ballplayer," and journey goals, the steps along the way, such as "I want to improve my footwork on defense." The journey goals make the destination goals possible.

To establish and reach goals, a player and a person must determine what they value, what is important to them, then establish those as a priority. If becoming a successful baseball player is the ultimate goal, then a player must set his priorities in life in order to reach that goal. It is not about mouthing the right words on what is important, it is about how the player devotes his time and energy. Giving lip service to a goal does not help reach an end.

You can understand what is most important to you by seeing where you devote your time and energy. If achievement is the value, it will take priority over playing with the Gameboy, hanging out in bars, making sure you see every new movie that comes through town, or fooling around with drugs. It demands mental toughness to establish priorities and stick to them.

Baseball players deal with three types of values: values related to how they play the game; team values; and personal values. Values related to playing the game include their personal approaches, preparation, and effort. Team values concern how the player functions within the framework of a team. Personal values are the core of who the person is and wants to become: Is he honest? Truthful? Does he make excuses?

Many attitudes grow from values. A player who values playing good defense is more likely to devote the extra time to becoming a good defender. A player who values hustle will be far more likely to run out ground balls or break up double plays. When Curt Schilling made the change from rambunctious youth to dedicated pitcher, it came because he changed his values about how he approached the game. Schilling possessed the natural ability to survive in the majors as an adequate pitcher, but his change in values led to a change in attitude that made the difference between stardom and mediocrity. The mental edge that comes with effective attitudes is born upon recognizing the value that is behind that attitude.

Acquiring mental toughness demands that a player confront his own values and determine what is important to him. These can be particularly tough decisions because they involve the commitment of time, concentration, passion, and energy that are not always in abundant supply. There will not always be enough time and energy for extra hours in the weight room plus an evening in the bars. There will be times players must choose among their needs and desires to reach a higher level. Pressures pull athletes in different directions, and making choices can be very difficult.

Establishing values becomes an effort for a person or player to determine who he wants to be, both on the field and off. This is what Curt Schilling confronted after his meeting with Roger Clemens—he was forced to decide whether he wanted to strive for excellence or maintain the ordinary. The values he chose helped him to grow both as a player and a person.

Values will change throughout our lives as we acquire more experience, learn to focus on our goals, and gain new priorities. We constantly reevaluate what is important to us, which is a natural process. This is sometimes done unconsciously, reacting to the events, personalities, or circumstances that surround us. The mentally tough player takes the advantage by recognizing the situation and keeping his values in order, and by occasionally sitting down to reconsider his values and how they apply to the current events in his life.

The combination of values and principles by which a person lives, plus the ability to sustain and practice these qualities, are what make up character. The legendary NFL coach Vince Lombardi said, "Mental toughness is character in action." That is a high measure for the value of building a character worthy of esteem. A person can make the conscious decision to improve his character by deciding to change his values and principles. The examples are numerous, from President Theodore Roosevelt, who began life as a sickly child and decided to build his future around a philosophy of vigor and positive attitudes, to Benito Santiago, who went from being considered one of baseball's bad apples to a legitimate team leader with the Giants and Royals after a car crash nearly ended his career and forced him to reconsider his values. Character can strengthen or erode, and it is a challenge for us all to build the character we want, to become the type of person we choose to be. At any point in a person's life, he can determine that he will become a better human being with qualities that will improve the way he plays.

VALUES RELATED TO PLAYING THE GAME

There is no mistaking it: playing in the big leagues is fun. Just about everyone you meet wants to give you something, women want to entertain you, fans are humbled in your presence, reporters from every publication—from your old high school newspaper to *Sports Illustrated*—want to write about how wonderful you are. There are so many demands for time that it can be rough to fit a little work into that dazzling social schedule.

In 1982 a few members of the Minnesota Twins learned just that lesson. Gary Gaetti, Kent Hrbek, Gary Ward, and Tom Brunansky were all in their first or second major league season, and they started good-timing and big-leaguing it—playing the role of half-hustle on the field by trotting after they hit fly balls and grounders, and by taking only a courtesy slide into second to avoid offending a veteran rather than busting hard to break up a double play. Hrbek, Gaetti, and Brunansky hit the party circuit hard, often arriving at the park the next day showing the signs of wear. All four would spend their time chatting up opposing players around the batting cages or quipping with reporters rather than concentrating on hitting or defensive drills. Life was good. Baseball was, well, not so good.

The issue came to a head in Seattle that June. The four young players went off on an all-day fishing trip before arriving at the ballpark smelling of salt and fish, looking as if they had not slept for a couple of days. The quartet stumbled through a miserable game.

After the game, one of the coaches pulled the four players aside for a little lesson in baseball. "We're a young team here, and you have a chance to show what you can do. If you were playing anyplace else, what you did tonight would be a ticket back to the minors," they were told. "If you go around kissing ass instead of getting ready to do the job, chances are you're going to screw up. Baseball doesn't owe you shit. When you get called up, if you think they owe you a job, you're wrong. You've got to earn the next time you play, you've got to deserve that next at-bat. If you don't get your acts together, you will be gone, history."

The gifted quartet took the discussion seriously. They sat down and took inventory of themselves and made a list outlining how they would play the game and behave in the future. Fans, reporters, family, friends, and the opposition might think they were A-holes in the future, but if that was the demand, they would pay the price.

The list that Gaetti, Hrbek, Brunansky, and Ward composed was:

1. **Be ready to play and be at my best every day**. If that means telling friends, family, etc., that I can't stay out after a game, and having them thinking and telling me I have a big head, so be it. I will be the A-hole, but I will be rested and prepared when I go to the park.

2. **Nothing or nobody will get in the way of or distract me from having quality practice and going through my pre-game routines properly**. If that means the fans get mad at me for not coming over to sign autographs, or reporters get pissed at me for not giving them the time and answers they want, that's okay, I am willing to pay that price. "I'll be an A-hole."

3. **Play hard all the time.** I will run out every ball, be alert, always back up, be ready and get great jumps on every pitch, always anticipate (never assume), give it everything I have until the wee hours in the morning if that is what it takes. When I go in to break up a DP, I'll take them out hard, because the next time I am coming in to break up a DP, I want them to remember it and be aware of my footsteps. No more "Mr. Nice Guy." I play to whip ass; to win. If they think I'm an A-hole because of the way I play, I'm willing to pay that price.

4. **I will be the intimidator, no one will intimidate me.** When they knock me down or drill me, I will get up, take my time, get back in, not allowing myself to be upset or distracted (they will not get in my head). Then I will be ready to put my "businessman's swing" on the next good pitch.

5. **No matter what happens, I will keep my poise and act professionally.**

6. **I will be a good teammate.** I will encourage, support, and make sure everyone is in the game.

The four young Twins confronted their own values. They had to decide what mattered most to them: whether all-day fishing trips and late-night escapades mattered more than winning ball games and building major league careers. From the time all four entered professional ball, they had heard coaches talk about those six points, but when they arrived in the majors, life became too much fun and they lost track of their values and priorities. On that day of reckoning, with fish scales under their fingernails, they recognized they must put their values in order if they were to remain big leaguers, and if they were to win.

They taped the list in one of their lockers, home and road, hidden behind clothing and uniforms on the hangers, where it could not be seen by visitors in the clubhouse. When any of them needed the inspiration, he would look at the list to remind himself just what he valued. The four would discuss the points among themselves after games, evaluating whether they had

The Minnesota A-holes (from left, Kent Hrbek, coach Karl Kuehl, Gary Ward, Gary Gaetti, Tom Brunansky) had to decide what mattered most to them.

succeeded on each point every day. As another reminder, they had T-shirts made up with OFFICIAL A-HOLE emblazoned across the front to remind them that they would accept being considered A-holes if that was what it took.

The improvement quickly became obvious, and other Twins saw and reflected the attitude. Rather than heading back to the minors or becoming accomplished deep-sea fishermen and party-hardy masters, all four went on to quality major league careers as the Twins contended through most of the 1980s.

The saga of the Minnesota A-holes is about players confronting their own values and deciding what matters most to them. All four recognized that becoming successful major leaguers meant far more than enjoying the good times that can accompany life in the majors. It is the same exercise that just about every ballplayer must confront again and again during his playing days, again and again during his life.

Each of the Twins' points represented a value related to playing the game. The first point presented the value of "Be my best every day." This can be far more difficult than it seems when fans, family, femmes, and the rest are competing for a player's attention. A player must learn to say no to invitations, hopefully politely. A mentally tough player must value his rest and preparation above good times.

The second point shows the value of quality practice. Success usually demands concentration on detail, and that comes from devotion to workouts.

The third point illustrates the value of playing to win, from the first pitch to the last, no matter the score. The Twins players recognized that running out ground balls and breaking up double plays can be the difference between winning and losing ball games.

The fourth point deals with an important essence of mental toughness: the decision that the player will be the intimidator and refuse to be intimidated. This can mean both boldness and restraint: glaring down an opponent and refusing to be glared down by another.

The Twins' fifth point emphasizes the value of maintaining poise and professionalism. The ability to roll with tough times makes for consistency.

The sixth point places importance on being a good teammate, which is the concept of team values.

The process of maturing as an athlete demands confronting one's values. When the four talented Twins faced their values, they came away with a purpose and a plan that would carry through their careers. Each individual player will have a series of values related to playing the game. These affect how a player prepares and plays the game, what he practices, how he works, and how he plays. If a player values being in top shape to optimize his ability, he will spend more time conditioning. If a pitcher believes he learns and improves from charting the opposition, he will pay closer attention to the chore.

If a player places a high value on hustle and intensity, he will play with commitment and pride. If a player does not consider these important, he will not play that way. If a player values proper execution—such as hitting the cutoff man and putting the ball on the ground on a hit-and-run—he is more likely to execute properly. If a manager or coach emphasizes certain aspects of the game, he places value on them.

During the 2002 season, Derek Jeter's statistics were not up to his previous highs, and he took a scolding from some writers. Jeter was undaunted. "I don't care about those numbers as long as I win," he told *New York Daily News* reporter Anthony McCarron. "There are ways to win that you don't get numbers for. If you hit a ground ball to move a guy over from second to third, and then the next guy hits a ground ball and gets an RBI, you don't hear about the guy who moved the runner over. I'm hitting second, and some of those other [big-name shortstops] are batting third. Part of my job is moving guys over and scoring runs."

Jeter places his highest value on doing the little things that make his team succeed, sometimes at the expense of his own statistics. He has consciously decided what is most important to him, and he remains true to that course. Many major league players today place a higher value on their statistics than on doing the little things that it takes to win. Even at the minor league level, some agents tell players to focus on improving certain statistics because it will help them in negotiating the next contract.

Since people are different, they are destined to have different values and value systems. One way a player can understand his own values is to examine how much thought he gives each aspect of his game and what he practices most. If his coach of-

Derek Jeter: "There are ways to win that you don't get numbers for."

fered him the chance to construct his own one-hour practice session, how would he do it? Would most of the time be devoted to hitting, say fifty minutes for hitting and only ten minutes for taking grounders? How much of the hitting practice would be spent on situational hitting? How much to playing long ball? Would the workout include baserunning and bunting?

Values related to playing the game include:

Work ethic. This is particularly important in baseball because it is a sport where repetition and training are critical for improvement. Natural talent can carry a player only so far before someone must learn the proper footwork or better throwing technique to play defense well. A player must ask himself if he is willing to devote the time necessary to improve to the next level.

Proper execution. The amount of value a player places on executing different skills and elements of his game will determine how much he focuses and works on them. For example, when a pitcher does not place a very high value on being effective with a change-up, he will not work at it and develop the pitch. When a hitter does not think it is important to know the strike zone and have good plate discipline, he will not have the determination that it takes to learn that skill.

Fortitude. This is the strength of mind that allows one to endure adversity and stand up to difficult tests. Colloquially it can be called guts or backbone. It demands backbone to stand up to a teammate who fails to hustle or is a bad influence on the team, or to a coach should it become necessary. Perhaps the most visible display of guts came when Dodger shortstop Pee Wee Reese stood up to his teammates and to opposing players in support of Jackie Robinson. His actions were those of fortitude and courage.

Tenacity. This means sticking through a task to completion. A player must ask himself if he is willing to fight through the frustration to learn a new skill or improve, or simply to remain motivated when things are going badly.

Taking responsibility. It is easy to avoid responsibility for flaws, errors, and mistakes by blaming others and making excuses. The big problem comes when you make those excuses to yourself. By taking responsibility for your actions, you assert control over what can be accomplished.

Enthusiasm. The player has an advantage if he can muster up the emotions to try to perform well in every game or workout. This is difficult—no catcher, for example, has ever enjoyed spending hours practicing blocking balls in the dirt. Enthusiasm may come easily during the big game at the end of the year, but it is often more difficult to muster on a rainy night in Waterloo in low A ball. There will be those days when the player wakes up feeling lazy, tired, or just out of sorts, and the mood carries over.

It happens to everyone. Enthusiasm is a discipline that has to be reinforced through difficult times. It is also a trait that virtually all professional coaches recognize and admire.

Competitiveness. Some of the desire to compete and test one's abilities against others may come naturally, but placing a high value on competitiveness increases the ability to compete.

Preparedness. This covers both body and mind. It means putting in practice time on the field and mental time off the field. For pitchers it can mean taking seriously the job of charting and watching opposing hitters when not pitching. For hitters it can mean watching films of both his own swing and that of opposing players. In modern major league baseball, most players highly value preparation.

Rest. Different people require different amounts of rest and relaxation. It is sometimes essential to get away from the rigors of public life to spend a day fishing to recharge, or simply an evening vegging out in front of the TV to relax. Or it can be vital to rest the body to help recover from the nagging injuries that are part of any baseball season. There is a difference between necessary diversion and laziness, and that is a line the individual must assess for himself.

Maintaining values is no easy chore. It can require a great deal of self-talk to build enthusiasm on a muggy night in Cincinnati. Or it can be difficult for some players to slow down long enough to rest a nagging injury. But if a player places a high value on such elements as enthusiasm, work ethic, and preparedness, he will work to make it happen. Mack Newton is a martial arts and fitness instructor in Phoenix who served as a mental coach and fitness adviser for the Chicago Cubs and now tutors players from several organizations. Newton will accept nothing less than full-bore enthusiasm from his charges. His daily classes begin by his asking a simple question to his students: "How do you feel?"

There is only one acceptable answer, and it must be boomed out with energy and enthusiasm: "I FEEL GREAT," the students must reply, whether they feel great, good, or downright downtrodden. It does not matter how Newton's students may really feel, it is about how they will build their enthusiasm to perform. While they are in his class or performing on the field, they will learn to take the mental edge of expelling their burdens and "feel great" for that period of time. It is an element of mental toughness to learn to muster enthusiasm for games in even the most dreary conditions.

Newton had to learn the hard way: he was a Vietnam combat veteran whose wounds forced artificial replacements for both hips. Despite the handicap, he returned to become a martial arts coach and a private trainer for professional athletes. "Every morning when I wake up, I say to myself, 'I feel great,'" Newton says, dragging out the "great" into five syllables. Through this mental exercise, he has managed to create an energy and enthusiasm that he carries through his daily routine.

Around baseball, an oft-used expression for building excitement is, "Fake it until you make it." The act of trying to build enthusiasm usually leads to real enthusiasm. Maintaining values and priorities can be difficult, but if enthusiasm and hard work matter to a player, he will work to make them happen.

Below are a series of positive attitudes related to playing baseball. Every player should ask himself how many of these value-attitudes are present when he is playing baseball, and if he is placing enough value on them.

I will hustle all the time, no matter the situation, and play with intensity. This attitude represents the value of playing with *enthusiasm*. Fans, coaches, and teammates all recognize and appreciate the player who plays hard all the time.

I will do what it takes to be prepared both mentally and physically for practice and games. This attitude represents *preparedness*. Schilling keeps a notebook on opposing hitters and reviews videos of hitters on his laptop to help him prepare for his turn in the rotation. He understands the value of going into a game with a plan of attack instead of just showing up and hoping to have a good game.

I will look and act like a professional during practice and games. This reflects the value of *pride*. Cal Ripken's reputation in baseball is one of dignity and class because of how he looked and carried himself on the playing field. Part of being a leader and a role model is setting a good example for others.

I can compete with anybody; no one is too good for me to beat. This reflects the value of *competitiveness,* which means playing to win every time. A true competitor believes in his ability to persevere and win the battle no matter what the situation is. In fact, when a competitor ends up on the losing side of a game, he feels he still could have won if the game had lasted one more inning.

I will be a good teammate. This places a value on being a *trustworthy* teammate, which means taking care of yourself on and off the field, taking responsibility to make the big play to help your team win, being a supportive teammate when you are not in the game or when you are playing poorly, and not being a disruptive force in the clubhouse or dugout with either your mouth or your actions.

I will make sure my body and mind are rested so I can play at my best. Being properly *rested* for games and practices is obviously essential for peak performance, but it is not always possible or a priority for players. For the student athlete who has homework and tests, he must simply do his best to be rested and grind out as much energy as possible during games. But for other ballplayers, it may mean deciding between turning in at a decent hour and getting a good night's sleep versus going out with the guys and partying well into the night.

Values become part of the package that makes up the person and how they are viewed by those around them. When Tom Glavine joined the New York Mets for spring training in 2003, teammates were quickly impressed by his work ethic. "That's all part of building up that winning tradition and respect that you want," Glavine told the *New York Post*. "You're not going to get respect from people unless you earn it, and you earn it by carrying yourself the right way as an individual and a team. You go out there, you hustle, you do what you're supposed to do, and when you win the game, well, you act like you meant to win the game."

TEAM VALUES

On a September night in Baltimore, near the end of the 1998 season, a little looper fell into left field, eluding Yankee left fielder Ricky Ledee, center fielder Chad Curtis, and shortstop Derek Jeter. Angrily, pitcher David Wells lifted his hands to his hips and peered into the dugout, showing 48,113 fans that he did not much like being let down by his defense. Jeter immediately stepped to the mound and told Wells, "We don't do that stuff here. That's not right and you know it. We don't do that if you give up a run. We're all out here trying. That was baloney." Wells apologized the next day, as Jeter told the story.

The championship Yankee teams of the late 1990s placed high value on what might be called teamsmanship, the collective responsibility of performing together as a cohesive unit and not showing up teammates. This is not valued as highly in some other organizations, but there is no question that the teamsmanship and chemistry of the Yankees is part of what led to consistent success during their streak of championships.

In becoming part of a team, every player takes on a responsibility to the team, a collective responsibility. This ranges from the obvious—attending games and practices—to more subtle aspects such as supporting struggling teammates. After reliever Byung-Hyun Kim allowed game-ending home runs in consecutive games to the Yankees during the 2001 World Series, teammates gathered around to console and support him. It was not because of long-standing bonds of friendship—Kim, a native Korean, could barely converse with the other players. It was because athletes become teammates on the field and in the clubhouse.

This can take on different dynamics, from support to confrontation. Being a good teammate can demand confronting a player whose poor preparation or attitude damage the team as a whole, and it means cheering your teammates' achievements. The Oakland A's make it a regular habit for all players to congratulate a teammate after a home run, a big play, or even properly executing to advance a runner. This was considered bush league in baseball just a couple of decades ago.

Team values include:

• I will be loyal to my team. That means I will play to win, not just to make myself look good.

• Being loyal means I will not show up my teammates when they make mistakes or fail to execute.

• I will know my job and attempt to execute it effectively. This means if I am told to bunt, I will take my best shot rather than fouling it off and hoping for the hit sign. Or I will give myself up to advance a runner.

• I am reliable. If I am expected to do something or be somewhere, you can count on me. I will make the adjustments that are necessary to execute consistently.

Perhaps the most basic team value of all is simply playing hard: running out ground balls, not standing at the plate to watch almost home runs bounce off the fence, and the like. "I always thought there was a certain way you play the game. You go out and give a hundred percent every day," Sean Casey says. "Dave Collins, a coach I once had, said, 'If you can't give your teammates four seconds down the line [running out a ground ball], you shouldn't be playing the game.'" It's really that simple: when a player gives away an out because he failed to hustle, he is cheating his teammates.

PERSONAL VALUES AND CHARACTER

Ruben Rivera had long been one of those can't-miss prospects who kept finding a way to miss. He was loaded with ability, but he could never put it together to reach stardom. When he came to spring training with the Yankees before the 2002 season, it was with a chance to revitalize his career and earn great financial rewards. During the early weeks, a scandal broke when gloves, bats, and other items began disappearing from his teammates' lockers and showing up for sale. It was discovered that Rivera had been stealing and selling the goods to a memorabilia dealer for a quick cash return. Rivera's actions outraged the Yankee clubhouse and left the players angered to distraction. Rivera was arbitrarily released.

In another incident several years ago, a highly renowned star went on the disabled list and skipped a road trip so he could concentrate on a daily therapy routine, vowing that he would approach rehab with intensity. When his teammates returned, they learned that the superstar had skipped every therapy session and that his condition had not improved. A delegation of players went into the manager's office and demanded their star be traded because he refused to do his part to make the team a winner.

Tim Johnson, manager of the Toronto Blue Jays in 1998, falsely claimed to have served in the military in Vietnam and regaled his team with dramatic war stories. When all this was found to be a lie, Johnson lost the confidence of his players and suffered severe public criticism from the athletes he guided. He lost the team, then he lost his job.

Character matters. Players learn—sometimes the hard way—that character makes a difference both on the field and in the clubhouse. Thieves, slackers, and liars do not earn the respect of their teammates and can find their careers short-circuited or derailed altogether. In the case of Rivera, he will forever carry a stain wherever his career takes him, and he can never really expect to gain the respect of his teammates. He threw away a huge opportunity with the Yankees in order to pick up a few quick bucks. Reputations take years to build and only minutes to destroy. When someone decides to engage in reputation-busting action, he may continue to pay a heavy price.

Character flaws and poor personal attitudes may disrupt an entire team as well as undermine an individual career. When a player's off-field actions become a primary topic in the clubhouse, it distracts from the task at hand—playing competitive baseball. If a player is arrested for drug possession, or caught in some other scandal, the entire team can be dragged down simply by being distracted and knowing that their teammate has let them down. At the college and professional level, this will involve media scrutiny and place the accused player's teammates in the difficult position of answering tough questions.

On September 9, 2002, Boston outfielder Manny Ramirez created a stir around the team when, after hitting a comebacker to the Devil Rays' pitcher, Ramirez simply turned and headed for the dugout. He didn't even pretend to run out the ground ball. The Red Sox were in the midst of a chase for a wild card playoff spot, and the lack of hustle by a $20-million-a-year player became a topic among both the players and the press. Ramirez apologized to his teammates, but the mutters continued among the team as it quickly fell from contention. If a player places his teammates in a position of making excuses—to themselves, the press, and management—for his actions, he is letting his team down.

Attitudes are built on character and values. It is easy to mouth effective attitudes but much more difficult to live up to the challenge of putting them into action. Character involves fortitude, tenacity, and inner strength to make those attitudes work to advantage. Character is built on a combination of principles and values, plus the ability to adhere to these principles. Principles are the great standards by which we function in society—for example, the biblical Golden Rule of "Do unto others as you would have them do unto you." That means, simply, treating those you meet with the same degree of respect and fairness with which you wish to be treated. Principles include honesty, truthfulness, fairness, honor, and courage. In this instance, honor means, basically, being in the right. Courage can mean both having the strength to meet challenges and to make amends after mistakes.

People can develop their character by dedicating themselves to principles and values. Almost all of us go through a period when we sit down and reevaluate our direction and our lives as a whole. Sometimes this is just part of the maturing process. Often it follows a life-changing event, such as being fired from a job, cut from a team or traded, or a traumatic experience such as a car crash, jail time, or the death of a close friend or family member. These evaluations, if honest, usually result in a change in our priorities. For Curt Schilling, that change came with the severe butt-chewing from Roger Clemens and Schilling's reevaluation of his direction.

Outstanding athletes face a difficult test in developing great character. Almost from childhood they are adored and feted, told they are wonderful, and treated as if they are superior beings.

When they reach maturity, they are then asked to be humble, respectful role models for children, when often they are just a few years beyond childhood themselves. What may be most amazing is that so many major leaguers actually do manage to develop superior character while living in this fishbowl. The likes of Schilling, Tim Hudson, Derek Jeter, and Luis Gonzalez prove that players can become outstanding individuals as well as great players. It is an enormous challenge to maintain the qualities that make up great character, but those who best meet that challenge will emerge as the successful leaders among their teammates and earn the highest respect in the game. Outstanding character is not always necessary in becoming a great player; it is almost always essential in becoming a great team leader, manager, or college coach.

In recent years on several occasions, professional and amateur athletes have run into trouble with the law for aggressive behavior off the playing field. Some highly competitive athletes see virtually everything in life in terms of winning and losing. They take mundane matters as a challenge to their manhood and refuse to compromise or even reevaluate for fear they will be deemed weaklings or losers if they do not get their way. At times the personal attitudes and feelings that help push them to be their best in athletics have a negative effect in their personal lives, even making them appear childish and petulant. If a player is to succeed as a person, he must learn to use his aggressiveness to his advantage rather than to his detriment.

To understand the importance of character, a player should look around at those he admires and see what accounts for his admiration. Does he admire a manager because he has been honest and fair? Does he avoid a teammate because he has been stealing from his locker? Does he respect a coach who promises to help with a workout, then bails out on him? Rarely will you ever hear a player express admiration for someone who tells grand whoppers and gets away with it, or lift a toast to a coach who shrugs off his workload. By determining the qualities a player finds admirable in others, an athlete can strive to improve himself and his own character.

Every player will face difficult issues when acquaintances try to lead him in a misdirection—doing drugs, cheating in school, or a multitude of other mistakes. Author and business analyst Larry Wilson sums up the problem by saying, "Peer pressure encourages people to do something in their best interest, not yours." Peer pressure does affect athletes, and it is important for players to realize that those who do the pressing usually have an ulterior motive.

Most achievers in any arena become aware of their principles and values, and regularly stop to organize their priorities, to decide what is most important to them at that time and for the future. Priorities can change as situations change—for example, marriage and children will force a change in priorities, as will a trade or moving from college ball to the professional ranks. Each player must understand his own values and determine priorities for them.

The early years of the new century have provided a public education in principles and standards. Several corporate leaders have been caught engaging in illegal and unethical business practices and have had their careers shattered. George O'Leary lost the football coaching job at Notre Dame when the university discovered that his resumé was highly exaggerated. Several journalists were caught faking their source material and fired from their jobs. Jayson Blair made up information in stories for the *New York Times*, leading to upheaval at the nation's most respected newspaper. Ruben Rivera faced humiliation for his thievery. Such public examples illustrate the risk people take when they engage in actions of dubious character. Even someone who has little regard for telling the truth should recognize that getting caught in a lie can have disastrous effects. A mentally tough player will be at a distinct advantage if he takes the time to list and understand the principles that matter to him, and to set priorities on his values.

General Norman Schwarzkopf says, "If it ever came to a choice between compromising my moral principles and the performance of my duties, I know I'd go with my moral principles." Maintaining principles demands mental toughness, and much of the respect we derive—from others and from ourselves—comes from our ability to stand by those principles we believe to be important.

ONE PLAYER ESTABLISHES HIS VALUES

Sean Casey had the advantage of a good upbringing and an early work ethic. Early on he learned that riding on his ability alone would not suffice, and he made every effort to get the most from his talents. Casey is one of those players who has his head screwed on right. This is about as good a reputation as a player can have.

"I think I really started learning work ethic when I was fourteen or fifteen," Casey says. "When I was a freshman in high school, I wasn't playing that much, and I complained to my dad. He said, 'Maybe you ought to work harder so they'll have to play you.' So then I used to go after school to the batting cages and hit. I hit and hit and hit. I saw that same work ethic in my father. He was a salesman for a chemical company, and he was always up early in the morning or working late to succeed at his job."

Even with that background, Casey has spent his college and professional careers reexamining the values and priorities that would lead him to achievement. From his teens he knew that he wanted to be not just a professional baseball player but a top-level player. He balanced that goal with the knowledge that he would need a secondary plan if pro baseball did not work, and he actively pursued his education. For Casey, accomplishment was about evaluating priorities and finding the path to his goals.

Casey grew up near Pittsburgh and played baseball at the University of Richmond before becoming the second-round draft pick of the Cleveland Indians in 1995. While his destination goal—the desire to play in the majors—remained solid, his priorities and journey goals evolved as he matured and as circumstances changed.

"Back when I was eighteen, nineteen, my priorities were different. I did what I had to do in school. My parents paid a lot of money for me to go to Richmond and do well in school. But I don't think I ever passed up going out and having a good time or going to a rock concert instead of studying for a test. There was a time when I was eighteen when I didn't do the things I should have done. As I get older, I realize that maybe I didn't do as well in my freshman and sophomore years as I did later because my priorities were different. When you get away from your parents, meeting new friends and enjoying college life, you make some decisions that maybe aren't the best decisions. As you grow older, the things that seem important in your freshman and sophomore years aren't as important in your junior and senior years. Instead of going out that night, you stay home and study. You're thinking, 'Next year, I've got to go out and get a job. I've got to be able to support myself. I've got to get my own place. I've got to really know in this accounting class how to do the numbers because I'll be using it before long.' I think that's where your priorities change. The first couple of years you're adjusting to college; it's a new experience. Your junior and senior years you're about to be done with college. Now it's for real."

Sean Casey: "I always looked for people who had their priorities where I had my priorities."

Casey played three years at Richmond before signing with the Indians. During the off-seasons he took classes to chip away at his degree, and he actually returned to college full-time after his 1998 rookie season with the Reds to earn his degree in speech communication. Considering the demands placed on professional baseball players, returning to college called for extreme self-discipline. During his rise through the minors, Casey gained another education in priorities. Minor league life holds many lures. Often the players become local celebrities of a sort, and there is always an opportunity to go out with teammates and new friends to explore the local nightlife. Many professional careers have fallen apart in the saloons of minor league towns.

"When you're in pro ball, you're on your own," Casey said. "Now you get a paycheck every month—not much, but you get a little bit of money. It's tougher for guys out of high school who are eighteen years old and have never been away from their families. They're going out, having a good time, maybe staying out late and having one too many drinks. All of a sudden they're playing 140 games. Now is when you have to get your priorities straight: Do I want to be a big-league ballplayer, or am I looking to hang out in the places I shouldn't hang out, with the guys I shouldn't be hanging out with?

"That was a big thing for me. I had to pick my friends. My father used to say, 'Show me your friends and I'll tell you who you are.' I think that's big with your teammates: show me your friends on the team and I'll tell you who you are. Who you hang out with is ultimately who you become. I always looked for people who had their priorities where I had my priorities."

For Casey there would be times when team bonding would become a priority. In Class A, every Thursday the team would get together as a team. "I'd make that a night to go out and enjoy the camaraderie off the field," he said. "There were other times I'd say, 'I've got to get ready for the game.' Sleep's so important in the minor leagues. Those bus rides are long, and there are days when you travel and you get off a fourteen-hour bus ride and your back's a little tight. The better you take care of yourself, the more you're giving yourself every opportunity to succeed."

An important part of Casey's maturation process was to learn to control his temper and stop making public displays of his failures. "In the minors, after a bad at-bat, I used to come in and throw my helmet; it was like the end of the world if I struck out. I realize now it's a long season—it's 600 at-bats, 162 games. One at-bat, one week, one month is not going to make or break your season. I may not have done as well as I wanted on that one at-

bat, but I'm not going to come back and go crazy. It's too stressful. As I get older, it's more of an effort to get all wound up. In
the minors you do stupid things. You come back and punch the
dugout. I'm lucky I didn't break a hand.

"Something else I learned was how stupid it is to swear all
the time. When I was coming up in the minors, every other word
was an F-bomb. In the Arizona Fall League in '97 there were
seventeen grandparents, seventeen eighty-five-year-old women,
and twenty scouts in the stands. Nobody was there. I'd make an
out and come back to the dugout and scream swear words at the
top of my lungs. My coach Jeff Datz said, 'Case, are you listening to yourself? There are fifty-four people in the stands and
you're screaming obscenities. It sounds kind of funny doesn't it?
It sounds kind of stupid.' I said, 'You're exactly right.' I thought,
'What kind of example am I setting? I can't get that at-bat back,
and I've got to move on.' Also, I knew that if I was going to be a
major leaguer, I'd be a role model on TV. Whether you like it or
not, you have a lot of little kids watching you and a lot of people
who look up to you. If I go out and swear my head off, some little kid thinks it's okay. Learning not to get so upset and cutting
down on swearing are two things that have changed a lot."

By understanding his priorities through the minor leagues,
Casey made a rapid rise and broke in with the Indians in a 1997
September call-up, before being traded to the Reds after the
season. The major leagues offered a new series of challenges for
a young player with the desire to be both a star and a good guy.
He also acquired new responsibilities—after his rookie season,
he married his fiancée, Mandi, then had a son after the 2001
campaign. He found himself in a juggling act, trying to come up
with enough time to do everything.

"My ultimate goal was to play in the big leagues. And one of
my other ultimate goals was to be married and have a family.
And now I have both of these. My relationship with my wife is a

lot of work, and my job—baseball—is a lot of work. So they kind of go hand in hand. It takes a lot of effort. I sit down with my wife and say, 'This is the off-season. I need to go out today: I need to hit, I need to lift, I need to take some ground balls. What time can we get together? We can meet for lunch, and I'll be home for dinner. Nothing that's good comes easily. If you want to have that relationship with a woman, and you want to be a big-league ballplayer and have some success in the game, you're going to have to prioritize. You can do both, but you'd better keep analyzing and learn to put them in one package."

One of the most difficult elements of being a major leaguer for Casey has been learning to keep his priorities in order. He believes deeply in community service, and he wants to use his position to help those around him. He has found it very difficult to refuse requests for his time.

"That was very tough for me because I want to help everybody, if I can. You wish there were forty-eight hours in every day so you could do so much more. But you can't do everything, and that's the tough part because there are so many people in need. It's tough to say no, but I know that at times I have to do it for the sake of my family. I would love to do every charity event, but my wife and son come first, and I have to make time for them. I have to make sure I get my rest so I can always play at peak efficiency. There are times when I do say yes, certainly. But there are also times where I have to bite the bullet and say no."

Major leaguers also come to understand a difficult reality: they cannot be everyone's hero every day. Often there will be a hundred or more fans waiting for Casey's autograph, and there is no way to satisfy everyone. "I'll try to sign as many as I can, but there is only so much time," Casey says. "I remember being that little kid who wanted the autograph. You try not to lose perspective—these people are here to see you, and you're the entertainment tonight. If you can go over and sign fifteen autographs, you're making fifteen people happy, and hopefully the others will understand. This is where you have to realize in your heart that your intentions are good."

One of Casey's first introductions to reality came in 1999. He was rushing out after a game so he could get Mandi on a flight back to her home in Charlotte, and he had no time to sign autographs in the Cincinnati parking lot after the game. "I walked to my car and said, 'Sorry, I've got to go,' but with everybody yelling at me, they didn't know what I was saying. The next day a reporter comes up to me and says, 'A person called one of the radio shows saying you're supposed to be the nicest guy ever, but you didn't sign any autographs when you left the park. You shunned a kid and you kind of waved them off.'

"It couldn't have been further from the truth. I didn't shun anybody. That's when I realized that I have a life too. I am a baseball player, which is great. But if you're a plumber or a businessman or an accountant, you all have lives. You all go home to somebody, or you all have families, moms, and dads. I was leaving work that day, and it just happened that I did not have time to sign autographs. When that whole fiasco happened, that's when it started to hit home: it hurt that the guy said that about me, but I realized that I can't please everybody. I had to do what I had to do. I think you learn that, and you try to please as many people as you can and hope the rest understand."

This is one of the most difficult lessons for major leaguers and stars in any field—that you must learn to make your best effort and recognize that not everyone will be satisfied. There is never a way to please every fan, every coach, every relative. All anyone can do is make his best effort and know that there will be a few lumps along the way. What Casey has learned is the importance of setting his priorities and using his time and effort to his advantage. Becoming a top-level major leaguer stands as one of his highest priorities, so he must make time to do the essential work and training that makes that possible. Being a good husband and father also ranks as a top priority, so he will use his time to that end. These challenges are faced by every player at every level in baseball—to learn to use their time and energy to best advantage. As Casey has learned, priorities change over time.

"I think you determine what your goals are, short term and long term, then you set a plan, then you have a vision. You put your plan together, and you say, 'Okay, if I do this, this, and this in the short term—if I go out and hit fifty balls off the tee and I have the correct technique; and I go run fifteen sprints; and I work on my form; and I take ground balls—ultimately in the short term I will make improvements. In the long term I have the vision of being an all-star big leaguer, or moving up a level, or whatever my goal may be. You have to have your goal. If I have a goal of having a wonderful marriage and being a great dad, I need to have my priorities straight. A lot of people think the grass is always greener on the other side—when you're married you want to be single, when you're single you want to be married. My sister once said to me, 'Have you ever heard the saying, the grass is greener where you water it?' That stuck with me, and whatever I do, I always make sure to water the grass I want to keep greener. If that means not going out with the guys and spending time with my family, that's what is most important to me. If it means taking extra grounders instead of going to the movies, that's what matters to me."

Casey has learned there is never time to grow lackadaisical. "It's a lot easier getting to the big leagues than staying there. Joel Skinner told me that in A ball, and I always kept it in mind. I wanted to stay there. I wanted to be one of the best hitters in the league. When you finally get through the minors, you have to prove yourself in the big leagues, and you have to work even harder. I think my work ethic has even gone up since I've been in the big leagues. If you don't produce here, there are guys out there waiting to replace you. If you don't produce in the minors, and you're a prospect, they give you a second chance, a third chance, a fourth chance, and a fifth chance. If you don't produce in the big leagues, they've got that prospect waiting, or a free agent. Somebody is coming to take your job. If you don't get better in the big leagues, you won't be around long."

And that is a basic understanding for baseball players at all levels. There is never a time to sit back and think you have it made, or someone else will be passing you up and taking your job.

Casey has spent the last decade trying to find ways to make the most of his talents. "I wasn't one of the fastest guys. I wasn't a flashy type guy. I knew I had to work hard. I think a big factor in why the Indians drafted me in the second round was that they saw a guy who wanted to get better and become a great player in the big leagues." To make that happen, Casey has been diligent in his work ethic and emphatic in establishing the priorities and values that would take him to the majors and keep him there. This attribute will prove important in every arena he approaches during his lifetime.

CHARACTER IN ACTION

One of the most stirring books in American literature tells the tale of a young Civil War soldier who runs away from his first battle, only to return to serve with valor in later conflicts. Stephen Crane's *The Red Badge of Courage* exemplifies the traditional American belief that we can all change our weaknesses and turn them into strengths; we can become the person we want to be rather than being stuck with our flaws. After fizzling in the post-season through most of his career, Barry Bonds shook the rap in October 2002, hammering the ball through the playoffs and hitting .471 with a .700 on-base percentage and four home runs in the World Series against the Angels.

We all have the option of making ourselves better. We can become braver, stronger, more educated. We can become better players by working harder and smarter; we can become better people by learning the consequences of our actions. The process begins by learning to understand yourself, to appraise just who you are, both as a player and a person, and to recognize both your strengths and your weaknesses. If you are consistently a half-effort player who hustles just enough to get by, that can be changed with resolve and a desire to bust it on every ground ball—as Sean Casey says, to give four seconds to your teammates. If you are a sloppy defensive player whose throws often miss the target, extra effort in footwork drills can make a big difference. If you treat your wife, girlfriend, or those around you poorly, developing a resolve to improve can create a better situation. From there, a player must decide what is important to him, what are his values.

The next step is recognizing the consequences of your actions. If you do not run out a ground ball, and it leads to giving away an out when a fielder flubs it but has time to recover, you have let down your teammates and possibly even cost your team a game. If you get caught cheating on your wife or girlfriend, you have let down your family. George O'Leary and Tim Johnson were caught lying, leading to public disgrace. Ruben Rivera was caught stealing. The process is quite simple: when you take an action, consider what could happen as a result of that action. If you do not like the outcome, you are probably better off avoiding the action in the first place.

We all have the opportunity to mold ourselves into better people, better players, better teammates, and better citizens. It may not always be easy, it may take painful self-analysis and repressing a few natural inclinations. But it is all right there. Everyone has the opportunity to make himself better if he wants to.

4

CONFIDENCE: YOU GOTTA BELIEVE

The kid center fielder from Alabama had fallen to just about the lowest point in his young life. After hitting .477 in Triple A and getting the call to the big leagues amid considerable media hoopla, everything seemed to fall apart. He started his major league career a mere 1 for 25, the sole hit being a home run. He was leaving runners scattered on the bases and making poor contact against good pitching.

So the rookie outfielder sat in the clubhouse and began crying quietly. A few minutes later his manager came down to join him, putting his arm over the kid's shoulder.

"What's the matter, son," manager Leo Durocher asked.

"Mr. Leo, I can't hit up here," the kid responded.

"What do you mean you can't hit? You're going to be a great ballplayer," Durocher said sternly.

"The pitching is just too fast for me here," the kid said. "They're going to send me back to Minneapolis."

Durocher pointed to his uniform and said, "Willie, see what's printed across my jersey? It says *Giants*. As long as I'm the manager of the Giants, you're my center fielder. You're here to stay. Stop worrying. With your talent you're going to get plenty of hits."

The conversation continued, then Durocher said, "You're the greatest ballplayer I ever saw or ever hope to see. But, Willie, you and your damn pull hitting. I don't know why you won't take the ball to right field. You can hit it into the bleachers here, over the fence, anywhere you want, yet you're still trying to pull the ball all the time. For you to do something wrong is an absolute disgrace. And I know you don't want to disgrace me, do you, Willie?"

The long, ugly string ended the next game with a pair of hits against the Pirates. And the kid center fielder from Alabama went on to become perhaps the best player in the history of the game, hitting home runs to all fields and brimming with belief in himself. There are occasions when even the likes of Willie Mays need a dose of confidence in troubled times.

Leo Durocher, a man of contradictions, could be a crabby misanthrope at times. But on that day in 1951 he pulled an act of master psychology by injecting Willie Mays with the confidence to believe he could play in the majors. Most professional players will not find many Leo Durochers during their careers, and they must learn to build their confidence through their own devices. "There is no substitute for confidence. When you get rolling you can ride it for a long time," veteran pitcher Tom Glavine says.

Baseball is the strangest game in that if you believe you can achieve, you are far more likely to do so. Extremely talented players languish in the minors, victims of their own self-doubts, while less-gifted players thrive in the majors. Attitude, confidence, and mental toughness become ingredients of success. Oakland A's player development director Keith Lieppman recalls a young pitcher who showed up in minor league camp in 1997, possessed of a magnificent two-seam sinking fastball and

Manager Leo Durocher of the New York Giants gave his kid
center fielder, Willie Mays, the confidence he needed.

another ingredient that was equally important. "After Huddy
had been here a few weeks, I sat down with him and told him
that he could pitch in the major leagues, and that he should believe in himself. He looked back at me sort of like I was crazy
and nodded his head. He already believed that he could pitch in
the major leagues and that he could be a big star there."

Tim Hudson came to the A's as a sixth-round draft pick, too
skinny and too short to draw much attention from major
league scouts. He had excelled in college, being named South-
eastern Conference player of the year at Auburn University,
but he still lasted through more than 180 selections in the 1997
draft because scouts questioned his stamina and strength.

What Hudson exudes is a quiet confidence—absolute belief without the need for boast or bravado. He does not have to tell anyone how good he is; he knows, and he backs it up on the field. He *believes* that when something goes wrong with his mechanics or delivery, he will find a way to conquer the problem. There is no fear of the opposition or self-doubt of his abilities. When then A's pitching coach Rick Peterson sat down with his rookie pitcher on August 19, 1999, to prepare him to face Pedro Martinez, the Red Sox, and the exuberant crowd at Fenway Park, Hudson just looked back at Peterson and said, "I've been waiting my whole life to play in this atmosphere," then went out and won the game.

Hudson learned early that if he did not have confidence in himself, no one else would either. "I was always a real small guy growing up. I was always a player who had to prove himself at everything, whether it was high school, college, or pro ball. It was almost like I was playing with a chip on my shoulder, with people not believing in me from the start." By being forced to prove himself over and over again, Hudson's confidence level expanded. "I almost believe that I can do anything out there on the field," he says.

Confidence is the basic internal belief that a person can and will succeed. A pitcher must believe he *can* and *will* throw that two-seamer on the outside corner; a hitter must believe he *can* and *will* drive the inside pitch. Consistent success is built upon a player's belief that he can perform successfully every time he steps onto a field. Only players with the highest level of confidence will have the mental toughness to emerge on top when they are challenged. When fans heckle a player, it is confidence that allows that player to ignore the taunts. Confident players are not inflicted with as much self-doubt or mental garbage that they must block out, because those doubt-inflicting thoughts are quickly dismissed or never enter their minds in the first place.

Tim Hudson has a quiet confidence—he
knows how good he is, and he backs it up
on the field.

So where does confidence begin? For some it comes in
childhood, from parents who teach their children to believe in
themselves. Then it is fortified through a series of successes. It
can be built on some stroke of good fortune, such as a four-hit
game against a good pitcher, which teaches an individual that he
can succeed in a certain area. Virtually every player who reaches
even high-school-level baseball has a basis of success from past
performances. Past achievements lead to the belief in future
achievement.

The Hudsons and Glavines learn to develop and maintain
confidence, and they learn to use it to their advantage. By

believing they can overcome difficulties, they become far more likely to do so. A confident player believes in his ability to make changes that will make him a better player; a player lacking confidence fears making adjustments because he questions his ability to succeed with the new style. When a player lacks confidence, he clings to what has worked in the past, hoping to make it work again, or he goes to the other extreme of making changes indiscriminately in the hope of discovering some magic formula. The problem is that nothing stays the same—pitchers learn hitters' weaknesses, or hitters learn to recognize a pitcher's breaking ball—and the past can never be repeated.

While players who reach any advanced level have built a foundation of confidence, this confidence can lapse as the competition becomes stronger and self-doubt eats away. When confidence wanes, a player's approach changes. He tries harder in every way: he thinks more; he puts more effort into his performance; he loses his discipline and patience; and he may become overaggressive or go the other way and become too passive. When a player senses a lapse of confidence, it is the challenge of mental toughness to reassert that confidence and renew his self-belief.

PREPARATION AND CONFIDENCE

In the bullpen and between innings, Greg Maddux spends most of his time working out of the stretch. The toughest pitches during a game come from the stretch, and Maddux wants to be ready, both physically and mentally. Knowing that he can make his best pitches from the stretch in the bullpen builds a confidence that carries over into the game.

Practice is a time to build confidence. A player learns that he can make the tough plays, hit a breaking pitch, and deliver a change-up during practice. Consistently doing it right in practice builds confidence that carries over into the game. If a player accepts sloppy performances in practice, he is practicing failure. Confidence is built upon the individual knowing he can do a task correctly again and again.

Players also learn that setting up a pre-game routine also helps build a comfort zone. While some of the personal rituals may seem almost superstitious—such as Wade Boggs's affinity for pre-game chicken—the use of routine delivers that sense of comfort that leads to confidence. "Whatever it was, whether it was eating a particular food, eating at 2 p.m., or getting eight hours of sleep a night regardless of the travel or hours being kept," Robin Yount said of the routine he maintained, "it worked. If I got six hours of sleep one night and ten the next, I was going to feel off or different. If I ate at 1 p.m. one day and 4 p.m. the next, I was going to feel different." Routine becomes an attempt to find the schedule and style that works best for the individual player. When that routine comes together, a player develops a sense of confidence from following a routine that has led to success in the past.

Before a player can establish a quality pre-game routine that will consistently prepare him for a game, he must do a self-evaluation of his habits. Yount continually evaluated his routine. "What did I do when I felt good? I did this, this, and this. So I did this, this, and this because I care what happens at the ballpark." Players will constantly make adjustments in seeking to discover the routine that works best for them. "So there are adjustments that go on before you get to the ballpark. There are adjustments that go on in the off-season as you learn what you need to do to prepare for the upcoming season," Yount says.

Being prepared also means being well conditioned. Added strength and stamina from workouts give an athlete confidence in his physical abilities to meet the challenges of competition. Fielding grounders, taking BP, and pitching on the side helps condition the body and gives a player a certain level of confidence that he can make the big play or break off a nasty curveball. Added strength from the weight room makes a player believe that his body is well tuned for competition and brings a sense of added power to his game.

One of the most striking elements of the Oakland A's three World Series teams of 1988–1990 was the workload assumed by the pitchers. Dennis Eckersley, Dave Stewart, and Bob Welch worked incessantly to ensure that they were always in the best possible condition. Before road games, Eckersley would run laps around the *outside* of the stadiums, leaving passing drivers to stare at a major league superstar sweating and puffing on the public streets. Being well conditioned helped the pitchers build a confidence that they could outlast their opponents and succeed. They made a conscious determination that they would not lose because their opponents were better conditioned than they were.

Yount reached the majors as a nineteen-year-old, after he had relied solely on his abilities to make him a high school star. When he became a pro, he had much to learn. "Playing daily at the professional level is a whole different animal than playing occasionally during the week while growing up. You have to get to know yourself and what it takes to play every day. You can get away with doing whatever you want when you are only playing twice a week, but it's going to catch up with you when you are playing every day for seven straight months. You had better have a routine if you are going to have any kind of longevity or success."

No one told Yount about routines or taught him to prepare for games. He learned on his own from trial and error at the major league level. He then attempted to repeat his routine as often as possible. "The most important thing for being at your best is preparation," Yount says. That belief in preparation helped carry Yount to a Hall of Fame career.

CONTROLLING WHAT IS WITHIN YOUR CONTROL

It may sound almost circular, but confidence breeds success, and success leads to confidence. The trick is to use success to build a level of confidence. Every player who reaches the majors can recall great performances in the minor leagues, so he knows he has the ability to achieve at the professional level. Every college player can recall prep success, and every high school player can feed off youth league gems. Successful players know they have excelled in the past, so they believe they are fully capable of doing so again.

A process of replay and pre-play enhances confidence. A player can replay past successes in his mind, recalling past successes that have led to his current level. The pre-play is the process of visualization, in which an athlete envisions every situation in his mind in order to prepare for what will actually occur on the field. Curt Schilling goes so far as to acquire his own personal computer program that plays his previous outings in order to help him prepare for upcoming games. In visualization, as we shall see, every thought should be positive.

Confidence does not always mean achievement—it means believing in the ability to overcome challenges and adversity. A confident player can fall into a slump and know that he will somehow find his way out rather than folding in despair; he can recognize that he needs to make a mechanical adjustment to his swing or his delivery, and have the confidence to know he will eventually succeed. Ozzie Smith began his major league career as a dismal hitter, but he combined confidence with an intense work ethic to get every bit out of his ability and become an offensive contributor.

Baseball players must learn to evaluate themselves based on what they can control, rather than on outcome. They must learn to measure themselves on the *process* that leads to getting a hit or retiring a batter: they are in control of the process, not the result. Players who evaluate themselves on the basis of results will have trouble pulling themselves out of tailspins because they are not even aware of the elements of the process that need improvement. Some players even become traumatized by bad results. Former Chicago White Sox manager Jerry Manuel told *USA Today's* Mel Antonen about Montreal Expos prospect Sergio Valdez, who had pitched lights out in the minor leagues. Then Valdez debuted against the Mets in 1986 and got pounded. "He was one of our top prospects," Manuel said. "But when he got to Shea Stadium, he couldn't get anybody out. He was shaken, and he never recovered. He became a journeyman." Former Stanford star pitcher Rick Helling came up in 1994 and went 3-0 in his first six starts with the Texas Rangers before being battered by the Angels. "Panic sets in," Helling told Antonen. "Instantly you start wondering if you are good enough. You think, 'Is this going to happen every night?' Or, 'Did I pick the right sport?'"

Learning to evaluate process rather than result is not nearly as easy as it seems. Fans and writers place enormous emphasis on statistics. Players constantly hear about their numbers from all directions, and accolades come from achievements. Add to that a player's desire to emulate someone like Luis Gonzalez in the 2001 World Series—getting the mega-hit with the game on the line—and it becomes clear how players become result driven. But evaluation is not about outcome. A player can only evaluate what he can control. A hitter cannot control whether Torii Hunter lunges into the gap to make a diving catch; a hitter can only control the elements that led him to hit the line drive. A pitcher cannot control whether some slap hitter reaches out of the strike zone to bloop a single to the opposite field; a pitcher can only focus on making the right pitch. This is baseball: there will be good fortune and misfortune, and a successful player must learn to ride with it and maintain the level of confidence that he can get the job done.

Even Greg Maddux had to learn this lesson. "I was worrying so much about winning and losing, about getting an out or giving up a hit, that it was affecting the way I was pitching. It was interfering with my ability to make pitches. Thinking exclusively about executing made a lot of sense to me, so I tried to do it. It's easier said than done, because you play this game to win. But at the same time you have to forget about that and concentrate on what it takes to win," Maddux said, as related in Harvey Dorfman's *The ABC's of Pitching*.

Hitters should evaluate themselves on:

- Quality of **preparation** before and during the game.
- Quality of **concentration**. Are you thinking too much? Is your mind clear? Are you rushing your thinking? Are you visualizing as much and as well as you can? Are you taking mental breaks?
- **Seeing the ball**. How well are you seeing the ball? Use a grading system to determine if you are getting your best look.
- **Pitch selection**. Take into consideration pitches you swing at, pitches you take, and your hitting plan—were they pitches you could drive? Even if they were in the strike zone, were they good pitches to hit?
- Quality of **takes**. Evaluate your balance and approach. Was your stride right? Were you on the pitch, even if it was out of the strike zone?
- **Effort level**. Were you working too hard, swinging too hard, or trying too hard? Were you smooth?

• Quality of **swing**. Was it a good swing? The pitch, the situation, and the count must be considered in this.

• Quality of **contact**. Did you hit the ball where you wanted? Did you get it on the sweet spot of the bat? Did you pop it up or top it, or did you hit it hard? The pitch must be taken into consideration in this evaluation.

• Doing the **job**. If there was a runner on second and no outs, your job would be to hit the ball to the right side to advance the runner. Or if the opposing pitcher gets two quick outs, your job is to make him throw pitches to avoid having a short inning. Evaluate also whether you knew your job and had the right plan to do it.

• Showing **poise** and **self-control**. Were you able to shake off negative emotions or frustrations and come back to take control of the situation? Did you avoid losing your cool after an umpire's mistake or a bad at-bat?

Pitchers should evaluate themselves on:

• Quality of **preparation** before and during the game.

• Quality of **concentration**. Are you thinking too much? Is your mind clear? Are you rushing your thinking? Are you visualizing as much and as well as you should? Are you taking mental breaks? Are you focused on the right things at the right times?

• Showing **poise** and **self-control**. What is your response after bad pitches, hits, runs, errors, or bad umpire's calls? Are you ready for the next pitch after something goes wrong? Be aware of your body language and the message it sends to your teammates and the opposition.

• Awareness of **game situations**. Are you getting the signs for pickoffs and bunt plays? Are you aware of your opponent's strategies in certain situations? Were you surprised?

• **Pitch selection**. Did you throw the right pitch for the situation? Were you committed to the pitch?

• **Delivery**. Have your mechanics been consistent, and is your arm slot correct? Have you had a consistent release point on all your pitches?

• **Execution**. What is the percentage of quality pitches you threw? Were they thrown how and where you wanted them?

• **Fielding**. Did you make the plays? Did you back up the bases and cover first on grounders to the right side?

Fielders should evaluate themselves on:

• Quality of **preparation** before and during the game. This includes anticipating all possible plays that may occur and how you will respond.

• Quality of **concentration**. Were you ready on every pitch? Or was your mind drifting elsewhere, such as to your last at-bat, as the pitch was made?

• **Execution**. Did you get good jumps? Did you approach the ball correctly and put yourself in a position to field the ball? How was your form in preparation for catching the ball? Did you catch the ball cleanly, without bobbling? Were you in position to throw? Did you make the throw?

• **Awareness of game situations**. Were you in the right place? Did you always get the signs correctly? Did you anticipate all possibilities?

• **Poise** and **self-control**. Did you avoid being distracted by negatives? Were you able to focus on the next pitch after making an error? How was your body language after an error?

• **Teamsmanship**. Were you encouraging your teammates and alerting them to possible situations? Were you helping to keep them in the game?

Similar evaluations apply to all facets of the game. Baserunners, for example, should evaluate their leads, jumps, and turn angles. They must also consider all their baserunning decisions, such as how well they read whether a ball will be caught or fall in for a hit. In all situations, players must evaluate how well they receive signs. Self-evaluation is integral to improvement. Knowing that you have done well in the various facets of the game builds confidence in success.

Strange as it may sound, confidence can begin with a personal decision to become more confident. A player can recognize that some of his problems are born in a lack of confidence, and make the conscious determination to rebuild his confidence. The process can be done with self-talk, even yelling it at the top of your lungs. Opposing players tell the story of watching Ted Williams walk into stadiums long before games and yell into the empty stands, "I'm Ted Williams, and I'm the best [bleeping] hitter who ever lived." He yelled it so much he believed it, and eventually so did everyone else.

A player can build confidence by telling himself over and over again that he is capable, that he can hit line drives or throw the tough pitch in tense situations. With a combination of self-talk, replay and pre-play visualizations, quality practice, and proper self-evaluation, confidence can be built. Every player must find what works for him, because baseball is a game where there are sure to be times when the ball keeps coming off the end of the bat, or the curveball refuses to break. Every player must learn to maintain his confidence in times of struggle. It will often be the difference between continuing improvement and stagnation.

Individual confidence can breed team confidence. When players believe in themselves and their teammates, they become far more likely to reach greater heights. If a pitcher believes his bullpen can finish a game, it allows him to pitch with a clear mind when he tries to escape a jam in the sixth or seventh inning. If a hitter believes the batter behind him can execute his job, he is less likely to try to hit those impossible five-run homers that will most likely result in a strikeout. The 2002 California Angels that defeated the San Francisco Giants in a seven-game World Series exuded team confidence. The Angels may not have been the most talented team in the majors, but they executed and played with extreme confidence.

When the 1969 New York Mets shocked baseball by winning the World Series, reliever Tug McGraw coined what would become the team's slogan: "You gotta believe." The Mets believed in themselves and their teammates, as did the Angels more than three decades later. Confidence is both an individual and team issue: you gotta believe in yourself, and you gotta believe in your teammates.

GOALS AND CONFIDENCE

Kids who fantasize about playing in The Show dream of batting .350, hitting 75 home runs, throwing a no-hitter, or getting the game-winning hit in the seventh game of the World Series. Not many kids go to the ballpark and dream of having a good at-bat or an excellent workout in the bullpen. Yet it is learning how to readjust smaller goals that makes the mighty dreams possible. The best professional players discover that goal-setting is about taking charge of those elements a player can control. A player cannot control whether he hits .350, but he can control whether he has a good at-bat and swings at pitches he can drive. A pitcher cannot control whether a batter gets jammed and bloops a hit, but he can control whether he puts in effective work in the bullpen and whether he maintains his concentration on the mound.

"Numbers—I never look at them. I don't like them," shortstop Nomar Garciaparra told *Baseball Weekly*'s Seth Livingstone. In September 1980, Kansas City's George Brett got the baseball world buzzing with the possibility of his reaching .400 for the first time since Ted Williams hit .406 in 1941. The Royals were in a pennant race, and Brett was hitting to win. "Every time up, I was just trying to give our club the kind of at-bat the situation called for," Brett said. But the night we wrapped up our division, I thought, 'Hey, I'm close enough. I'm going to go for it. I'm going to try to hit .400.' That was the day things fell apart. I didn't have many good at-bats when I started concentrating on getting hits."

Unrealistic or inappropriate goals become a huge burden on confidence. By trying to hit .400, Brett wound up hitting .390. One of the most common examples of unrealistic goals at the professional level is the player with borderline power who tries to become a home-run hitter, only to find himself lingering in the minors as a nonhitter. Goals, set properly, can be a boost to success. But the wrong goals can also be a major detriment and lead only to frustration.

Focusing on the job at hand, and on the elements that a player can control, leads to reaching the great goals. Reaching, then excelling, in these individual points builds a player's confidence. The secret is the specifics: do the individual elements correctly and they will lead to greater achievement. The individual, specific goals—journey goals—are what lead to reaching the highest goals—destination goals. Only by mastering the journey goals can you reach the destination.

HOW CONFIDENCE CHANGES

It would be ideal for a player to maintain absolute confidence through his playing days, believing in himself through every at-bat or while delivering every pitch. It simply does not work that way. Most players run into peaks and valleys, where confidence disappears and they may begin to question whether they even belong on a college or professional field. This most often comes as a result of perceived failure when they base their self-evaluation strictly on results and statistics, elements that are beyond a player's control. Four line-drive outs may lead to an O-fer, but it should not lead to a loss of confidence. Players are best served by building a strong foundation of confidence based on the execution of fundamentals.

Levels of confidence can differ for everything a player does in the game. He may hold high confidence in his ability to hit one pitcher while completely lacking in confidence against another. A pitcher may lose confidence in his best pitch after someone hits it, then begin muscling up and throwing with too much effort, or even abandon that pitch for the rest of the game. Confidence levels change constantly, even from pitch to pitch during an individual at-bat. Pitchers usually have more confidence in their ability to retire the eighth and ninth hitters in the lineup than they have against the third and fourth. The count affects the confidence level of both the hitter and the pitcher. For example, with no balls and two strikes, the pitcher's confidence usually soars while the hitter's diminishes, because both know that the pitcher can throw any of his pitches in that situation. With two balls and no strikes, the hitter knows the pitcher must throw a strike, and he can lay off a pitch he does not like. The pitcher's confidence diminishes because he knows he has to hit the strike zone, and the hitter is probably sitting on a fastball. Even if the pitcher does decide to try to trick the hitter with his second- or third-best pitch, he is probably not as confident of being able to make a good pitch as he would be with the fastball.

Such uncontrollable elements as sun, wind, lights, and playing field can also alter confidence. An infielder can feel very confident before a game, but then a ball taking a bad hop in front of him can lead to concern about more bad hops. He loses confidence in the field and in his ability to catch the next ground ball.

Virtually all players must fight through confidence dips that tend only to make bad situations worse. It is difficult to maintain perfect confidence at all times: hitting against Randy Johnson or pitching to Barry Bonds tends to drain the opposition's confidence. This is one of the challenges of baseball. Mentally tough players are aware of their moments of high and low confidence and work to repair any problems when confidence sags. Here is a list of factors that often lower confidence:

• **Not being prepared physically.** Knowing in your heart that you have not worked as hard as you should or practiced every possibility that may come up in a game will always leave some doubt in your mind about being at your best.

• **Not being prepared mentally.** Whenever you are in a situation that you know you have not mentally prepared to face, or have not anticipated, your confidence will suffer.

• **Feeling overmatched.** Any time a player faces a situation where he thinks, "He's better than I am," confidence will decline. Even by thinking, "This guy's really good," and questioning whether you are up to the challenge can lower confidence.

• **New situation.** Being placed in a new situation often creates doubts. It could include any number of possibilities—a new team, a new park, a different position, the post-season, being traded. When you are placed in a new situation, you often do not know what to expect, and you must learn to carry the same level of confidence. A player must remember that even though the situation changes, the game is still the same: the bases are still 90 feet apart, and the mound is still 60 feet, 6 inches from the plate.

• **Dwelling on past failures.** Spending too much time reliving an error or swinging at a bad pitch makes confidence fade. Players must learn to visualize success; mentally recall the situation and visualize yourself succeeding in the same place where you failed.

• **Worrying.** Worry is a mental rehearsal for failure. Worrying means thinking about what can go wrong or imagining bad results. When we worry, we go over things again and again in our heads. These thoughts come to dominate our mind and, consequently, become a guidance system. Worrying must be distinguished from analyzing potential outcomes—worriers dwell on the negative while analyzers evaluate possible outcomes.

• **Fear**. When a player fears embarrassment, humiliation, failure, injury, or just about anything else, it serves as a major obstacle to confidence. Fear comes in degrees, but even a slight amount of fear erodes confidence.

• **Doubt**. When a player is uncertain about some part of the game, it is impossible for him to have confidence in his actions. If a pitcher doubts the pitch called by the catcher, it leaves the hurler lacking confidence in that pitch. He may also wonder if he can throw the pitch where he desires, or if the catcher can block a pitch in the dirt. If doubts cloud a hitter's mind, he may wonder whether he can catch up to a certain pitcher's fastball, or whether his swing is right. A defensive player may question his ability to make a certain play.

• **Perfectionism**. Being a perfectionist can be motivating, but it can also be deadly to confidence. Players who see themselves as perfectionists tend to dwell upon negatives and upon elements they cannot control. They often tell themselves: "I'm awful, I can't believe I'm that bad." A perfectionist who focuses on results is destined to become angry, frustrated, and negative, because no one can control results. Other than trying harder, this sort of perfectionist does not know how to fix a problem. But there is a positive perfectionism: the player who focuses on the process. He learns to identify what part of his game needs fixing and goes about finding the solution. He remains positive and learns to use his perfectionism to advantage. A positive perfectionist may strive for perfection, but he does so with the realization that such goals will not always be attained.

• **Lack of self-support**. Many players fail to stop and pat themselves on the back for their successes. There is an emotional need to stop at times and praise yourself for what you have done well. There is also a need to keep this under control and maintain a balance where the negatives are not washed away by internal excuse-making. An effective self-evaluation includes both back patting and constructive criticism, in balance.

• **Poor self-evaluation.** This is one of the greatest causes of low confidence and can also lead to false confidence. It is natural for people in all fields to evaluate themselves on outcome and results, but in baseball, players cannot control the result, only what leads to the result. Hitting a line drive that a defender dives to catch and flailing at three bad pitches may both result in outs, but a player must learn to appreciate the difference between an unsuccessful result and a poor effort.

Because it is easy and natural to fall into work and thinking habits that can lead to lowered confidence, a player must constantly be aware of what he is doing to himself. Awareness is the first step in making changes that will build confidence.

FALSE CONFIDENCE

In the late 1970s several of the big linemen from the Minnesota Vikings made the trip to the old Metropolitan Stadium outside Minneapolis for a little showing off. They had boasted publicly that they could come over to the Twins' park and scorch a few batting-practice home runs, and they really believed they could. It looked so simple from the stands, after all, that big strong guys should be able to knock balls over the walls with ease. So they came, and they swung. And they swung. And they hit a few little dribblers but nothing remotely close to the wall. They lacked the skill and experience to follow through on their brag.

This was false confidence without dire results, other than a little ribbing. The linemen assumed that something that appeared so easy would be easy. For baseball players, the consequences can be more severe when false confidence occurs on the diamond. False confidence may replace work ethic—a player may think he is so good that he does not need to do the extra work and mental preparation that is required for success; he may think that he has the game figured out and will not have to produce the intensity that characterized his game in the past. For many years the "sophomore jinx" was a staple of baseball, where a young player might come up for a big rookie year, then falter in his second season. At times this occurred because the player refused to adjust. He was determined to stay with what had worked in his rookie year—as happened to Mark McGwire later in his career. At other times it occurred because a player simply grew overconfident in his abilities and failed to follow the work ethic that carried him to the majors in the first place.

False confidence can show up in different ways. When former Cy Young Award winner Mike Marshall pitched for the Twins during the late 1970s, he displayed a peculiar type of false confidence. When a hitter roped a line drive on a fat pitch for an out, he would later analyze the pitch: "That's right where I wanted to throw it and right where I wanted him to hit it," Marshall would say. When a hitter lined a double into the gap, Marshall would say, "He hit it right where I wanted him to. I can't believe we didn't have somebody playing there."

Marshall's false confidence got in the way of his ability to evaluate his performance, then make the adjustments that would help him improve. Not only was he basing his evaluation on his result; he was assuming results that did not occur and blaming his manager for failure. This is the extreme danger with false confidence: that it will lead to a belief that preparation and evaluation are unnecessary; that a player already has all the answers and does not need coaching or improvement. This flaw occurs in all areas of life, for example with doctors or lawyers who fail to prepare for a case because of their overwhelming belief that they can just wing it and get the results they desire.

False confidence also got in the way of heralded prospect Aaron Holbert, the Cardinals' first-round draft pick in 1990 and the designated heir to super-shortstop Ozzie Smith. "Being a bonus baby, I took things for granted and let it go to my head," Holbert told *Baseball Weekly*'s Lisa Winston. "I never put forth my total efforts, mentally or physically." Holbert spent more than a decade battling through the minors after starting with the mistaken belief that success would come easily.

One of the finest lines in baseball is the difference between a can-do attitude and false confidence. With a can-do attitude, a player believes in himself and works intensely to make those beliefs possible. Rickey Henderson carried a belief bordering on arrogance that he could do anything on the baseball field, then he worked intensely to make that happen. Henderson's extreme confidence forced him to live up to his expectations.

A truly confident player is unafraid of making the adjustments that will lead to improvement. He will have the confidence in his ability that he can shorten his swing and still drive the ball, or that he can deliver all his pitches from the same arm slot and maintain maximum effectiveness. A player striving for mental toughness must stop to evaluate whether he carries with him a can-do attitude that leads him to greater achievement, or a false confidence that interferes with success. The key point of evaluation is to determine whether this attitude causes a player to prepare more or prepare less. Mentally tough, can-do players put in that extra preparation that leads to achievement.

CONFIDENCE IS A CHOICE

Self-evaluation is never easy, and understanding one's own confidence level is difficult. Some players seem confident on the outside, but inside they cringe with self-doubt. Others may never say a word, but confidence seeps through their souls. Players have a distinct advantage if they can learn to evaluate and understand their confidence level, then recognize when it dips or leaps into false confidence that may influence their work or mental preparation. Once a player learns to do this, he recognizes a key ingredient in achievement: confidence is a choice. When a player takes charge of his confidence level, he learns to take advantage of a major mental ingredient that leads to achievement. In doing this, he takes a mental edge.

Starting pitcher Cory Lidle put together a solid 2001 season for the Oakland A's, then got off to a miserable 1-8 start in 2002 before starting to put it back together in the second half as he began recognizing his problem: "I had to rededicate myself. After last season, I think I thought I was just going to roll back and start off where I ended up last year. Obviously, that's not the case. Now I'm coming up with a plan and making my pitches," Lidle told *Oakland Tribune* reporter Joe Nolan. The right-hander then began a course of intense preparation, mentally and physically, keeping notes on opposing hitters and locking himself mentally into every game, every pitch. Lidle made the transition from solid high confidence in 2001 to false confidence and then to no confidence before making the climb back to a proper confidence level.

Since confidence levels fluctuate, players must constantly check themselves to make certain they have not lost confidence or drifted into a false confidence that will mess up their preparation. Once a player learns to be confident, he can learn to restore his levels of confidence when he catches himself sagging. It may sound difficult, but this is a learned behavior that is used by top-level professional players. Certain behaviors can be seen consistently in confident players. What follows is a comparison of behaviors between players who lack confidence and those who have it.

Confident Players	*Players with Low Confidence*
1. Positive visualizations and feelings.	Replay failures and do not properly visualize.
2. Positive attitudes / Attitudes work together.	Negative and/or conflicting attitudes.
3. Good concentration / focused.	Thinking too much / scattered / mental game falls apart.
4. No worries.	Worry about everything.
5. Have emotional control / are cool.	Emotions off kilter / get down.
6. Feel in control.	Believe they have no control / hope for success.
7. Appear in control.	Display poor body language.
8. Stay within themselves.	Try harder / extra effort / cautious / careful.
9. Relaxed and loose.	Anxious and tight.
10. Patient.	Impulsive / impatient / hurrying.
11. Have a plan and stick to it.	No plan / deviate from plan without sound reason.
12. Handle negatives positively / move on.	Overreact to negatives and worries.
13. Take responsibility / no excuses.	Make excuses.
14. Focus on what they can control.	Worry about the outcome and what they cannot control.
15. Goals centered on what they can control.	Goals set toward stats and results without a plan for achievement.
16. Have peace of mind.	Worry about what others will think about their performance.

When a player catches himself engaging in actions that diminish confidence, he must immediately decide to change his behavior. If a player makes an error and finds himself reliving the mistake, he must drive out the negative thoughts and visualize making the play successfully. If a pitcher gives up a hit then finds himself sulking back to the mound with his head down and his shoulders slumped, he must immediately make a conscious decision to pick up his body language to recapture his confidence. With every behavior that indicates a fading of confidence, a mentally tough player will learn to battle adversity by choosing to regain his confident thinking and behavior.

Perhaps the most difficult part of self-evaluation is learning to be honest with yourself. When a player fails to be honest with himself, he colors his evaluation and cheats himself. This only works to keep him from making the necessary adjustments that are the key to improvement. Mental toughness demands the self-discipline for proper self-evaluation, without being either too hard or too forgiving. Being too hard can result in the perfectionism that is impossible to reach; being too forgiving leads to a failure to recognize the problems that demand making adjustments.

YOU CAN'T WORRY ABOUT WHAT YOU CAN'T CONTROL

Miguel Tejada never had many advantages in life. He grew up in impoverished surroundings in the Dominican Republic, then signed with the A's in July 1993 and came in contact with the coaches who would help shape his future. Early on he learned the importance of quality practice—practicing at high intensity. He put pressure on himself to make every play correctly, field every grounder, and learn his craft. Because of the intensity, quality, and volume of his work, he built a confidence level that

Miguel Tejada made a mental correction
that got him back on track to be an
outstanding shortstop.

helped him believe he could make the plays at shortstop well
enough to become a first-rate major-leaguer.

During his rookie year of 1998, Tejada hit a blip. He fumbled
too many routine plays and amassed errors. He grew frustrated,
but he never lost his base of confidence because he knew that he
had been able to make every play during practice. He knew he
had the skill and ability. The next spring he called over one of his
former minor league coaches for a little chat. They went through
his pre-pitch mental preparation and found something missing.
While Tejada prepared with self-talk—telling himself he wanted
the ball hit to him—he had stopped visualizing having the ball
hit in his direction and seeing himself make those tough plays.

With one quick mental correction, he got himself back on track and developed into an outstanding shortstop.

Confidence builds success, and success builds confidence. Tejada built his base of confidence upon his successes in practice and carried them over into games. He *knew* he could make those plays; it was just a matter of finding the lost ingredient.

One of the favorite adages of modern baseball coaches is, "You can't worry about what you can't control." To be mentally tough, a player must understand just what he can control and must build his confidence around those elements. Confidence comes and goes, and a mentally tough player must learn to dig deep into the reservoirs of his soul to reassert his confidence in the toughest situations; he must learn to make the choice to be confident. Believing in achieving is one of the first steps to getting there.

5

THE CONCEPT
OF COOL

It was, perhaps, the ultimate high-pressure situation. With the Boston Red Sox down three games to none in the 1990 American League Championship Series, Roger Clemens took the mound against his nemesis, Dave Stewart. Clemens and Stewart had a history—the Oakland A's ace held a staggering 8 to 1 advantage against Clemens in head-to-head meetings, a mastery that had been played heavily in the press. Stewart had outdueled Clemens in the playoff opener, and they met again in the game that could determine the series. All the pressure was directly on the strong shoulders of the Texas transplant to Boston.

From the beginning, Clemens had trouble establishing a strike zone with umpire Terry Cooney. Clemens usually got the calls just off the black for strikes, but Cooney refused to give away either the inside or the outside. Clemens walked two hitters in the first inning before escaping without a run scoring; in the second inning came his personal nightmare. Carney Lansford and Terry Steinbach hit back-to-back singles, and left fielder Mike Greenwell's throwing error left runners at second

Roger Clemens excels at many aspects of
mental toughness—but has also been known
to blow his cool.

and third. Mark McGwire grounded out to score Lansford, with
Steinbach getting caught at third. Clemens then walked Willie
Randolph, missing on close pitches just off the black.

The game seemed to be collapsing around Clemens: defensive gaffes, strict umpiring, and Stewart pitching for the other
side. Clemens then began the strangest behavior. He appeared
to stage a conversation with his glove while on the mound. John
Peale, a film messenger for the Associated Press, stood behind
the screen, in hearing range. He reported Clemens as saying,
"You son-of-a-bitch, you don't know where the strike zone is."
Umpire Cooney responded, "What?" And Clemens said, "I'm
not talking to you, you son-of-a-bitch." Clemens then followed
with a stream of profanity.

Stewart said he could hear the whole thing from the A's dugout. According to Stewart, Clemens said, "You get your big fat bleeping ass back behind the plate and call the balls and strikes." When Cooney stepped forward to say, "What did you say?", Clemens repeated it.

In big-league baseball, an umpire will not tolerate being shown up or cussed at loud enough to be heard in the dugouts. He knows that if he allows this, he will lose control of the game. Cooney lifted his arm and ejected Clemens, only the fifth time a player had been thrown out of a post-season game.

Roger Clemens, one of the greatest pitchers in the history of the game, had blown his cool. He lost his temper, and in doing so he damaged his team. While Clemens excels at many aspects of mental toughness, there have been times in his career where he has been, simply, uncool.

"I can't imagine what he was thinking," Stewart said after the game. "He's got to realize his importance to his club and keep himself in the game. He's got to show more self-control. Maybe he was thinking he'd spark his club, but it struck me as an inopportune time to get kicked out. I mean, my importance to the A's is about the same as his to the Red Sox, and I'd never allow it to happen."

The emotional circus of a baseball post-season tends to bring a higher level of intensity for players and fans, since a championship hangs on performance. One win could be the difference between squirting your teammates with champagne or quietly cleaning out your locker. Playoff games and other pressure situations force desires and fears to the forefront of a player's mind, and, in a flash, emotions can steer a player away from disciplined habits and routines into spontaneous, result-driven actions void of rational thought. A hitter who swings through a face-high fastball for strike three with the go-ahead run at third base knows not to swing at that pitch—and rarely even flinches at it—under less pressure-filled circumstances. Because he wants nothing more than to drive in that run, his discipline is lost in the moment. For Clemens, his desire to win in the worst way overwhelmed his composure and his ability to control his thoughts and adjust to his situation. Understanding why something like this happens is the first step in developing habits to become a clutch performer.

Dr. Daniel Goleman, in his 1995 book *Emotional Intelligence*, says that your mind has two parts: the *emotional mind* that feels and the *rational mind* that involves awareness, thinking, and comprehension. Goleman also concludes that emotions have the power to take over your thinking and behavior, which explains why some very disciplined athletes, such as Roger Clemens, can lose their self-control in important ballgames.

When the emotional mind is in control:

Awareness is lost. Ballplayers lose awareness of their own intensity level and do not realize they have physically begun trying too hard. Pitchers overthrow. Hitters squeeze the bat and overswing. Defenders overrun balls. Players are mentally unaware that their intensity level has risen to an unproductive level. Awareness of what is going on during a game is also lost, as players become distracted with too many thoughts and feelings. In game two of the 2000 World Series between the New York Yankees and the New York Mets, Mike Piazza broke his bat on a foul ball. Clemens, now a Yankee, jumped off the mound to field the ball but picked up the end of Piazza's shattered bat instead and fired it up the first base line as Piazza ran past. This incident nearly started a brawl because Piazza thought Clemens was throwing the bat at him. Clemens swore that the act was unintentional and that he was merely trying to throw the bat toward the bat boy on the on-deck circle. "I had no idea Mike was running," Clemens said after the game. "I guess it came close to him. I came back to the dugout and I said, 'I've got to get control of my emotions and calm down.'" In Clemens's defense, Yankee manager Joe Torre asked, "Why would he throw it at him? So he could get thrown out of the game in the second game of the World Series? Does that make any sense to anybody?" The umpires understood Torre's defense and did not eject Clemens from the game. But when a player's emotions are in control of his common sense, he is not clearly seeing or understanding the events surrounding him.

Thinking becomes irrational. The emotional mind will lead athletes into thinking about things they should not be considering. After making an error on an easy, two-hop ground ball, an infielder replays the negative image over and over in his mind and begins to feel that he does not want the next ball hit to him. The infielder anticipates an error on the next play instead of a clean catch. When the error becomes the dominant thought in his mind, the player greatly increases his chances of making another error on the next play.

Comprehension is lost. Emotions interfere with a person's ability to comprehend what is happening around him and to figure out solutions. Thinking becomes defensive. He fails to make adjustments to his game because he has no clue that he has performed poorly or done anything wrong.

Judgment is lost. Decisions made under emotional duress will not be as good. A person may say or do things he later regrets. A pitcher stares down an infielder who made an error on a routine ground ball that would have gotten him out of a jam. The pitcher's action starts a verbal confrontation between himself and the fielder at an inappropriate time.

A person is more inclined to act impulsively. A batter abandons his hitting plan and swings for the fences at the first fastball he sees, regardless of its location.

In response to emotional or physical challenges, the human body has an "emergency preparedness system" that often reacts like a shot of adrenaline. As a person undergoes stress, whether emotional or physical, the body prepares for the *fight or flight* reflex. All athletes can relate to the physical signs of the *fight or flight* reflex: the heart beats quicker and harder; breathing become shorter and more frequent; the hair on one's arms and neck stands up; perspiration increases; and the liver releases glucose for quick energy, which many often mistake for a release of adrenaline. As a result of these physical changes, an athlete can experience emotional consequences during clutch moments. Timidity or overaggressiveness are often the result when an athlete does not manage and control the physical and mental changes that occur under pressure.

The rational mind is a key to overcoming emotional moments that threaten to disrupt performance. When the human body reacts to emotional stress, the player must be aware of the physical changes in his body and refocus his thoughts and energy to the task at hand in order to control his physical performance. Players who do not let their emotions run on impulse, who focus more intently, often experience some of their best performances. By consciously controlling their thoughts and the speed at which their thoughts are coming and going, athletes can begin to channel the energy boost that their bodies feel to a level that enhances their performance.

When the rational mind is in control:

Awareness is sharp. The rational mind allows a person to live in the present instead of in the emotional past or desired future. A ballplayer is fully aware of the situations occurring in the game and can plan for different scenarios. A player is also in touch with his effort level and emotions and has a sense of control over himself.

Thinking is clear and focused. Dave Stewart talks of organizing his thoughts and putting them into compartments. He is in control of his thoughts instead of his thoughts controlling him.

Comprehension improves. Ballplayers are able to figure things out and make physical and mental adjustments as situations change during the course of a game.

Sound decisions are made. Judgment is not clouded by a flood of emotions.

Everyone's intensity level for maximum performance is different. Some all-stars play with a nonchalant, relaxed demeanor, like Jim Edmonds, and some play with an angry intensity, like Randy Johnson. Most major league players are somewhere in between with their intensity, in the style of Derek Jeter or Alex Rodriguez. Regardless of a player's intensity level, emotions must be managed to focus and play the game properly at each individual's game rhythm.

According to some of the personality assessment tests given to prospective amateur players by various major league scouting departments, some individuals are born with a low inherent anxiety and are genetically wired to handle stress more calmly than others. Although those individuals have an easier time staying cool in the clutch, they feel pressure, anxiety, fear, and anger like everyone else. This chapter will offer methods to improve your game when emotions are running high.

COOL IN THE CLUTCH

One of the strongest attributes of mental toughness is being able to get the job done when the game is on the line. Being cool in the clutch is often what distinguishes great major league players from everyone else. Yankee shortstop Derek Jeter has a knack for making the big play or getting the big hit at the crucial moment. "If Derek Jeter wasn't always in the right place at the right time," Jason Giambi said of his Yankee teammate, "I'd call it a fluke. But he is. The guy's just plain clutch." Part of Jeter's mystique is his ability always to look relaxed and confident, whether it's playoff time or a spring training game. He gives the same effort with the same rhythm to all his actions, and a bad call or an error rarely unnerves him. Clutch players like Jeter take the attitude that they want to be in pressure situations and that they play at their best when the game, or the season, is on the line. A tremendous part of being a clutch performer is wanting to be in the game when its outcome is decided, and to be the one who is responsible for the game's finish.

Pressure situations do not occur only in the eighth or ninth innings of a ballgame. There may be turning points in a game from the first inning on, or any time a player senses an urgency or a need to perform *right now* for any reason. A player's desire to succeed has a greater impact on what is perceived to be a pressure situation than the actual game itself. If a player believes he must have a great game today in order for the manager to still like him and put his name in the lineup, then every pitch, play, at-bat, and game situation will have importance and pressure. The player could be in a blowout game with his team winning 12-2, but if he has not yet recorded a hit, he may believe that he will be riding the bench unless he hits a home run in his final at-bat. Certain situations do have the potential to be clutch moments because their outcome may decide who wins or loses, or they may cause a shift in a team's momentum. But, ultimately, the pressure a ballplayer feels individually stems from the desire to succeed in that moment in the game. No desire, no pressure. If the outcome is irrelevant to the player, he will not feel there has been anything lost. That said, every great athletic performer has a strong desire to succeed.

When a player is said to "choke" in the clutch, fear of failure is not the only reason for a poor performance. Some athletes who choke have such a burning desire to win that they try too hard and self-destruct, losing their focus, discipline, and game plans. Great desire and competitiveness are characteristics that every elite athlete must possess, but without self-awareness and discipline they can lead to failure. Here is a list of how athletes choke:

Overaggressiveness is the most common form of choking. The desire to succeed this instant is so great that patience and discipline are lost, and the player's effort level goes out of control.

Being too careful or cautious occurs when a player's focus is on not making a mistake or looking bad. A player is slow to react because he is afraid of doing the wrong thing and often waits too long to make his move. A pitcher might aim the ball and squeeze it rather than having a smooth release. A hitter flinches at a hanging curveball, not really sure whether he should swing or not.

Loss of focus and concentration. A player becomes result-oriented, thinking about driving in the go-ahead run or not letting a hitter get a base hit, without formulating a plan of how to accomplish that result.

Increased muscular tension from either trying too hard physically or from nervousness. He gets tight.

"Brain-locking" is a term used to describe a player's emotions overwhelming his thoughts, at which point he stops reacting to, or even recognizing, what is going on around him. A batter takes a called third strike right down the middle with two outs and the bases loaded. A pitcher fails to cover first base on a ground ball to the first baseman, and the hitter is safe.

Failure to stick with the plan. A player becomes impulsive and gambles with his play.

Fear of failure. Players who want to win but doubt themselves may think, "I do not want to be the guy who loses the ball game."

A natural assumption is that the most physically gifted athletes are the best clutch players because of their superior talent. Although physical talent is always a plus, the "blue-collar" baseball players—such as Craig Counsell, David Eckstein, and Pete Rose—who have proven themselves under playoff pressure dismiss that myth. Until the 2002 World Series, Barry Bonds was known for choking in the playoffs. He had struggled badly during his previous playoff appearances, with both the Pittsburgh Pirates and San Francisco Giants, but in 2002 he hit seven home runs and had thirteen walks in thirteen playoff games. Bonds was noticeably more patient at the plate than he had been in the past. His mental game had matured, and he grew cool in the clutch.

Performing in important moments requires the ability to focus on and execute a plan despite the emotions and distractions surrounding you. Following is a list of ways a player can improve his ability to focus in clutch moments and control his emotions and physical excitement when the desire to succeed is running rampant in his mind and body.

Confidence in yourself and your ability. In a clutch moment, you must believe that you are the better competitor than your opponent. You must *know* you will succeed. Being prepared for your opponent with a plan of attack will help give you confidence. Reflect on previous successes and let them elevate your confidence level. Your body language and posture must exude and reinforce the confidence that you are feeling. If you do not believe you can succeed, you will be right, and it will show in your posture (head hanging, shoulders sagging, lifeless movements). See yourself as a winner, not as someone hoping to win.

Do not mistake nervousness for pressure. Everyone feels nervous to some extent, especially in potentially game-changing moments. It is normal to experience butterflies in your stomach and extra tension in your body during games. Learn to play past the nervousness. Develop the skills that will help you concentrate and focus more acutely.

Have a plan for handling nervousness in a clutch situation. You can tune the TV to any big-league game and see a hitter step away from the batter's box to stretch and take a couple of practice swings, or see a pitcher step off the mound and use the resin bag or retie a shoe. These routines allow the player to refocus between pitches and temporarily escape the pressure.

Desire to be on the playing field in clutch moments. Derek Jeter, Curt Schilling, Pedro Martinez, Shawn Green—all want the opportunity to decide the outcome of a game. They realize they may fail but instead choose to focus on the positive side of playing to win.

Accept that success does not have to be pretty. Luis Gonzalez of the Diamondbacks is a World Series hero for his broken-bat, bloop single that drove in the winning run in the bottom of the ninth of game seven of the 2001 World Series against the Yankees. Mental toughness is about finding a way to get the job done for the team, no matter how it looks. Games rarely end on a home run or a pitcher striking out the side.

Slip into your routines, focusing on the process and not on the desired result. Wanting to make the perfect pitch or hitting a screamer into the gap will not make it happen. Being result-oriented will only fuel your desire and increase the pressure to perform that you are already feeling. Instead, focus on your approach, on what you need to do to make the pitch or have a great at-bat. Your routines for preparation before games and between pitches gives your mind a positive focus on something you can control. You have no control over an umpire's call or a great play. Have you ever noticed that you are more nervous before a big game, possibly experiencing nausea, muscular tension, and worry, but that once the game begins and you fall into your routines of playing the game, your body and mind relax? Next time you feel pressure to achieve a result, immerse yourself in the routine of playing the game and focus on what you can control.

Breathe. This sounds simple enough, but when your body's fight-or-flight reflex kicks in, your breathing rhythm gets out of synch, often leaving your body slightly depleted of oxygen. Some people find themselves holding their breath under stress; in others, their breath comes quicker and shorter, both of which can lead to more rapid, more erratic thoughts. You can slow down your thoughts and relax your body by performing *cleansing breaths:* slowly inhaling air from your belly up to the top of your lungs and releasing the air through a relaxed mouth. Do not force the air out through pursed lips but instead prolong the exhale to clear your mind and relieve tension. Consider the breathing technique and how relaxing it feels. Doing this two or three times will help oxygenate the body and slow down your thoughts so you can focus on one thing at a time. When you are done, step back into the moment with your attention on what you can control. Slow stretching movements will also help to slow down breathing and thoughts. Cleansing breaths and slow stretching are two of the best and most common ways of handling nervousness. They should be included in any routine for calming yourself in clutch situations.

Talk to yourself, or mumble, in order to fine-tune focus and block out distractions. By talking out loud to yourself, or mumbling, it becomes difficult for distractions to enter your mind. "This is the opportunity I've been waiting for. I love challenges." "See the ball, nice and easy." "Stay back, and put the ball right in the catcher's mitt." This is the most effective way to control your thoughts when your mind starts racing.

Play with the same intensity all the time; do not try to turn it up a notch when the game is on the line. Some professional athletes feel they can turn it on when they really want to perform well, but the question then becomes: If it helps to turn it up a notch, why not play that way all the time? The fact is, it does not help to try harder, because most athletes are better in nonpressure situations, such as during practice or when the bases are empty. Players who achieve consistently in the clutch are also the ones who are just plain consistent. They discipline themselves to give the same effort throughout an entire game, regardless of the score. A player's energy level sometimes gets a boost from the excitement of the moment, but players who are consistent in the clutch recognize the added energy. They manage themselves by slowing their breathing and their thoughts, which calms—but does not remove—the adrenaline-like buzz the body feels. Most players want that extra energy because they feel it makes them stronger and quicker, but if it is not managed it can lead to overaggressiveness and out-of-synch mechanics.

Prepare for pressure situations by putting pressure on yourself in practice. Have the same high standards in practice that you have for yourself in games. Allot some time in practice to put on your game face and practice with the same mental and physical energy you use in games. For a pitcher, it could be having a mentally intense bullpen session. Both Roger Clemens and Greg Maddux react to poorly executed pitches in a bullpen in the same manner and intensity they do in a game. In effect, they are also practicing how they mentally handle a poor pitch in game, and how they plan to fix it and refocus on the next pitch. Lazily shagging fly balls in the outfield or playing Home Run Derby with your hitting group does not prepare you to play a game or handle clutch situations. When it is your turn to practice, whether you are taking ground balls from a coach or stepping into the cage to hit, put on your game face. Do not practice your practice habits; practice how you will play the game.

Play fearless. Play to win. Too often, teams take a lead into the late innings and after playing aggressively for five or six innings, they suddenly become timid or cautious. They lose the drive to continue pouring on the runs. This occurs when a team begins playing *not to lose* the game. They are winning now, but they do not want to lose, so they start trying to play perfect baseball, instead of relying on the relaxed, aggressive style that got them ahead to begin with. Whether you're ahead or behind in the late innings, playing without fear requires the discipline to push any thoughts of losing out of your head and remain focused on playing to win. The 2002 World Champion Anaheim Angels had a fearless reputation in late-inning games. Their "rally monkey" would make an appearance on their scoreboard, the fans would stand up and yell, and if an Angels player got a base hit, the feeling of, "Uh-oh, here they come again," would often affect opponents and fans alike. There can be no fear of losing if you are to remain loose, relaxed, and focused in tight games.

Do not dwell on the past. Thinking about that day's 0-for-4 at the plate while stepping into the batter's box in the ninth inning with the score tied will not help you succeed. Likewise, being full of yourself after hitting a couple of home runs will not help when it's your turn to hit in a tie game. What will help you succeed is staying focused on your game plan and having the right approach for the situation. If you are 0-for-4, learn from that experience and adjust your plan to try to fix the part of your game that broke down. Or if you had four quality at-bats but have no hits to show for it, have the discipline to trust your game plan. Play in the moment. Do not be distracted with thoughts of the past or future.

In 2002, Rice University stood two outs away from beating Notre Dame to advance in the College World Series, clinging to a tenuous 3-2 lead. The Irish's 5-foot-8 senior leadoff hitter, Steve Stanley, came to the plate knowing it would almost certainly be his last minutes in a Notre Dame uniform if he failed to reach base. Stanley responded with a line-drive triple, then moments later scored to tie the game before teammate Brian Stavisky hit a walk-off home run to give the Irish a 5-3 win. This was about as clutch as it comes.

"When the going gets tough, that's when the best athletes rise to the occasion," Stanley said months later. "My father [Mike Stanley] coached me when I was younger, and he always said, 'When the game's on the line, we want Steve at the plate. When it counts, we can count on Steve to do something to help us.' I love to rise to the occasion; I love to get that chance to come through. I want to keep having that persona."

Angels rookie reliever Francisco Rodriguez found himself at peace in the showcase of the 2002 World Series. Despite spending most of the year in the minors, he emerged as a dominant force in the post-season, putting up a 5-1 record and allowing only four earned runs in 18-2/3 innings. "I felt completely at ease," he said during the World Series. "I had complete control of my pitches. I'm trying to do nothing but have fun out there. This is a job I like. . . . I'm young, and I have the heart to do this job."

Being clutch begins with the desire to be The Man in the biggest situations, and follows with learning to command the tension rather than having the tension take control. By mastering these skills, every player can improve his performance in tension-packed situations.

GRINDING IT OUT

"Grinding it out" is an oft-used expression that refers to a player's ability to generate mental energy and drive to accomplish a goal when circumstances give him an excuse to go through the motions or quit. A player who "grinds it out" plays with enthusiasm and hustle when he is ill, when it is raining, when his team is being blown out of a game, when he is exhausted, and when his friends and teammates have stopped playing hard. While playing under pressure usually involves having to calm yourself down when desire and emotions create too much tension and energy, "grinding it out" involves the opposite tactic—generating energy and drive when there is a lack of stimulus.

Baseball's all-time hits leader, Pete Rose, was called "Charlie Hustle" for the way he played the game. He ran the bases hard all the time, not just when he felt good or considered it important. Coaches and managers at every amateur and professional level rave about the player with mediocre tools who busts it every day he steps onto the playing field. With a typical minor league season of 140 games, and the majors playing a 162-game schedule, a player who grinds it out becomes a valuable commodity to a team. The 2002 Angels were successful, in large part, due to their team concept of hustling all the time regardless of the score. Major league scouts were surprised to see David Eckstein as the Angels' shortstop and leadoff hitter, considering how his arm is far below average compared with those of other shortstops around the league, and his limited natural talent on offense. But Eckstein proved his critics wrong with his relentless hustle and earned his teammates' praise throughout the regular season and playoffs with his style of play and his knack for getting the job done.

Athletes who have the mental toughness to grind out performances under less than optimal circumstances rely on certain qualities: discipline, determination, playing injured or ill, and competitiveness are among the most important.

Discipline, as it relates to athletics, means doing what has to be done, when it has to be done, the way it should be done, and doing it *that* way all the time. Mentally tough athletes are disciplined athletes. Tiger Woods, Michael Jordan, Wayne Gretzky, and Alex Rodriguez did not get to the elite level of their sports by cutting corners in their workouts or by slacking off in games when they did not feel 100 percent. Instead they raised the standard for performance and effort in their respective sports by persevering in all different situations. Golf legend Arnold Palmer said in a *Los Angeles Times* article: "What I am saying is, a guy who knows where he is going and what he wants to do and builds up to that point . . . he's got to really have himself fixed for bad breaks, weather delays, or whatever the conditions might be. It's easy after you lose to say, 'Well, I got a bad break.' But that doesn't mean squat." Having the discipline not to give in mentally to distractions and other obstacles is essential to the athlete who wants to grind it out.

Another essential quality of grinding it out is determination. In order to push yourself physically, you must have the mental determination to complete a performance with life and energy. A grinder does not stop playing to win while there are still innings to be played. There is no quitting mentally or physically. Playing the game the way it should be played *all* of the time means just that. A mentally tough player does not stop playing as well as he can simply because his team is losing 13-5. Big innings have befallen many teams in the late innings after they took what they thought was a comfortable lead. The determination to hustle down the first base line in the top of the fifteenth inning on a routine grounder to the shortstop, in case the first baseman bobbles a poor throw, is what grinding it out can do for a club. No one will know the final turning point of a game until the game is over. Sometimes the deciding moment occurs in the first inning, sometimes it's the last play of the game. Being determined to play hard all the time will put constant pressure on the opposition and place you and your team in a position to take advantage when the opposition makes a mistake.

Playing with injuries and illness is also an essential quality of grinding it out. Some major league players do not want to play if they are not 100 percent, because it may affect their batting average or ERA. But many players, such as a Cal Ripken, a Darin Erstad, or a Tim Hudson, do not succumb to built-in excuses, even if the reasons may be legitimate. They are determined to play to the best of their ability despite how they feel. Some injuries and illnesses demand missing time at work; those instances are not in dispute. But once an athlete is cleared to play by medical personnel, and there is no longer a physical question of being able to play and compete, it becomes a matter of mental toughness as to who plays and who does not. In a long baseball season there will always be strains, pains, pulls, bruises, headaches, and viruses that work their way through a clubhouse. The players know who wants to play and who wants the time off that the ailment offers. Grinding it out with injuries and illnesses requires that you know yourself—what you can and cannot play with—and get good medical advice. Once you make the decision to play the game, you give the best possible effort with no excuses.

Competitiveness is also needed to grind out a performance. Competitive athletes enjoy challenges. They enjoy overcoming obstacles and proving critics and doubters wrong. They enjoy playing in big games, making great plays, and physically pushing themselves to be stronger and faster. But some athletes lose their competitive edge in the ordinary, routine details of playing their game. A batter who grinds it out pushes himself to remain competitive when running from home to first base after hitting a ground ball to the second baseman. An outfielder gives full focus on a routine pop-up and plays it properly. A pitcher hustles off the mound to cover first base on a ground ball to the right side of the infield. A shortstop keeps his eyes on the ball and remains alert for bad hops while fielding. The ability to remain competitive in attending to even the easiest, smallest details is often the advantage in winning games. Teams beat themselves every day by failing to execute routine plays.

Performing with a grinder mentality sometimes requires having to generate emotions and intensity to get up for certain games, practice drills, or even going to the gym. Routines are often the foundation for getting your mind to a certain place. Getting to the locker room, getting dressed, stretching, and doing any drills necessary to get your skills ready for a game all help in preparing the mind and body to perform. Some players also have Walkmans to play their own music that gets them in the right mood. An inspirational talk from a coach can motivate. Watching video of good performances can excite a player to perform at his best. But once the mind and body are ready to perform, it requires the player's discipline, determination, and competitiveness to grind it out for the entire game, practice, or other endeavor that requires full attention and effort.

DEALING WITH UMPIRES

Without a doubt, dealing with umpires requires mental toughness. Most on-field exchanges with umpires are over controversial calls, where anger, frustration, and other emotions rise to the surface. Sometimes it all happens very quickly. What needs to be understood is that umpires make mistakes. They will miss calls that are pretty obvious to everyone else in the ballpark, just as a ground ball going through a player's legs is an obvious error. The umpire can make only one team happy with his call. It will help a player emotionally to accept that bad calls are a part of the game, and to move on to the next pitch instead of fighting the call. The game will continue with or without the angry player.

Once a questionable call is made, a player has only three choices: 1) Suck it up, keep his mouth closed, and get back to business. 2) Say his peace and move on, quickly refocusing on the next pitch, whether on offense or defense. Or 3) Let his emotions run wild, losing focus and concentration and possibly getting ejected.

One example of not keeping cool is the Carl Everett incident of July 15, 2000. In the midst of an all-star-quality season, Everett blew his cool. Plate umpire Ron Kulpa pointed out to Everett that his back foot was outside the chalked batter's box and too close to home plate. Everett began arguing and quickly lost control of his emotions. Filled with rage and excitement, he first bumped the umpire with his chest and then head-butted him while continuing to yell at him. Eventually he had to be restrained by coaches in order to get him away from the umpire. For his inexcusable behavior, Everett was given a ten-game suspension without pay by the commissioner's office.

At the time of this incident, Boston was battling the Yankees for first place in the American League Eastern Division. During Everett's absence the Red Sox began to slip out of contention and never got back into the race. Had Everett's rational mind taken control when he felt himself start to scream, he would never have made contact with the umpire. He might still have argued with passion and gotten thrown out of the game, but he would not have chosen to lose more than $100,000 in salary and jeopardize his team's playoff chances because an umpire asked him to keep both feet in the batter's box. That was not a rational act.

Players who let bad calls fester in their mind begin to see the umpire as an adversary. When that happens, those players start to question every close call and may even feel they have to change their game plan because the umpire is so "bad." A pitcher may feel he has to throw every pitch right down the middle to get a strike call. A hitter starts swinging at any pitch remotely close to the strike zone. And the umpire usually gets blamed for their poor performance.

Mentally tough players do not lose their cool to bad calls. They may get angry and say their peace, or they may converse with the umpire to get a better feel for what he is seeing and calling that day, but they keep battling and making adjustments. The only time it may help to argue, or present your side of the call, is when the umpire is humble enough to admit—at least to himself—that he may have made the wrong call and is willing to listen to an argument and ask a fellow crew member for assistance. Otherwise, arguing with umpires is just blowing off steam, which could distract the umpire from his focus on the next pitch if he gets too emotional and angry.

The mentally tough player takes responsibility for his actions and knows when he is approaching the breaking point of losing his rational thought after a bad call. The team player does not want to jeopardize his team's chances of winning by getting thrown out for an impulsive action, although we have all seen players lose it and later express remorse for their actions. Letting emotions fly in an argument should be a rare occurrence, not a repeated behavior. Even great players sometimes reach a point of frustration for one reason or another, and say things that will get them thrown out of a game. But they usually recognize it and make a conscious decision to do so.

Managers get thrown out of games more than anyone else, and at times they do so with the intent of motivating their club. Players like to see their manager argue on their behalf over close calls, and sometimes it has a rallying effect on the team as they band together in an us-against-them mentality. But arguing too many calls, too frequently, not only wears on an umpire's patience, it can also lose its motivating effect and become a distraction to the manager's players. Sometimes a team can be seen laughing at its manager as he gets tossed from yet another game.

Keys for dealing with umpires include:

1. **Accept that bad calls are part of baseball**. As long as there are human umpires, there will be disputed calls. As a hitter, you will have strikes called against you that are four inches outside. Pitchers will throw breaking balls that fool the umpire as well as the hitter. But there will be calls that go in your favor too. During his playing days, when a call went against Mark McGwire, he said to himself, "That's okay, that's baseball." And he was right. Watch any sport on television and you will see calls by officials questioned. Once you are able to accept that there will *always* be disputed calls, you will be able to hold back your emotions more effectively and consistently.

2. **Be self-aware**. Know the signs that indicate when your emotions are beginning to impair your judgment. If you start feeling aggressive toward the umpire and want to verbally abuse him or her, chances are you are losing your cool. There are also physical signs, such as veins pumping in the neck and temples, and hair rising up on the neck.

3. **Keep your rational mind in control**. If you want to keep your composure, slow down your thoughts by taking a deep breath. Speak with a low and even tone of voice. Excited people yell.

4. **Pick the times you choose to discuss calls with umpires**. If you voice your opinion on every close call that goes against your team from the first inning on, umpires will start to tune you out. Save your arguments for those times you want to be heard the most: when you have a chance to make the umpire think about how the call may have altered the game.

5. **Take the viewpoint that all umpires care if they make the correct call**. Umpires do not want to look bad or be embarrassed by blatantly obvious missed calls. It is a rare instance when an umpire reverses his own call, but if you make a

good argument, you may get him to ask another crew member for assistance. This is actually becoming more common; there are more calls being reversed by this procedure than there were ten years ago.

6. **Do not get personal when arguing with an umpire**. You can say, "I saw it this way. . . ." But if your argument is, "You stink!" or "You're blind," you can expect to get tossed from the game. The point is, to make a difference in the way the game is called, make an argument that makes sense. Some umpires will occasionally let you know that they missed it, or will say that they will be in a better position to see the play next time. That may not appease your frustration at the time, but you have accomplished something that could favor your club in the future.

7. **Dialogue with an umpire should be done with a purpose**. A hitter, a pitcher, or a catcher may want to talk to an umpire to get a better understanding of the strike zone. A good way to open a dialogue with an umpire without making the ump defensive is to say, "I saw the ball inside," or "I saw it [the pitch] hitting the corner." The umpire may respond by saying it was close, or "It was just off the plate," but you should get an idea of how close it was for the umpire. If you refrain from making an accusing statement like "That wasn't a strike; it was below my knees," the umpire is less likely to get defensive and retort with an attitude. If you are the hitter having a conversation between pitches about a call, you should avoid looking back at the umpire, which lets everyone know you are questioning his call. Look down at the ground or out to the playing field while talking about calls. And do not ask the umpire, "Where was that pitch?" You will lose credibility with the umpire if you let him know that you are not seeing the ball well.

8. **Discuss calls with an umpire between innings, when fans, teammates, and opposition are not paying such close attention**. An umpire is more likely to be open with you

about his decisions if the spotlight is not on him. An umpire is taught to stay in control of the game. If he thinks you are questioning his play-calling ability in full view of everyone, he may be short with his responses or get defensive.

Emotions are part of baseball. A player must learn to know himself and his body's signals when he begins to lose emotional control, so that he can defuse the emotional mind and retain rational thought. A player who allows an umpire's call to knock him off his game damages his team's chances of winning. The challenge is to learn to use emotions to advantage, taking that burst of energy and turning it into motivation, then getting back into the game with the next pitch. Remaining cool has its rewards, and staying in the game to continue competing is one big reward.

INTIMIDATION

During his playing days, Bob Geren gained a reputation as a top defensive catcher, but he was not known for his hitting skills. While playing for the Yankees in 1980, Geren ran into one of the true challenges of his career against Texas Rangers ace Nolan Ryan.

"We were going into Texas. I knew Nolan was going to be pitching, so I figured I had the day off because I was being used exclusively against left-handed pitchers," Geren recalls. "Even though I knew I wouldn't be playing, I had a lot of family and friends in the park. When I came to the park, I didn't bother to look at the lineup card; I knew I wasn't playing. When I was told I was in the lineup, I was shocked. I hadn't hit against a right-handed pitcher all year. I thought, 'Why me? Why tonight against Ryan?' I had never faced Ryan, and he wasn't any fun to face even for the guys in the lineup every day. Ryan not only threw the ball as hard as anyone, but he had that nasty curve and a bit of a mean streak. If you had good swings at him, he would brush you back in a minute. I'll be honest, *I was intimidated.*

"My first two at-bats, I struck out on six pitches. I had no chance. I was on deck for my third at-bat when we had runners on first and second with Roberto Kelly hitting [and two outs]. The count went to two balls and no strikes (on Kelly) when Nolan surprised everyone by throwing a curveball for ball three. I thought, 'What's going on here?' If the runners were on second and third with first base open, I can understand him not caring if he walked Kelly to get to me, but not with runners on first and second. On the 3-0 count, he threw another curve. Now I was totally embarrassed in front of all my friends. Nolan showed he had no respect at all for me. I got mad and determined. I guess that helped me focus, because on the first pitch I lined a single to center field, driving in two runs. I was still upset when I came to the plate the next time; I hit a home run with a man on, making it four RBIs on the day."

Geren learned quickly that being intimidated allowed no chance for success. He also learned the power of attitude and emotion. His anger overpowered his fear and intimidation of Ryan. As he said, "It helped me focus."

Intimidation is a part of all competitive sports. When one athlete or team is trying to beat its rival, intimidation is used to try to gain an advantage. It involves the use of fear. If a player feels threatened by an opponent, he could have a fear of failure, or a fear for his own safety, such as being hit by a pitch or taken out by a hard slide. More important, intimidation causes a loss of concentration and focus; if you are intimidated, you spend more time thinking about that than focusing on your responsibilities. Sometimes the threat is real, sometimes it is imagined, but if you—the player—feel intimidated, the effects will be real. Intimidation is physically responsible for an increase in both tension and anxiety, which is a formula for failure during competition.

There are many ways athletes can be intimidated during competition:

An opponent can intimidate. If an opponent has a reputation or history of winning and projects so much confidence that a player or team feels beaten before the game even starts, intimidation is present. The Oakland Athletics in the late 1980s and early 1990s intimidated with their physical size—the Bash Brothers of Jose Canseco, Mark McGwire, Dave Parker, and Dave Henderson. A pitcher may be intimidated by a long home run off his best pitch. Many pitchers have been known to scrap an effective curveball or change-up after it has been hit hard once or twice. Many hitters are done mentally for an at-bat or a game after being hit by a pitch or knocked down by a high and tight fastball. If the pitcher is a little wild with his control, hitters will not be comfortable in the batter's box, especially if the fastball is in the ninety-plus mile-per-hour range.

Managers and coaches can intimidate. If a coach or manager yells at a player, that can be intimidating. If a player is embarrassed in front of his teammates, family, or stadium crowd after a visible tongue-lashing, fear and insecurity can overwhelm the player into submission and defeat.

Game situations can intimidate. A clutch situation where the game's outcome could be decided by the next pitch or swing can be intimidating. Bases loaded, two outs, and a tie ballgame in the bottom of the ninth inning—there's a lot of responsibility in that situation.

Stadiums/location can be very intimidating. Imagine walking into Yankee Stadium for the first time to play a game. The fans are loud, the crowds are huge, and the stadium is filled with history. Many rookies and veterans get unnerved in the "Bronx Zoo."

The mentally tough do not get intimidated; they *are* the intimidators. Most intimidation in professional sports is from the "projection" of confidence by the intimidator. Think of Mets' ace pitcher Pedro Martinez, whose reputation for winning, his ninety-six-mile-per-hour fastball, and his remarkable change-up are a source of frustration for many major league hitters. Most hitters who face Martinez know before play ever starts that they will be in for a tough game. He shows no fear on the mound and openly challenges hitters with his best stuff. If you do not believe you are better than your opposition, you have been intimidated into thinking you cannot win. And if you approach a game with an attitude that you cannot win, you have lost your focus and your confidence. Pedro Martinez *is* an intimidator.

To be an intimidator requires the right attitude. You cannot hope to succeed; you have to know it and feel it. Everyone, at one time or another, has experienced the feeling that you *know* you are going to get the big hit right now, or you are going to get this hitter out. Those feelings were a projection of your attitude and helped you succeed in a clutch situation. Intimidation is all about attitudes and perceptions, and the mentally tough player always sees himself winning in any situation. Fans recognize the excitement when two intimidators face off against each other: Barry Bonds versus Randy Johnson, or Pedro Martinez versus Alex Rodriguez. Attitudes are a mental edge.

Here is a sampling of positive attitudes dealing with intimidation:

- I will not be intimidated. I AM THE INTIMIDATOR.
- The competition is not a factor in my approach.
- If you knock me down, I will get right back up and be focused, holding my ground in the batter's box. I cannot be intimidated.
- I will not let the situation intimidate me. I'll just keep playing my game.
- I am a winner. No matter what happens, I will find a way to succeed.

- I cannot be intimidated. I will not show fear or nervousness. I will be calm and cool, and stick to my game plan.
- I will respect the great players, but I will not be intimidated in their presence.

In competitive sports, those who are most successful over time will always have an aura around them. The New York Yankees, the Los Angeles Lakers, Tiger Woods—all hold a mental advantage over their opponents before the game even starts. The feeling—and to a certain extent the truth—they create is that they are the odds-on favorite to win every time, and their opponents have to beat them. Whoever steps on the same field, court, or course with them had better bring their best game to have even a chance of winning. That perception unnerves players who lack the confidence in themselves that they can be less than perfect and still win. In other words, they feel they are not on equal ground physically or mentally with the best in their sport, and anything less than perfection will result in a loss. That perception will defeat those who lack the mental toughness to stay focused and play their game until the fat lady sings. The fact is, underdogs can and do win. The Angels beat the Yankees in the 2002 American League playoffs and went on to beat Barry Bonds and the Giants in the World Series. The New England Patriots beat the St. Louis Rams in the 2002 Super Bowl. Tiger Woods does not win every tournament in which he plays. If an athlete cannot look into the eyes of a competitor and see himself winning, he will never be in a position mentally to capitalize on the chances his opponent gives him. BE THE INTIMIDATOR.

PLAYING IT COOL—ACTING PROFESSIONALLY

Maintaining composure in adverse moments is an act of emotional control and discipline. Respect comes to those who can stay calm and keep their wits when they are under stress. Submitting to rage and disappointment is viewed as a weakness, as evidenced by crowd reaction to the disgruntled players who give fans the middle finger after receiving a barrage of insults during the game. It demands a confident, disciplined, poised athlete to deny himself an act of prideful defense in lashing back at verbal abusers. Pedro Martinez revealed to reporters almost a year after the fact that he was taunted by Cleveland Indians fans at Jacobs Field as he prepared to pitch in relief for the Boston Red Sox in game five of the 1999 American League Divisional Series. Martinez said he was showered with racial slurs by some fans and received one death threat. "I remember being told when I was warming up, 'You are going to be shot.' They were calling me 'beaner' and saying, 'Go back to your country . . . you don't belong in this country.' That came from fans who probably just wanted me to get out of there. They said so much discriminating stuff to me, it would sound unreal. It was the first time I had ever heard such things, and I heard them here in Cleveland." Martinez managed to maintain his composure and pitched six no-hit innings in the win against the Indians.

Playing it cool and acting professionally requires confidence and the ability to block out distractions. Martinez filtered out the fans and focused on his game plan. He had the self-confidence to know that what the fans were yelling at him was untrue and not worth paying attention to. He knew that some fans come to the ballpark with the belief that a twenty-dollar bill buys them the right to be a jerk, and he refused to be intimidated by complete strangers who were trying to get into his head and distract him from the duty at hand. The Cleveland fans produced exactly the opposite result of what they desired—their taunts only served to make Martinez more focused on his game. He used his emotion to advantage and dominated the game.

Ultimately there is no better way to quiet critics than with a solid performance on the field. Yelling back at a rowdy crowd, making an obscene gesture, even starting an on-the-field brawl cannot quiet a crowd or the opposition like a victory or a great performance. When Hall of Famer Reggie Jackson was still playing, it was known throughout the American League that if a pitcher knocked him down with a fastball seemingly on purpose, Reggie made the opposition pay with his bat. Jackson became the intimidator, and pitchers feared provoking him. He knew how to slow down his breathing in moments of excitement and calm his mind in order to focus on hitting his pitch. He stayed within himself during the most challenging moments.

Anyone can surrender to his emotions and fight back when he feels threatened. But it takes courage, discipline, and confidence to handle adversity in a professional manner. Grinding it out and hustling when exhausted, staying calm under pressure, dealing with umpires and intimidation, surviving unmet expectations, and turning the other cheek all require a sense of cool in order to stay focused on the task at hand: to play baseball to the best of your abilities every time you set foot on a baseball field and under any circumstance. That is a player of character, and a player who is mentally tough.

PUTTING ON THE "BLINDERS"

The coolest team in baseball during the late 1990s was the New York Yankees. Led by such players as Derek Jeter, Bernie Williams, and Mariano Rivera, they dominated post-season play with a businesslike approach. In *Joe Torre's Ground Rules for Winners*, Yankee manager Torre writes this about his team's mental approach: "Players who are involved in a postseason series—whatever the sport—get constant questions about winning the championship. When they start thinking championship, they get distracted from the business at hand—today's game. I tell players to put blinders on, whether they are up or down in a series. If they are down, the blinders keep them from getting overwhelmed. If they're up, the blinders keep them from losing their focus. Too often, teams with the lead in a series suffer a big letdown the moment they lose a game. Maybe they've been too busy celebrating the championship that hasn't yet happened. Players should be so wrapped up in playoff games that they won't realize that they won the championship until someone taps them on the shoulder with the news: 'Hey, it's over. You won it.'"

Torre's Yankees failed to keep this mind-set in 2004. After taking a 3-0 lead on Boston in the American League Championship Series, the Yankees lost four straight, the first time in Major League postseason history that a team had failed to win after being ahead three games to none.

Baseball is not a sprint, it's a marathon. The individual games and the season demand a sense of continued cool to avoid panic and ultimate collapse. Temptations abound in baseball for a player to lose his composure, then lose his game. Umpires, opponents, and fans all can get into a player's head and throw him off his game. The challenge of mental toughness is to translate those emotions into productive energy, as Reggie Jackson and Pedro Martinez have, and make cool into a personal credo.

6

FOCUS AND CONCENTRATION

In Dave Stewart's mind, he had been through nothing less than an emotional rape. During four seasons with the Texas Rangers and Philadelphia Phillies, his confidence had eroded and he had lost direction on how to pitch. By 1986 he found himself at Triple A Tacoma, an unfocused twenty-nine-year-old with a superior fastball that lacked command of the strike zone.

"I was concentrating on all the bad things that happened to me instead of thinking, 'It's just an out, you can get out of this inning.'" Stewart says. "The years in Texas and Philadelphia, the experience was so hard on me that it emotionally raped me of what I'd learned with the Dodgers. I was so used to hearing something negative from the people who coached me or managed me that I just thought, 'What will happen next?'"

Stewart had lost his focus. The lessons he learned coming up through the Dodgers organization were lost in negativity and apprehension of failure. Stewart threw two pitches to the backstop that evening in Tacoma and scarcely resembled a major league pitcher. Later that night he sat down with Karl Kuehl for a little talk. During the conversation, Kuehl learned that Stewart had earned a black belt in karate. He asked if Stewart had tried to transfer the focus and mind-set demanded by karate to pitching. "At that time I told Karl I didn't think the two were related," Stewart recalled in 2002. "As I started thinking about it more and more, I realized one of the main parts of being involved in martial arts is being able to center thoughts, so actually the two did relate. What I learned to do was to slow things down and to keep things very, very individual. You take everything in its individual place and put it in its individual slot. I kept taking each event one at a time. The arts helped me control and keep myself emotionally together. I think that's the biggest part of the process: keeping yourself emotionally together. Once I learned to control myself emotionally—not let situations take me over— I became much better at that time."

The next year A's pitching coach Dave Duncan taught Stewart the forkball, and the combination of an improved repertoire and masterful concentration turned Stewart into one of the great pitchers of his generation. He rolled off four consecutive twenty-win seasons and led the A's to three straight appearances in the World Series, then pitched for the Blue Jays' 1993 world championship team. An element of Stewart's intense focus became the famed "death stare," an ominous glare toward the batter that could melt glaciers. No matter the situation, Stewart gave the same facial expression. He never showed fear, never showed surprise.

"That's the process working," Stewart said. "Some people go into a different place or zone. It was constant mental preparation. As you pitch, you go through different highs and lows, but you can't allow things to overtake you."

Everyone has experienced the problem of losing focus. You can be playing third base thinking about your last at-bat and forget that a ground ball may be headed your way. You can even be in

Dave Stewart's masterful concentration
helped make him one of the great pitchers
of his generation.

the batter's box when alien thoughts come creeping through
your mind. It happens in school when you lose track of the pro-
fessor's lecture; it happens at the office when you kind of float
away and wish you were playing baseball instead of working up
the current report or preparing an analysis. The ability to focus
is an essential skill for success in just about any arena.

The key to focus is mental discipline, in the same way that
Dave Stewart learned to focus on the mound. Sometimes focus
just seems to come naturally, when it almost magically shows up
and every ounce of our being is into the task at hand. At other
times it seems that no matter what we try, thoughts and distractions prevent us from focusing. A baseball player plagued with
distractions will not perform at his peak level.

Distraction can take a multitude of forms. It can mean thinking about problems at home, getting caught up in comments from the stands, or rethinking the last at-bat. In generations past, major leaguers taunted opposing players with bench jockeying to try to break their concentration. That continues today to some degree in some college conferences, but it has been nearly eliminated at the professional level. Yet teams still try to play emotional games with the opposition—getting into their heads. While managing Double A Quebec City in 1972, Karl Kuehl played the game against opposing pitcher Joaquin Andujar, making little comments about how, "The ump's squeezing you today," or "You had more fastball the last time we saw you." Andujar struggled miserably against Kuehl's team until the playoffs. When Kuehl made his first get-in-his-head comment from the third-base coaching box, Andujar looked over, wagged his finger, and smiled. "Not today, Karl," he said. Andujar had caught on to the game and learned to toughen his approach. Veteran major leaguers will still toy with opponents' emotions in this way, and mentally tough players will learn to block it out.

Strange as it seems, in baseball perhaps the most common form of distraction is the game itself. The learning process involves putting together many minor mechanical tasks, and thinking about these mechanics interrupts concentration. If a hitter is thinking about whether his hands are starting late, it can interrupt his focus on the task at hand. That is why mechanical corrections must be done during practice so that they become natural when they are taken into the game. When the game begins, focus must be on the task at hand.

"You can never let up, and that applies more to concentration than the actual throwing of the ball," Tom Seaver said in *The Edge,* by Howard Ferguson. Once concentration lapses, it can be difficult to regain it. When a pitcher chugs along dominating a game, then suddenly runs into trouble, often the reason is that he has lost his focus and begun making pitches that are too hittable, or off the plate for walks. Most successful players learn to keep their concentration at a high level at all times. Some have developed the ability to concentrate by studying the mental processes associated with getting focused.

When Tony La Russa managed the A's, he developed nine points in a game when a pitcher is most susceptible to losing focus. They are:

1. In the first inning, when a pitcher is attempting to find his rhythm and stuff.

2. In the fifth, when a pitcher can grow nervous trying to secure a win.

3. In the seventh, when a starter begins to sense that his job is done and it is time for the setup man and closer to take over.

4. In the ninth, when a pitcher begins thinking, "Just three more outs and the game is over."

5. After a rain delay, when the pitcher's tempo and rhythm are disrupted.

6. When the pitcher begins nearing his pitch-count maximum and knows it is his last inning.

7. After your team's pitcher has a quick inning, throwing perhaps five or six pitches, meaning the opposing pitcher does not have his regular rest between innings. An extra-long rest between innings can also cause problems.

8. When a pitcher is working from the stretch with men on base; some pitchers fail to practice from the stretch or can become distracted.

9. When weather conditions, such as wind or light rain, serve as a distraction or an opportunity to make excuses for failure.

The pitcher's challenge is to develop the mental toughness to overcome these points of potential weakness. The opportunity for wise hitters is to learn these times when pitchers become vulnerable and exploit the pitchers' lapses.

FINDING YOUR ZONE

The ultimate concentration comes when a player is in what is called "the zone." This is an almost undefinable realm where the world seems to slow down around you and your concentration is so intense that everything is magnified: the ball seems bigger to the hitter; every muscle works in harmony for the pitcher. With "the zone" comes an almost unthinking confidence and belief in success. It is an almost magical experience that at one time or another is shared by most athletes at all levels. Why it comes and why it goes defies explanation.

When players are "in the zone," they say:

• Their mind is clear. They are not thinking.

• There is no self-consciousness. They are not thinking about themselves or how they are going about their tasks.

• They are relaxed and calm.

• There is no concern about outcome: they are not worried about results.

• They are focused, with only one element on their mind.

• They are totally confident and trust themselves to get the job done. When a player trusts himself, he feels no need for extra effort mentally or physically.

• Their actions are effortless and unconscious—it just happens.

• Their thoughts are in the present, not thinking about something that happened in the past or may happen in the future.

• Everything is positive.

While entering "the zone" seems to have no logical explanation, losing "the zone" usually comes because of several specific reasons:

• Trying harder and becoming more intense mentally.

• Giving more effort, swinging harder, trying to throw the ball harder or break it more sharply. When all is going well, everything is effortless. That feeling tricks the player into thinking he can do even more with a little more effort. With more effort, "the zone" disappears.

• The player becomes self-conscious and begins thinking about how it is happening instead of just letting it happen.

• The player's emotions take charge. A different situation, a bad call by the umpire, less pressure or greater pressure, frustration—all can drive a player out of "the zone."

• Thinking about the past or worrying about the future, rather than playing one pitch at a time.

• The player's confidence level drops. If expectations are not met, doubts creep in. Or if a player begins wondering, "How long can this last?"

• A player begins consciously trying to continue his successful performance. The difference is that before, the player was not thinking, he was just doing it. By adding the thought process, the player becomes self conscious and changes the process.

• Negative thoughts creep into the mind.

Major leaguers will discuss "the zone" with reverence and respect, wishing they could always be in that special place. Just about everyone understands that "the zone" itself is almost mystical and comes of its own accord. All anyone can do is attempt to enhance his concentration and make himself more likely to find a zone, if not *the* zone, then *my* zone. "My zone" is a player's attempt to replicate the sensations that come from being in *the* zone by creating his own personal zone. It may not be as sharp or productive as "the zone" itself, but it creates a situation in which success is more likely and "the zone" will appear more often. It also leads to improved concentration.

It seemed an odd ritual when Reggie Jackson came to the plate. At times he would begin mumbling to himself. Catchers would come to learn that when Jackson started mumbling, it meant he was locked in and focused. In contrast, Yogi Berra would come to the plate and chat with the catcher. "I didn't want to think," Berra said. "Afterward I couldn't even tell you what we talked about." These were the ways Jackson and Berra found their own personal zones.

In other words, they found a way to ignore the distractions of the ballpark—the taunting fans and yelling opponents—so they could direct their focus on the task at hand. When Tony Gwynn stepped into the on-deck circle, he reached a point beyond distraction and carried it into the batter's box. "Even somebody I respect can yell at me and I won't hear it, because I've zoned out all those sounds," Gwynn said.

Pedro Ramos, a star pitcher of the 1950s, told *We Played the Game* author Danny Peary, "When I got on the mound, I didn't even know how many people were in the stands. That's why fans never bothered me in opposing cities. If they did boo me, I never heard them. Even if they cheered, I didn't look up past four or five rows. I didn't care which ballpark I pitched in. I didn't care if the mound was high or low. I didn't talk to the groundskeepers to fix the field for me, as many pitchers did. I just concentrated on pitching."

This is one of the secrets of big-time players: they have learned to concentrate in such a way that they can create their own version of "the zone" almost at their own direction. A psychologist might call the process self-hypnosis in that the players have learned to direct all their energies and attention to the task at hand.

As with just about everything else in baseball, the process of reaching *my* zone requires practice—a plan of concentration. It can be done at home as shadow baseball: imagining situations and replaying them again and again through the mind. It becomes almost like a song being played through the mind, where the rhythm and beat stay the same, time after time. Many players find *my* zone by beginning with control of their thoughts through self-talk and visualization—they tell themselves that they expect full focus. They repeat the process by keeping their thoughts in the same order and at the same speed; as a soft chant, saying to themselves, "Nice and easy" and making it quieter and quieter to slow the rhythm and focus their minds. They maintain the same level of emotion and intensity—the beat of the song inside the head does not change. You can see disciplined major league hitters do this when they enter the batter's box, repeating the same routine time after time as they direct their concentration. Gary Sheffield pumps the end of the bat toward the pitcher. Hall of Famer Joe Morgan used to come to the plate and flap his back elbow as he zoned in. Many hitters will step to the plate and take the same number of practice swings as they focus their concentration and become locked in. Top pitchers also have their routines before they step on the mound and after they get their sign. Each player must develop his own method of locking in and finding *my* zone, bringing physical movements in synch with thinking.

When a player develops his plan of concentration, he takes control of the situation. He determines just where to direct his focus and how to use it to his advantage. A concentration plan is a mental routine that includes: evaluating the situation; receiving signs; fine-tuning the approach to meet the demands of the moment; self-coaching on mechanics; relaxing, visualizing; and a final dominant thought.

The final thought should put the player on target and dominate all other thoughts in his routine. This should be the most powerful thought in the sequence, carrying the exact point a player must take to the point of action. That may be "See the ball" for a hitter, or "Nice and easy" for a pitcher. A player must develop the discipline to make that final thought dominate, otherwise it may slip through his mind too quickly, lost in the flurry of activity, and lose its place to an earlier thought. The amount of time and emotion given to an attitude during the concentration routine will increase its strength and impact. A hitter can go to the plate determined to be aggressive yet knowing that his most important thought must be "See the ball well." If the hitter is unable to discipline his thoughts so that "See the ball" becomes dominant over "Be aggressive," the likelihood is that he will be aggressive without seeing the ball well.

The goal is for the final thought or attitude to dominate and control the player's approach. To make certain that happens, a player must have a plan: a concentration routine. He must control the speed at which his mind works—he can speed his thinking or slow it down at the appropriate times. He can take more or less time between thoughts. He must pull out the appropriate senses and emotions with each element of his approach. All routines should begin with situational evaluations and attitudes, then finish with approach attitudes.

There is no single magic concentration routine that will work for every player every time. Each player must develop what will work for him. The routine will need periodic adjusting and fine tuning, but the fundamentals will remain the same. A pitcher may choose to focus on his release point at the end of his routine and achieve excellent results. In the next game, however, he may recognize that focusing on release is no longer working. He changes his focus to staying back, and he slips into a perfect groove.

Once a player learns to direct his focus and concentration, he can avoid the distractions that get in the way of success. When he begins to use a concentration plan, his mental routine will fall into place. As he repeats it time after time, the routine will become automatic and natural. The process will begin to flow effortlessly, without thought. When this happens, it will help the player find his personal zone.

FOCUS FOR PITCHERS

From the first pitch of the game until a pitcher is sitting in the clubhouse with an icepack, it is critical to remain focused. Those sporadic bursts of wildness, or mistake pitches down the middle, often result from a lapse in concentration, where the mind briefly takes a holiday on the mound. Every pitcher must develop his own formula for concentration and find what works best for him. This involves setting a regular pattern of thought processes between pitches. There is no universal right way; it's a matter of testing and learning. For example, most veteran pitchers believe that mechanics should be dealt with before stepping on the rubber, but former major leaguer Matt Keough says some pitchers benefit from focusing on their mechanics during the delivery process itself. In this case the pitcher will focus on one key, such as release point or staying back, while making his delivery. Every pitcher must find the routine that works for him.

While the basic concepts of focus and concentration are the same throughout athletics, there are some subtle differences between the ways that pitchers and hitters must focus. Hitting is reactive: a hitter must have a clear mind so he can better react to the ball's movement within just the split second he has to act. Pitching is proactive: a pitcher formulates his plan of what he wants to do with the ball and where he wants to throw it. The pitcher controls the tempo of the game and establishes the rhythm of its flow.

Pitchers should intensify their focus before they step on the rubber. This begins by developing a routine to use between pitches. The routine becomes normal and happens almost automatically.

A sample routine for pitchers begins before stepping on the rubber. The steps are:

1. *Evaluate the game situation.* Consider the score, inning, outs, runners on base, and whether those runners have speed.

Ask such questions as: What is the other team's strategy going to be? Is this a bunt situation? Who is on base, and can he steal? Who covers second on a comebacker? How will I attack this hitter?

2. *Self-coaching.* Think about game tempo, mechanics, and adjustments.

3. *Pause and relax*, taking a break before going to work. Breathe. Exhale, trying to let as much air as possible escape your lungs. Think about the breath, feel it going out. Relax your neck and shoulder muscles. Slowly blink your eyes. This is a relaxation exercise to help a pitcher regain his comfort level and helps return his mind to the present situation after planning the future. This also ensures that the pitcher is starting from the same place mentally and physically on every pitch.

After stepping on the rubber, the pitcher begins the next phase of preparation:

1. *Get the sign from the catcher.* Again visualize the pitch searing from your hand to the catcher's glove, moving like a laser beam. When the catcher calls for a pitch that you had not visualized, stop and consider it. If you do not agree, shake him off. If you decide to throw the pitch, take the extra time to visualize the pitch. If you make the mistake of rushing yourself and not taking the time to get a good strong image in your mind, your chances of success are not as good.

2. *Plan.* Visualize what you will do with different types of balls hit back at you. Visualize the pitch you are going to throw, feel your delivery with the correct level of effort, and imagine the flight of the ball from your hand to the target. Do not visualize the hitter, just think "Me and the glove." Visualize what you will see and feel. Some pitchers will use the catcher's shinguard or mask as a target and visualize hitting that.

3. *Pause, clear your mind, exhale, and pitch.* At this point, thinking and preparation must be complete, and execution fol-

lows. This is the point to let it happen; let it flow naturally. As you pick up the target, visualize the flight of the ball for the final time.

After every pitch comes an evaluation process. If the pitcher is satisfied with the previous pitch and its result, he knows it without thinking about it. If he is dissatisfied, he should stop and consider what adjustment needs to be made. If the pitcher does not pause to mentally correct an error, he is likely to repeat the mistake the next time he throws the same pitch. After considering the previous pitch, the pitcher must immediately clear his mind to focus on the next pitch.

When a pitcher recognizes that his mental routine is not right, or when he has been distracted in the routine, he must stop and start over. When a pitcher rushes his mental routine between pitches, it results in rushing his delivery and often leads to diminished control and throwing less effective pitches.

The routine between innings can be critical for pitchers since it is easy to lose focus while sitting in the dugout. A long inning, or his team putting up several runs, can cause a pitcher to alter his thought processes. Most pitchers need to stop and take a break from the intensity, then begin focusing again. "With two outs, I'd start getting myself ready to pitch," says former major leaguer John Farrell, now the farm director for the Indians. "If you try to wait until you cross the foul line to get ready, it's too late." Early in his career, Farrell says, he would think about doing post-game interviews or have other irrelevant thoughts filter through his mind that would lead to distraction. As his career progressed, he grew more disciplined and developed his routine of returning to his game face with two outs.

Concentration and focus are essential for pitchers. When a pitcher loses focus, he often loses the strike zone and fails to throw each pitch with determination. In his role as a pitching coach, Dave Stewart will talk with his pitchers and ask them,

"How do you feel when you have finished pitching a game?" The pitchers usually respond with "Worn out" or "Kind of tired." Stewart tells them, "When I pitched, I was exhausted after every start. I'd come in and go to sleep on the trainer's table. That was because I put everything into every pitch." Stewart learned to make every pitch he threw an exercise in focus and concentration, to such a degree that he would be both physically and mentally drained when the game ended. This is the level of concentration that helped make Dave Stewart a legitimate superstar during his glory years. He wants the pitchers he coaches to aspire to the same level.

FOCUS FOR HITTERS

The moment Mark McGwire stepped into the on-deck circle, he placed both hands on his bat and almost never let go until he hit the ball. This was part of McGwire's concentration ritual, finding his zone. Every hitter must find a way to exclude the distractions that surround him; the process becomes individualized. Here are the basic needs:

The first phase of preparation, the thinking phase, is done outside the batter's box. This allows a player to know just what he is trying to accomplish, whether it is to advance a runner or reach base to lead off an inning.

1. *Evaluate the game situation.* Consider the score, inning, outs, runners on base, and anything else that might dictate game strategy.

2. *Look at the coach and receive the sign.*

3. *Self-coach.* Give yourself any needed directions or reminders about mechanics. Do not just talk to yourself about it but picture yourself doing it. Stepping out of the box and getting it right on practice swings will provide the strongest reminder. For example, if you want to stay back longer and stride more

softly, get in your stance, imagine a pitch coming, stay back, and take a slow, soft stride.

4. *Develop a plan.* This process includes four steps: 1) define your job; 2) visualize the pitch you want or expect to receive; 3) visualize the location of the pitch; and 4) visualize hitting the ball where you want to hit it. You will be most effective picturing the ball leaving the pitcher's hand, following it all the way, and seeing the ball leave your bat. Do not make the mistake of just seeing the ball in the hitting zone and seeing it go for a hit.

5. *Pause, clear your mind, relax, and clear your lungs by exhaling.* Think about and feel the breath escape. This helps clear the mind. The momentary relaxation will return you to the present after planning for the future.

The second phase of preparation comes after stepping into the batter's box. This is where the thinking stops and the action begins, where focus is strictly on the moment. It is vital that the hitter not think in the batter's box; his head should not be filled with distracting thoughts.

1. *Get loose and comfortable.* Use a regular setup routine that can include swings or relaxation actions. For example, Nomar Garciaparra goes through a toe-tap routine when he enters the box.

2. *As the pitcher is getting his sign, look at him, but do not focus on him.*

3. At this point, *keep your mind clear* by using what major leaguers call a "key." This is a word or short phrase that will prevent distractions. A key may concern seeing the ball, such as "Pick it up out of his hand," or "Stay on it." Or it may deal with mechanics, such as "Stay soft" or "Stay back." The key may vary depending on who is pitching, such as "Quick hands" against a hard thrower and "Stay back" against a breaking-ball pitcher. Or the situation may dictate the key: with two strikes it may be "Play pepper—put the ball in play." Whatever key you choose,

say it softly and slowly, as if you are coaxing a puppy. Say the key as the pitcher begins his windup. Stop using your key about three seconds before the pitch. Should the pitcher delay and force you to wait, or hold the ball in the stretch, you must repeat your key. Repeating your key in this way will keep any unwanted thoughts from popping into your mind and keep your mind clear. You cannot think and hit at the same time. Using your key with proper timing will keep your mind clear.

4. About the time the pitcher separates his hands, without thinking, *shift your eyes to the release zone*. This will become a natural action that can be developed during batting practice.

5. *Decide to swing or take*. The pitcher pitches, you see it and decide whether to allow your swing to continue to the ball or to stop and take the pitch. A good hitter approaches every pitch as if he will hit it, then stops if it is not to his liking.

6. *Evaluation*. After every pitch, whether you swing or not, you should have a mental response. If that response is positive, the thought passes quickly and you can return to the first phase of preparation for the next pitch. But if the response is negative, you must take the time to consider it. If it is something over which you have no control, forget it. If it is something that can be improved, figure out how to do it the next time. This entire process should take only a few seconds. Then prepare for the next swing.

If the mental routine is interrupted at any time, the hitter must start over. If the routine does not feel right, or it is moving faster than usual, the hitter should start over, calling time out if necessary.

FOCUS ON DEFENSE

In no area of baseball is the importance of focus more obvious than on defense. Relatively ungifted athletes become outstanding defenders through their ability to focus, and highly talented players fumble away their careers because of lack of focus. One of the most common questions concerning an infielder is whether he can make the routine play. This is an issue of maintaining concentration from start to finish, focusing on the ball all the way into the glove, then continuing the concentration process. Many great defenders turned average or even below-average ability into successful defense through their ability to focus: they visualized themselves making all types of great plays, then practiced hard to make it possible. They prepared mentally to know how to make every play.

No place was this more clear than in the 2001 American League playoffs where Yankee shortstop Derek Jeter made what seemed an impossible play. After the right fielder overthrew two cutoff men on a play to the plate, Jeter picked up the ball near the first base line and made an underhand shovel pass to the plate to throw out Oakland A's runner Jeremy Giambi. Afterward Jeter said that coach Don Zimmer had suggested that the shortstop function as a third cutoff man on such throws, and Jeter had been prepared mentally for even this unusual possibility. Jeter's acute awareness of everything that occurs on the field is a product of mental preparation and focus. Jeter has practiced and mentally prepared to be ready for everything he can imagine occurring. This is pattern recognition—a player recognizes a pattern of events, then is prepared for what happens next.

Hall of Fame third baseman Brooks Robinson had poor speed, but his mental preparation gave him a huge edge. He could sometimes read the direction of the ball even before it was hit. Robinson learned to watch hitters—how they reacted to different pitches and where they would hit certain pitches. When he saw the same pitch coming in a game, and when he saw the hitter approach the ball in the same way, he could anticipate where the ball would be hit.

To gain the mental edge on defense, the process is to develop a mental routine that will be repeated between every pitch. Visualize making plays in every direction—diving, scooping balls on the run, fielding balls hit straight at you and in each direction, over-the-head leaps, and catches at the wall. During the days when many fields had artificial grass, third baseman Mike Schmidt even anticipated balls hitting a seam in the Astroturf, then making the play on the bad hop.

The process of preparation is to see the entire play, start to finish. Visualize the pitch connecting with the bat, the flight of the ball, and the ball entering the glove. The player visualizes himself being smooth, having his feet in the proper position to catch the ball and make the throw, then effortlessly throwing a strike.

Improvement can come quickly and dramatically on defense by learning the basics of focus and concentration.

OBSTACLES TO GOOD CONCENTRATION

One big problem with concentration is that it can be blown quickly. Getting it back becomes an ordeal of mental toughness. It is a challenge to players to avoid losing concentration. Here are a few indications that concentration is not at the proper level:

• *Thinking too fast or too much.* Thoughts begin racing through the mind, jumping from one subject to another out of proper sequence without completing the previous thought. When this happens, the traffic going to the brain becomes a blur and is impossible to sort.

• *Thinking about something at the wrong time, or thinking about irrelevant issues.* For example, the moment the pitch is delivered is not the time for the hitter to be thinking about mechanical adjustments.

• *Holding focus too long.* After a player clears his mind and locks in, he usually has about five or six seconds of intense concentration before some other thought pops into his mind to cause distraction or divide his attention.

Some of the cat-and-mouse games between major league pitchers and hitters are designed to break the opposition's concentration. It is a matter of experience and mental toughness for a player to learn not to be distracted by a pitcher or hitter who is playing amateur psychologist with his opponent.

THE ART OF VISUALIZATION

Over the last decade there has been much talk of visualization, making it sound almost as if it is some New Age art form. It is not. Rather, alert coaches have recognized that top players engage in off-the-field mental preparation and have refined and gathered their ideas under the term "visualization." This is the cornerstone of concentration, because it mentally prepares the athlete for success by envisioning a positive outcome.

Visualization is far more than just a daydream of fantasies and future accomplishments: it is a tool of preparation that can be used to program thoughts, feelings, and actions for future games. Few young players understand the concept of visualization, let alone how to do it properly in a manner that will benefit them in an actual game. Proper visualization can be described as a virtual-reality movie with you, the visualizer, as the star. When most people daydream about sports, they see themselves being the hero of the game. They may see themselves as the star pitcher striking out Albert Pujols for the final out of the World Series, or hitting the game-winning home run off Randy Johnson to win the League Championship Series. They may even see themselves after the game accepting the

MVP award, saying they will go to Disneyland, and chatting up Jay Leno. These daydreams are all well and good and may even provide a temporary feeling of determination and confidence, but they lack several key ingredients that can actually help a player maximize his performance on the playing field, at his current level of competition and at future levels.

It is essential to understand that visualization is a key component of preparation. Unless you are relying on pure luck, you preface an action by first having an image of what it is you want to do, how it should look and feel, and what the result should be. It may not be a strong mental image, but you do have a mental understanding of what it is you need to do, or what the finished product should look like when you have completed the task. For example, say you live in Sacramento, California, and you intend to drive to a relative's house in Greeley, Colorado. Do you just hop in a car and start driving in any direction and hope you get there, or do you consult a road map for the route you want to take? Without proper directions, you may end up in Wyoming or Arizona before you realize that you are lost. You may get lucky and find Greeley, but without a plan your margin for error is large. Visualization provides a mental plan for your actions in athletics.

Athletes who visualize do so for three reasons: 1) to follow a routine that helps maintain their current level of play by reinforcing all the positives in their performance; 2) to help make adjustments when they are not performing well, or when they are learning something new, by mentally rehearsing what they want to see and how they want to feel during their performance; and 3) to help prepare for specific opponents and/or elements. Visualization is a key element of anticipation. A by-product of visualization is increased confidence. Think about it: if you mentally rehearse positive experiences over and over, you feel better prepared and have a sense of what to expect and how to react in the situations you have been playing in your virtual-reality movie.

Confidence in athletics is directly related to your expectations of success for a given situation. If you are a hitter who has dominated a specific pitcher in the past, you will expect to hit him hard again. The opposite is also true—which is where visualization can help. If you are 0-for-15 with nine strikeouts against a certain pitcher, you will not have as much confidence when you face him again. Ask any left-handed hitter who has ever faced five-time Cy Young Award winner Randy Johnson just how confident he feels when he steps into the box against the 6-foot-10 southpaw with the 99-mile-per-hour fastball. Visualization can help you make adjustments in situations where you have not been successful in the past without having to wait for that situation to arise again.

To make visualization work effectively, a player must make the situation seem as real as possible, imagining it to be as if he is in that situation at the moment. The process begins by finding a quiet place, then shutting your eyes for fifteen or twenty minutes so all senses can be incorporated. You then see yourself in your game environment: You are wearing your uniform on the field where you are competing. Your team is there. You can make it a day game or a night game. There could be twenty people in the stands at a high school game or thousands in a college or professional stadium. Whatever you see, sense, or are aware of when playing a game in the situation you are preparing for, you want to incorporate that into your visualization, the movie in your mind.

Experience the visualization through your own eyes, in the same way you see things happening when you are playing. Incorporate the feelings of your actions during your personal virtual-reality movie. During competition, you know what you are doing mechanically by how it feels. You make adjustments during games by how things feel to you, like taking too long a stride or trying too hard—muscling-up on a ball. You should know from experience what your best performance felt like and incorporate those perfect mechanical feelings into your vision. You can enhance your physical feelings by actually performing while visualizing. A hitter can take a bat to his bedroom and perform his swing as he visualizes pitches coming in. A pitcher can stand in his room and perform "dry mechanics" without a ball while visualizing the game in front of him.

Do not just visualize the execution of your performance. A hitter does not start his movie when the ball is released from the pitcher's hand and end it after the ball has been hit. Instead, he includes the routines that he performs during the game that help him prepare for action. A pitcher should include his bullpen in his visualization, because that is where his physical involvement in the game begins. A pitcher would also want to include thoughts between pitches; the routine of stepping on the rubber and looking for signs (some pitchers wipe the rubber clean with their foot before stepping on it); his last thought and breath before making any movement; and then the execution of his pitch. A pitcher should feel his delivery exactly the way he wants it and see the pitch out of his hand, with the hitter reacting the way he wants him to in a game. A hitter would want to include his on-deck routine, walking up to home plate, pausing to get the signs from the coach, turning back to the plate and performing any physical routines such as adjusting batting gloves and checking the defense for positioning, stepping into the batter's box and getting comfortably into his stance while repeating a hitting key to focus on his objective, and then seeing the pitcher move into his delivery. A hitter should see the ball out of the pitcher's hand and all the way into the hitting zone exactly the way he wants it, and feel his movements into the pitch. He should feel the ball strike his bat and envision where it goes on the field. Include running the bases and feel the satisfaction and confidence that comes after hitting the ball hard, then making a good slide or beating a close throw.

Control your thoughts during your visualization. Players who experience untimely, distracting thoughts in the batter's box or during their delivery can practice playing with a quiet mind on every pitch during visualization. If distracting thoughts pop into the mind during visualization—such as recalling a strikeout against a certain pitch or pitcher—immediately stop the process and start over from the beginning. In visualization, a player can perform perfectly every time.

Use past successes for the basis of your visualizations. Everyone has had a great performance he can remember—how it looked and felt when he hit a screaming line drive or when he made a perfect pitch to strike out a tough hitter. Those memories should be used as a foundation for visualizations, because a player does not have to imagine how it felt or looked—he has already experienced it. Michael Jordan has said that his memory of his game-winning shot at North Carolina for the NCAA championship was a source of visual preparation for many of his game-winning shots in the NBA. That was the first time he had made such a dramatic shot with a title on the line, and because he did it and could remember what it felt and looked like, it gave him the confidence to do it in the NBA.

Using past experiences as a source for visualizations can also help prepare for a specific pitcher, team, or environment. For instance, a hitter preparing to face a pitcher and team he has played before has a strong memory of that confrontation and can actually relive those at-bats in his mind. The hitter reinforces all the positive images—the pitcher's mannerisms on the mound, his delivery, picking up the ball out of his hand, and hitting it hard. If there were negative experiences in the past, such as striking out or popping up a fat pitch, change the image to a positive one, such as hitting the ball hard into the right-center-field gap or taking a curve in the dirt. It is important to include the feel with the vision, using all your senses to live the experience. This is where the hitter can take real images and tweak them to make everything perfect. It does not have to be just about mechanics; a player can change all his behavior in all areas. If you are the type who loses his cool when an umpire makes a bad call, which messes up your performance, you can visualize yourself reacting calmly and staying in control, then coming back to hit a line drive. A player can create a plan of how he wants to react in any situation.

The strangest part about visualization is that it works. Players are amazed at how frequently they will visualize a scenario, then see it play out the same way in real games. Visualization sets up mental preparedness to deal with situations, and it creates a confidence and expectation of success.

Robin Yount, a 1999 inductee into the Hall of Fame with 3,142 hits and two American League MVPs, said that during the best year of his career he took the time to visualize every single day. "Before I would go to the ballpark," Yount said in an interview, "I might lie down on my bed and visualize this guy and take ten to fifteen at-bats off him before I'd face him that night. But it takes a while to face a guy enough to lie down on the bed and take some at-bats off him." Yount added, "It was amazing how often that year [1989] I would see, visualize, these things happening in my hotel room before I went to the park, and it was scary almost, how many times, after replaying things in my room, they actually happened that night. You got that pitch that you just played in your mind in your room, and you hammered it. . . . It's like I'm standing on second base thinking, 'Man, that's the same thing I saw in my room two hours ago.'"

In his room, Yount would close his eyes and see the pitcher and the pitch, then hit the ball the way he wanted and where he

Robin Yount: everything about his personal
"movies" was positive.

wanted. "I'm watching a movie. I am seeing it clearly. I was doing it, as far as I was concerned—feeling the sound of the
crowd. You get the feel of the stadium. The buzz is going on. I
felt all of that when I was back in my room playing what
I wanted to happen later that night. I would run the bases. I
would hit the ball and run the bases, and maybe I would slide
into second. The crowd was cheering. All of that stuff was going
on." Everything about Yount's "movies" was positive. At times,
however, Yount would visualize an at-bat in which he would
swing and miss at a curve, as he had in a game. When that happened, he would open his eyes and get off the bed to "slap himself around a bit," because that was not what he wanted to

remember or program himself to do. He wanted to see himself hitting the ball hard, so he would stop and start over. "It's funny," Yount said, "because those negative images want to creep in there. I don't want to see the one where he blew it right by me and I swung and missed."

During the game, Yount did not visualize as he did in his room before games. Instead he would play a quick "scene" to prepare him for a specific pitch. He would think about getting a fastball away and hitting it to right field, but he did not take his mind into a "movie" and away from the game. Other hitters, such as Mark McGwire, visualized all the time. During McGwire's home-run chase with Sammy Sosa of the Cubs in 1998, the year Big Mac hit seventy homers, he was on camera constantly during games and could be seen in the dugout before an at-bat with his helmet on, a bat in his hands, and his eyes closed, visualizing what he wanted to see, feel, and do with certain pitches. If he needed to, McGwire would even do it between pitches outside the batter's box. When and where you visualize is a matter of personal preference and what works for you.

There are five points during a game day when visualization can help you prepare for a game. Most players visualize before they get to the ballpark, because it is easy to find a quiet spot for uninterrupted time. The next opportunity is at the ballpark, before getting loose or while stretching with the team. Instead of playing a long movie, players visualize a few pitches, at-bats, or defensive plays. On the bench during the game is another opportunity to visualize. A player can take what is going on in the game and play a few scenes or short movies, using a previous pitch sequence to a hitter, an at-bat, or a defensive play as focus.

Another opportunity to visualize is during the game between pitches. A pitcher may step off the rubber, a hitter may step out of the batter's box, a defender may walk away from his ready position and play a quick scene or sequence of scenes to prepare for the next pitch. This is where visualization can help a player focus on his game plan by reinforcing what he wants to do with the next pitch. It can help a hitter anticipate what may happen next: with two strikes a hitter may visualize himself taking a tough slider in the dirt for a ball, hitting the hanging slider hard into the gap, or hitting the fastball away to the opposite field. It also provides a way of making adjustments during the game.

It is also important to visualize after the game, recalling everything done well and adjusting what can be improved. If a player is having difficulty seeing himself doing something specific, he can take a strong memory of someone else and put himself in their place, creating the feelings for the images. For example, a pitcher can imagine being Roger Clemens, repeating his delivery in his mind but replacing Clemens with himself. Every young player imitates the stances and deliveries of famous major leaguers; this is the same concept, adding the feelings and emotions of competition.

Between pitches in a game, there is a sequence to how you, as a player, should visualize. First **pre-play** the image that you want to happen with the next pitch. Pre-play is essential for anticipation and quicker reactions, and if you need to give yourself a quick mechanical reminder, this is the point where you can do so. But make your mechanical reminders first so that you can always finish with thoughts about the ball. A mechanical reminder for a hitter may be as simple as stepping out of the box and taking a couple of practice swings, emphasizing the correction he wants to make, such as swinging down on the ball. A hitter pre-plays the pitcher delivering his pitch and tracks it all the way into the hitting zone while feeling his stride and approach into the ball, finishing with solid contact of the pitch and hitting it where he wants to. A hitter may want to visualize taking tough pitches that he does not want to swing at—especially if he is in a rut swinging at certain pitches—as well as seeing the pitches he does want to attack. A pitcher's pre-play includes feeling his delivery of a pitch and seeing it from his hand all the way through the strike zone, with the pitch moving or breaking the way he wants it to. A defender visualizes a ball hit to his left, to his right, and right at him. It is important for a defender to visualize the pitch being thrown, the hitter's approach, and the bat angle at contact the way he does in a game; this will help to pick up clues where the ball will be going before it is even hit, so that the defender can lean into his first step more quickly.

Next comes the **play** itself—what actually happens.

Then you **replay** the performance, making any corrections necessary with your action if you did not like the result, such as a missed target by a pitcher, an off-balance swing by a hitter, or a poor throw by a defender.

Before the next pitch, you start the process over and **pre-play** what you want to happen in the next moment. The pre-play and replay visuals should take only three to five seconds each.

This should not be a time-consuming routine but rather a quick vision to reinforce a positive action or anticipate an upcoming pitch or batted ball. When this routine becomes habit, it provides a rhythm to your game that helps you prepare in a consistent manner. The result will be more consistent positive actions and thoughts.

"Visualizing and clearing your mind, that's the key," Barry Bonds told a group of Little Leaguers in 1993. "It's so easy to get caught up in baseball, even at your age, the excitement of it, and the thrill of it, and having your parents there—you can get caught up in it. So if you can just take a few minutes, and just sit down and relax and really visualize positive things. . . . Today we have [pitcher] John Smiley. I will do everything I can to visualize his pitching motion so that I can pick up that baseball at the point of release."

Visualizing is not something that comes easily for a lot of people. As Robin Yount points out, "It sounds silly, but it is hard to get yourself for a half an hour every day to lie down on the bed before you get to the ballpark and play that [game]. You have to really work at it, unless it is part of your routine." Mc-Gwire said that his career took off when he began visualizing more frequently. He understood that being mentally prepared for each pitch had more to do with his success than his strength, which was important but not as crucial. Mac hit 49 home runs his rookie season, when he weighed closer to 200 pounds than the 245 pounds at which he finished his career. He could always hit a ball out of the park, but being prepared for each pitch of each at-bat through visualization helped him become one of baseball's all-time greatest power hitters. Visualizing gave him a plan of attack for his at-bats and a sense of "been there, done that" in his mind, so he was confident of how he was going to re-act to specific pitches and thus became extremely consistent. He just did not miss many mistake pitches over the middle of the plate. That was a matter of his being prepared for action, rather than how many pounds he could bench press.

SEEING THE BALL

It seems so simple, and at some time almost every player and coach will use the line, "See ball, hit ball." But seeing the ball is not something that can be relegated to chance. This is a critical element of everything that is hitting. The most important part of hitting is seeing the ball. A hitter may have a perfect swing, but if he is not seeing the ball well, he might as well be trying to hit while wearing a blindfold. The act of seeing the ball is an exercise in concentration—it is more an element of the mental game of baseball than simply a physical act. And consistently seeing the ball well demands mental toughness.

Many hitters are so mechanics-minded that they obsess about their swing or stance when their real problem is seeing the ball. A coach may question whether the hitter is seeing the ball well, only to have the query brushed off as unimportant. Hitters often undervalue the importance of seeing the ball and simply take it as a given that they are seeing the ball well, or at least well enough. This is not satisfactory. Good hitters learn to see the ball consistently as well as they possibly can.

Ted Williams became a maniac about seeing the ball. He wanted the longest possible look at every pitch. It was an important ingredient in what made him one of the best hitters in the history of the game. "Everybody tells you that a right-hander should never drop down and throw sidearm to a left-hander," Williams said. "But I hated it. It would take me just a fraction of a second longer to adjust my eyes to the arm angle, and I wouldn't get as long a look at the ball."

Robin Yount tried to train his eyes to track the ball from its origin to the plate in the hope that when he stepped into the box, his eyes would automatically go to the release point and pick up the ball. He would never have to think about this, it would just happen as a natural process. "I think it worked, because I became a better hitter over time," Yount says.

"My biggest issue in hitting was seeing the baseball," Yount said. "If I could pick up the ball early, if I could see it leave the hand, I knew the pitcher was in trouble. So I started in the dugout. If I was the third guy up, I was down as far into the dugout as I could be where I could get the best angle, and from that point I am sitting there concentrating, watching the ball leave his hand. That's all I watched: watching it leave his hand from the corner of the dugout, watching every pitch. Is he coming out of the same slot? Does he have about the same timing whenever he is in the stretch?

"Next I'd go to the on-deck circle. Same thing, every pitch. I take a couple of swings with the lead bat. Get down on one knee. And now all I'm doing is concentrating on where the ball is coming from. And then I take that to the plate. And hopefully between there [the dugout], there [the on-deck circle], and then home plate, I was visually locked in to where I needed to be to have the best chance of hitting the ball hard."

As Yount developed into a veteran star, he grew obsessive about seeing the ball and found new ways to develop his abilities. He did not limit his work to hitting-related activities: he found other ways to keep his focus on seeing the ball. "Every time a ball came my way—whether somebody threw it to me playing catch, whether it was hit to me off a fungo, whether it was shagging batting practice as it was leaving the bat, whether I was standing in the outfield or I was on the infield—I started working to train my eyes to see the ball. Wherever it came from, at the earliest possible moment. Whenever I was playing catch to warm up, I found myself concentrating on watching that guy throw the ball to me, watching his release point. When I was playing shortstop and the first baseman rolled my ground balls between innings while the pitcher was warming up, I was trying to watch it leave his hand. When the second baseman threw me a double-play throw, I tried to watch it leave his hand. I figured that if I constantly worked on seeing the ball from the instant it originated from anywhere, it had to help me in the long run to see the ball leave the pitcher's hand without consciously having to do it. I think the conscious thing is what screwed me up."

Yount took seeing the ball to levels beyond what most players could ever imagine, and he became one of baseball's great hitters. This is an area of action where the hitter has enormous control of his own destiny. If a hitter makes every effort to get a good view of the ball, he will optimize his ability to hit. It is really that simple. In past generations of baseball, more pitchers would vary their arm angle to make it difficult for hitters to pick up the release point. In modern baseball, however, the emphasis is on pitchers finding a consistent arm slot for their delivery.

When a hitter's eyes are tilted, seeing the ball becomes more difficult.

This makes an Orlando "El Duque" Hernandez more difficult to hit because hitters are not used to seeing different angles from the same pitcher.

Seeing the ball is a combination of physical and mental processes, mixed with an intense determination to build a mind-set for the importance of getting a good view of the ball. Before you deal with the mental elements, the physical pieces must be in place.

When the hitter takes his stance in the batter's box, his body is at such an angle that it is difficult to get a head-on look at the ball. Some hitters have such a "closed stance" that they can barely see the ball from their back eye, limiting their depth perception and making hitting even more difficult. When a hitter leans too much from the waist, his eyes can tilt, making it more

The hitter must find a stance with good, level eye position.

difficult to judge the flight of the ball. Seeing the ball becomes even more important as hitters advance though high school and into college or the pro levels, since they will be seeing better and better pitching. It is vital for the hitter to find a stance with good eye position that allows him to see the ball well enough to become an effective hitter.

The object is to pull all the physical elements together to find the best way to see the ball. Before anything else, a hitter must find a stance with good head and eye position. The hitter should be off his heels, with knees slightly bent. He should also develop a stance that gives him confidence in his ability to get out of the way of pitches thrown at him. More and more, this is why many hitters start from an open stance: their head is completely square to the mound with both eyes on the pitcher. This has many advantages, but the disadvantage is that it requires extra movement during the swing.

Once he has a stance that provides the best opportunity to see the ball, the hitter needs to develop consistent eye movement. He should develop the same routine with every at-bat, starting from the moment he steps into the batter's box. Here is a sample routine that is used by many hitters:

1. Step into the box and look at the outside corner of the plate to make sure you are in the right position in the batter's box.

2. As you look up, your eyes should take the same path to the pitcher every time.

3. While waiting for the pitcher to start his delivery, look at the pitcher.

4. When the pitcher starts his delivery or goes into his stretch, look at the pitcher's hat (or chest or belt). This look should be relaxed, not concentrating intensely.

5. About the time the pitcher separates his hands, look to the release area with sharpened focus. You should already know the pitcher's window—his release area—before stepping into the box. Many young hitters see the window off the pitcher's shoulder. Experienced hitters learn to move the window back to where the pitcher's hand first appears behind his head. At times they are able to pick up the ball in his hand before the forward movement begins. This allows them a longer look at the ball.

By following this routine, the hitter will not be disrupted by the pitcher's motion since the hitter is not looking at the motion. Even if the pitcher bends at the waist, like Mike Mussina, or hesitates in his delivery, like Keith Foulke, the hitter will not be disrupted by the motion because his focus is on the release zone rather than on the pitcher himself. The idea is to use a sort of soft focus at first, then shift the eyes to the release zone and intensify concentration as the pitcher reaches the release point. Against a herky-jerky side-armer, a hitter may want to soft-focus on the pitcher's waist, then shift his eyes straight across to the release area. On a side-armer this is usually at about waist level. A hitter wants to watch the flight of the ball from the release, without being distracted by the pitcher's motion or other movements.

Strange as it seems, one of the big problems hitters have in seeing the ball is learning to keep their eyes open. Some hitters become so intense that the muscles around their eyes contract, causing them to squint as the ball comes closer. Hitters must learn to relax their eyes while keeping them wide open during the flight of the ball. And hitters must learn to move their head with the pitch, rather than just following it with their eyes.

The hitter should attempt to keep his eyes level to the ground, rather than tilting his head. And he should track the ball to the point of contact, keeping his head at that point of contact at least until the bat points at the pitcher during the follow-through. Many young hitters make the mistake of shifting their eyes too quickly, losing the contact point with the bat. It is natural for the eyes to jump to the part of the field where the ball is hit, but good hitters learn to control this instinct.

One question that has become increasingly important to hitters is the use of contact lenses or glasses. Most modern major leaguers prefer contacts because they offer an uninterrupted field of vision while the nosepiece in a pair of glasses interrupts the field and can cause the hitter to experience a momentary loss of vision. A few hitters have experimented with wearing sunglasses during bright day games, and most have found them less than satisfactory. These are decisions each individual hitter must make in finding what best improves his performance.

Once the physical elements of seeing the ball are in place, then comes the mental part. This is every bit as important as the physical, and hitters must deal with the mental issues in order to optimize their ability to see the ball. They are:

1. **Fear of being hit by the ball**. Fear is a distraction that divides attention, and a hitter who fears being hit does not get a great look at the pitch. Such pitchers as Pedro Martinez and Randy Johnson know they can instill fear in a hitter, and they use it to their advantage. When a player fears being hit, the first inside pitch leaves his mind scattered and his thoughts divided: he is so concerned with avoiding getting hit that he is not focusing on seeing the ball. This problem plagued Hall of Fame catcher Gary Carter, who found his own solution. First, he admitted his fear, then he learned to get out of the way of the ball. "When I developed confidence in my ability to get out of the way of ball, my fear disappeared," Carter wrote in his book, *The Gamer*. Overcoming the fear of being hit makes seeing the ball easier, which will actually improve reaction time and help in getting away from tight pitches.

2. **Doing two things at the same time**. Hitters often complain that the best pitch comes when they get the take sign. What actually happens is that they get their best look at the ball when their coach tells them not to swing. On the next pitch, when they do swing, they do not see the ball as well. This is because when the hitter knows he is not swinging, he has only one thing to do: look at the ball. When he has the green light to hit, he has two tasks: see and hit. This divides his attention and makes it more difficult to focus on the ball. A veteran big-league hitter learns the skill of keeping his mind clear and focusing to maintain an intense view of the ball while swinging. Keeping the mind clear and seeing the ball while swinging is best developed during batting practice.

3. **Thinking too much**. Additional thoughts create a distraction and do not allow the hitter's eyes to work as effectively. When a hitter starts thinking in the box, his focus shifts to what

he is considering rather than on what he is seeing, which leads to distraction. Internal thoughts overwhelm what the player is hearing or seeing.

4. **Trying too hard, mentally or physically.** The harder a hitter tries, the smaller the ball appears. Excessive effort or tension can cause the hitter to squint and not see the ball as well.

5. **Swinging too hard.** Suddenly trying to turn on the power will always cause the hitter to pull his head and eyes off the ball. Upon recognizing a fat pitch, or while trying to catch up to a fastball, the temptation is to take the big hack, which usually results in the big miss or a poorly hit ball. A smooth start, then powering on gradually, not only enables the hitter to keep his head and eyes on the ball, it also enhances his bat control. Professional hitters learn the skill of being quick, under control, and smooth.

6. **Beginning the focusing process too early or too late.** Timing is involved in focusing. When a hitter's eyes get to the release area too early or too late, it makes it more difficult to see the ball. Too early leads to too long a period of concentration; too late does not allow a full view of the flight of the ball or provide enough time to fine-tune focus.

A hitter improves his ability to see the ball by evaluating how well he sees every pitch. The path of the ball is divided into three zones: the release, the middle, and the contact. From the side, the zones would appear like this:

├ ─ ─ ─ ─ ─ ─ ─ ─ ─ ─ ┤ ─ ─ ─ ─ ─ ─ ─ ─ ─ ─ ├ ─ ─ ─ ─ ─ ─

Release Zone:	**Middle Zone:**	**Contact Zone:**
Seeing the ball leave the pitcher's hand.	Following the ball in the middle region, where you begin to read the speed of the pitch.	From the grass to the point of contact.

A hitter should develop the habit of reviewing how well he sees every pitch, even grading his view of the pitches. This would mean an "A look," in which he sees the ball as well as possible; a "B look," in which he sees the ball satisfactorily—well enough to make contact but not enough to develop consistency; and any poorer look, in which the hitter will be fortunate to make contact.

When a hitter does not have his A look, he identifies the zone or zones where he could have seen the ball better. Anything less than an A look must be repaired immediately, and the only way to make the repair is by identifying the zone where the problem occurs. Identifying the zone and focusing on that area allows for the problem to be corrected.

Below are illustrations of how much of the flight of the ball the hitter might miss:

1. When the hitter takes for granted that he will see the release, and focuses on tracking the ball or the contact zone, he will miss the first four to six feet.

| ⊢-------------------╀------

2. When the hitter's concentration is on seeing the release and seeing the ball in the contact zone, he will miss several feet as his eyes jump ahead. This is the most common zone where hitters lose the ball, and most do not realize it because they saw the ball coming out of the hand and later in the contact zone.

3. In the contact zone, hitters often do not see the ball well because they do not follow the ball with their head and eyes, they do not keep their head down during the swing, their swing

The path of the pitch is divided into three zones.

pulls them out, or they look up too soon to see where the ball has been hit. Hitters cannot solve their individual difficulty until they identify the problem. They must learn to understand what occurs in each zone.

Release point. Many pitchers telegraph what pitch is coming by changing their release point for different pitches, by leaving their fingers up when throwing the change-up, or by varying armspeed between fastballs and off-speed pitches. This allows hitters to read what the pitch is and recognize the speed. At times a hitter seems to recognize this telegraphing without being able to pinpoint the reason, seemingly by intuition. When this happens, it is best for the hitter simply to trust in himself and not try to figure out why.

When the hitter does not see the ball in the release zone and picks it up later, the pitcher has a great advantage, almost as if he were pitching from 55 feet, because the hitter is only seeing the final 50 to 55 feet rather than the full 60 feet, 6 inches. Picking up the ball late does not allow the hitter as much time to make the necessary judgments on the pitch, speed, and location. Greg Maddux says, "I have built my game around changing speeds because hitters can't read the speed of the pitch." In fact hitters can and do read the speed of a pitch, but it is only possible when they pick up the ball immediately upon release and get the best possible look at the pitch.

Middle zone. After the ball has been released, the ball enters the middle zone. This is where the hitter gets a better read on the speed and location of the pitch. This is where the early movement begins on fastballs, and where breaking pitches begin to break. In this zone, hitters begin to recognize the spin on a pitch. Slow curves and splitters can be seen about thirty feet away; breaking balls with a tight spin will become recognizable late in the middle zone; four-seam fastballs will appear white; and a red blur will be seen with two-seamers because of the visibility of the stitching.

Recognizing the spin becomes an almost unconscious process, with the mind absorbing the information. Some hitters, such as Tony Gwynn and Sammy Sosa, say they do not see the spin. Probably they have become so tuned in to the pitch that their minds process the information without them actually realizing what they are seeing. Hitters who question whether or not they see spin can simply get in the batter's box and concentrate solely on watching the spin as the ball comes in. If the hitter still cannot see the spin, he can try standing two feet behind the catcher. Eventually the spin becomes visible. Every player is capable of seeing spin on pitches; it's just a matter of mental toughness to learn to recognize the spin in order to see the ball better and become a more effective hitter. With experience and practice, this becomes almost an unconscious process, the reaction occurring without thinking about it, and the awareness coming after the fact.

Contact zone. The last ten feet is where some fastballs move most and where breaking pitches angle across the plate.

This is the place where many hitters have a tendency to pull their heads and eyes from the ball as they launch into their swings. When the swing pulls the hitter's head and eyes from the ball, it changes the path of the bat, taking it off the ball. Every hitter can improve his ability to see the ball. It is, first of all, a matter of recognizing that seeing the ball is an element of mental toughness, not something that can simply be left to chance; that a hitter must become aware that seeing the ball is the most essential ingredient in hitting and not just a given. Here are several tips to improve your ability to see the ball:

1. **Visualize seeing the ball the way you want to see the ball.** By visualizing, the hitter tells his mind and eyes how he wants to see the ball. All the elements of visualization are used, including all parts of the at-bat—seeing the pitcher release the ball and following it from zone to zone. During a slump, visualizing seeing the ball is a critical element to escaping problems. A hitter can recall how he saw the ball when he was getting his best looks, then use this in his preparation. Hitters can visualize the ball appearing bigger, see the release more clearly, and make the pitches seem slower.

2. **Clear your mind: thinking and hitting must be separated.** A hitter must plan or engage in self-coaching outside the batter's box, then clear his mind before returning to the box. Once in the box, his mind must be kept clear by repeating his key about every five seconds. The hitter must not think, rather he must program himself to let his eyes take over. If a hitter is thinking about mechanics in the box, it becomes virtually impossible to gauge the speed of the pitch. He loses the sharp focus needed to make that evaluation.

3. **Trust your eyes.** A hitter must not be too intense and try to force the action. He will see as well as possible when relaxed and just looking.

4. **Change your game plan**. As long as baseball has been played, the conventional way to escape a slump is to hit the ball to the opposite field. Slumps most often occur because of over-aggressiveness and not seeing the ball well. Hitting the other way helps a hitter keep his head on the ball because the point of contact comes later. Trying to pull the ball makes the hitter more likely to lift his eyes off the ball in the moment before contact.

Too many hitters think of seeing the ball as just a natural element of the game, not a result of intent or a plan; but the great hitters learn that improving their ability to see the ball makes them a better hitter. Robin Yount's simple process of watching the pitcher before coming to the plate best illustrates the emphasis a great hitter places on seeing the ball. Following this procedure, or creating one that works for you, will help you become a better hitter. The challenge is for every hitter to develop the ability to get his best look at the ball in every at-bat.

PRESSURE AND THE PRESS

Late in the 2003 season, with his Red Sox fighting for a wild-card playoff berth, Kevin Millar sprung his cool. In a column he wrote for the website MLB.com, Millar said, "It's almost to the point where the media is waiting for you to fail. The radio shows, the TV shows, the newspapers want you to fail. You almost get that sense."

From Millar's standpoint, he'd had enough of listening to the sports talks shows and reading the papers talk of the Curse of the Bambino—how the Red Sox had not won a World Series since the 1918 trade of Babe Ruth—and the devastating power of the Yankees.

"It baffles me that all the media and all the fans want to bash the Red Sox in August," Millar told the *Boston Globe* on August

21. "There's a lot of baseball left. There are going to be negatives, but why not jump on this team's back and have fun with it
and pull for this team and write good things about this team, because when this team is in the wild card or [wins] the division title, this is going to be a fun team to root for.

"I love this team and I love this city, but some of the things
you see and read, it's like, 'Uncle, turn the page.' It's a new team.
It's 2003."

Several Red Sox players stopped talking to the press, and
others echoed Millar's complaint about the media's incessant
negativism. It all became a big topic of discussion in the New
England press, on the sports talk shows, and on the many internet chat rooms that now proliferate. Players, fans, and reporters
all discussed the topic with passion and emotion.

Dealing with the press is not easy. An athlete is expected to
perform on the field, then become a public relations specialist
the minute the game ends, popping out pithy quotes and building interest in the team. It's often uncomfortable, but it's one of
the duties that accompany athletics. Publicity is part of the
game. The fans who follow the games are the reason for those
big salaries and massive attention. Publicity will be a true pain
at times, but it is a necessity. And dealing with the press is one
of the more difficult challenges for mental toughness, for players from high school to the major leagues. Whether the problem
is getting caught up in the adoration or the objections, players
must learn to deal with media attention and with the positives
and negatives that surround celebrity status.

Striving for success will inevitably lead to criticism. The answer is simple: Get used to it and learn to live with it. Develop
a thick skin that is not penetrated by inexpert criticism. A player
will never be as good as his most positive press adorations, and
he will never be as bad as the rips he will read on the internet.
Fans are fickle: they will love you when you are going well, and

admonish you when you are going poorly. That's just the way it is, and those who enter the public spotlight are destined to face scrutiny and criticism, whether they are politicians, entertainers, or athletes.

Players can gain the advantage by developing a plan for dealing with the media. They must determine what they want to say and what they choose not to discuss. If they really do not wish to talk about their theory of plate discipline for fear of giving an advantage to opposing pitchers, they should make that decision. Will Clark once told the press that he was able to sit on a certain pitch because he read the lips of a pitcher-catcher discussion and knew what was coming. That led to all those mound conferences that now take place with the players using their glove to shield their mouth. Clark's explanation of his success led to the recognition of his canniness, but it also prevented him from repeating his achievement. Players must determine what they want to reveal and what they want to keep private.

Enormous salaries paid to star athletes have led to further complications in dealing with the press and public. When players are bringing home multi-million-dollar paychecks, fans expect to see players perform at their highest level. When a fan is forking out a day's salary to take his family to a ballgame, he will not appreciate half-effort from players, just as players would not appreciate using a rare off-day to see a singer slog through a poor performance. Some fans believe they are making an investment in the team when they purchase a ticket.

Media attention can become a major distraction for a player and a team as a whole. For a player to learn how to maintain his focus, he must first understand the role of the press. Journalists—print and electronic—are not boosters for a team. The role of the press is to serve as a conduit between the fans and the team: asking the questions that the fans want answered and reporting the news that surrounds the team. If a player gets in a bar fight, that is news that must be reported. If the players lose faith in their manager, or the manager loses faith in a player, that must be reported.

Sports are public relations operations, where financial success has much to do with media attention by creating interest in the teams. Interest translates into higher attendance, better TV and radio ratings, and greater endorsement and appearance deals for individual players. When a player stops talking to the press, he is simply not doing his job. He is not helping draw interest to his team, which would lead to greater financial success.

The challenge for a mentally tough player is to learn to deal with the press without being distracted by it. Part of the job of a reporter is to ask questions that players do not want to answer—they may not even want to hear them. If a player is doing poorly, he certainly does not wish to discuss the rigors of life in a slump. If a player is doing well, he does not wish to stop and analyze every aspect of his improvement for public consumption.

Roy Smalley began the 1977 season with a spectacular first half, hitting nineteen homers and driving in big runs night after night for the Minnesota Twins. After playing in the All-Star Game, the media peppered him with questions about his sudden breakthrough success. Smalley thoughtfully responded to all the questions, explaining in detail the adjustments he had made as well as every move he made at the plate. After voicing and analyzing these explanations, he became a slave to his approach: he became so conscious of his every move that he lost the focus and fluidness he had displayed through the first half of the season.

Yankees catcher Jorge Posada had a different approach. When he hit a hot streak in August 2003, the *New York Post* asked him why it was happening. "I don't want to talk about it," Posada said. "Every time I talk about it I go [horse-bleep], so I will stay away from that."

Posada's comment was humorous enough that it satisfied the press while not forcing him to analyze his play. Not great reading, but nothing that caused antagonism. Former major league center fielder Dave Henderson often avoided questions he did not wish to answer by telling jokes to reporters.

The key for players is to learn to control the interview, not be controlled by it. If a player wants to dodge a question, Posada's response tells the story. If a player is comfortable answering a question, then give the answer. There is a distinct advantage for a player who cooperates with the press: he will be better received by fans and less likely to face continual intense criticism. If a player can face up to the press and the public, he is far more likely to gain their respect. Players who hide from the media after a rough game often lose the respect of the press and the fan base.

The bigger the stage, the more a player's words will be magnified. In media centers like New York and Boston, almost any utterance will become fodder for columnists and talk-radio hosts. If a player can learn to accept the situation and even maintain a sense of humor about it, he is more likely to prosper in the public eye than to endure distress and distraction. This begins with attitude. Reliever Alan Embree, part of the 2003 Boston team, told the *Boston Globe* how he viewed the intense media and public scrutiny in Boston: "Everybody wants to make it into such a negative thing, but I don't see it as a negative. They boo you when you're bad because they want you to do good. It's nothing personal. They don't hate you. They hate the fact you failed that particular night. How you handle that depends on a guy's particular makeup. I've been booed and cheered, I've gone through the highs and lows, and I've survived, I'm still on a very good ball club. I can deal with being booed in Boston, where the fans are great fans, so passionate. It's not like getting booed in San Diego. If you get booed in San Diego, you're pretty close to the end."

A player must learn to deal with the press and public in a way that works for his own style and skills. Most of all, he must learn not to be distracted either by positive attention or by bitter criticism. It is not easy to develop a thick skin, but you need one to persevere in the public arena.

FOCUS AND CONCENTRATION ON THE FIELD

It took Dave Stewart nearly eleven professional seasons to learn to become a focused and directed pitcher on the mound. Once he developed that ability, he became a demon of the art. For a half-dozen seasons, Dave Stewart ranked among the very elite pitchers in the game. Robin Yount's improved focus helped carry him to an MVP award. The same principles apply at every level of the game, and players who develop their abilities of focus and concentration are destined to become more effective players. The mentally tough learn to remain focused when those around them crumble to distraction, and it is the focused athletes who thrive during the toughest times. These are not secrets that have emerged from the sports fields alone. Generations of young men have read Rudyard Kipling's inspirational poem "If" and received the same basic message. It is for the athlete to learn to put the principles into practice.

"If"
by Rudyard Kipling

If you can keep your head when all about you
Are losing theirs and blaming it on you;
If you can trust yourself when all men doubt you,
But make allowance for their doubting too;
If you can wait and not be tired by waiting,
Or, being lied about, don't deal in lies,

Or, being hated, don't give way to hating,
And yet don't look too good, nor talk too wise;

If you can dream—and not make dreams your master;
If you can think—and not make thoughts your aim;
If you can meet with triumph and disaster
And treat those two imposters just the same;
If you can bear to hear the truth you've spoken
Twisted by knaves to make a trap for fools,
Or watch the things you gave your life to broken,
and stoop and build 'em up with wornout tools;

If you can make one heap of all your winnings
And risk it on one turn of pitch-and-toss,
And lose, and start again at your beginnings
And never breathe a word about your loss;
If you can force your heart and nerve and sinew
To serve your turn long after they are gone,
And so hold on when there is nothing in you
Except the Will which says to them: "Hold on";

If you can talk with crowds and keep your virtue,
Or walk with kings—nor lose the common touch;
If neither foes nor loving friends can hurt you;
If all men count with you, but none too much;
If you can fill the unforgiving minute
With sixty seconds' worth of distance run—
Yours is the Earth and everything that's in it,
And—which is more—you'll be a Man, my son!

7

MAKING
ADJUSTMENTS

It began under the March sun at Tempe Diablo Stadium. Angels manager Mike Scioscia had a point to make, and he did it with a little gentle needling, telling his switch-hitting first baseman that he needed to find a way to become more productive from the right side.

"What are you doing joking around in the cage?" Scioscia asked when he saw Scott Spiezio batting right-handed. Then Scioscia grew serious. He told Spiezio that he was not getting the job done right-handed, and he would have to make an adjustment. "Basically, what he was telling me was that if I didn't make an adjustment, I wasn't going to bat right-handed at all," Spiezio said. "I adjusted to it pretty quickly."

Once Spiezio recognized an adjustment had to be made, the rest came easily. "The idea was to take my base hits, keep the ball on the line, and keep the ball up the middle," he said. "If the pitcher makes a mistake, I'll be able to pull it, but basically keep the ball on the line and up the middle. It was more of a mental adjustment than anything else."

So Spiezio worked with hitting coach Mickey Hatcher for about five minutes, changing his approach from trying to pull every pitch. Then he took his changes into the cage. By the time the season began, Spiezio evolved into a dangerous line-drive hitter from the right side. In 2001 he hit .239 with a .312 slugging percentage from the right side. In 2002 as a right-handed hitter he batted .368 with a .539 slugging percentage, the best average in the American League against left-handed pitchers. He always seemed to be in the middle of the many post-season rallies that carried the Angels to their World Series win over the San Francisco Giants. Spiezio's adjustment was almost miniscule, but it changed his career and helped carry the Angels to a championship.

For all the tools and talent in the world, what makes a top-level player is the ability to make adjustments. Opponents will forever be finding ways to exploit weaknesses, and players must constantly adjust if they are to survive the rigors of professional baseball. Extremely talented players get left behind in the minor leagues because of their inability to make adjustments, while less-tooled players advance and thrive in the majors because they are very good at adjusting. Pete Rose lacked above-average major league tools, but he had a marvelous ability to adjust quickly. He finished his career with the all-time record for hits.

Late in 1983, his final season, Carl Yastrzemski came to the field early one day to take extra batting practice before a game in Minneapolis. One of the Twins' coaches cornered him and asked why the superstar would do extra work with his career winding down to conclusion. "I have some adjustments to make," he said. "I found out, even my first year up, no matter how good I was going, if somebody would get me out a certain way, I knew word would get around the league just-like-that. I'd

Scott Spiezio had to find a way to be more productive from the right side.

better find a way to plug up that hole. Even if it meant opening another hole, I had to plug it up right away."

After hitting a record-setting 73 home runs in 2001, Barry Bonds decided he needed to change to stay ahead of the competition. He expected to be pitched around even more than in the past, and he wanted to maximize his run production. "He said, 'I'm going to go up the middle and go to left field more,'" agent Scott Boras told *Los Angeles Times* reporter Jason Reid, recalling a luncheon with Bonds in early May. Bonds caught the opposition off guard and wound up winning his first batting title in 2002 by hitting .370. He also contributed 46 home runs in carrying his San Francisco Giants into the World Series.

There is simply no way around it. *Every player must make adjustments to succeed and improve. Once he has succeeded, he must continue making adjustments to continue succeeding.*

Improvement is a product of change, and to get better a player must adjust. Some players make adjustments better or more quickly, and that's what enhances their success. Yastrzemski made them all the way to the Hall of Fame. Spiezio's adjustment helped his team to a World Series championship.

Making adjustments is not about simply keeping up or staying ahead of opponents. It is also about a player striving to reach his potential. "How good can you be? The only way to find out is to do it," said Hall of Fame shortstop Ozzie Smith. "You don't know what you are reaching for; you just keep reaching."

There is no easy formula for making adjustments. Players can make good adjustments, and it may revitalize their careers, as with Spiezio. Players can make bad adjustments that can lead to even worse problems. Some players make too many adjustments, some too few. It is a maze of complexity that demands intense mental toughness in order to develop an effective plan of action.

FAILURE AS AN EDUCATION

Everyone fails. And baseball players must learn to handle failure if they will achieve success. Even Randy Johnson and Curt Schilling make fat pitches and lose games, and Barry Bonds made outs 63 percent of the time during his stellar 2002 season. The best pitchers have days when they get shelled; the best hitters miss hanging curves. It happens, and if players beat themselves up, they will only compound the problem.

Rather than viewing failure as an end in itself, baseball players must learn to live by the basic belief that failure is an education. It educates you by telling you that something is not working, that it is time to try something new, time to make an adjustment. Spiezio learned this lesson when pitchers found his right-handed hitting weakness on the outside part of the plate. He made an adjustment, more in attitude than in mechanics, and it led to an outstanding season.

Baseball is a game of constant adjustment. Situations change from season to season, game to game, pitch to pitch. There will be major adjustments and tiny adjustments. In the course of a single at-bat, a hitter will recognize how the pitcher's ball is moving, or a pitcher may notice a hitter leaning too far over the plate. As the count changes, attitudes and strategy change.

Barry Zito seemed to have everything figured out when he won the Cy Young Award after the 2002 season, putting together a 23-5 season for the Oakland A's. Then came 2003, and circumstances seemed to change around him. Zito struggled through much of the year and in early September owned an 11-12 record. He realized that something was wrong, and he had to make an adjustment. "I was trying not to make a bad pitch instead of trying to make a good pitch," Zito said. "When you just say, 'Okay, I'm going out there and do my thing,' that's when you do it." The change in attitude led to a mental adjustment, and Zito went on a tear through September, winning all three of his decisions and finishing the season with a 3.30 ERA, seventh best in the American League. By recognizing the problem, Zito was able to change his thinking and return to his Cy Young form.

Ideally, players should always want to learn and improve, even when everything is going well. But when a player recognizes that something is going wrong and his productivity is falling, that's the time he needs to ask himself, "What can I learn from this?" "What can I do differently to get the result I want?" It may be the time to approach coaches and ask for suggestions. It's the time to evaluate what is not working, in order to determine what could solve the problem. Coaches often repeat the old baseball adage, "If you keep doing what you've been doing, you'll keep getting what you got." It is foolish to imagine that the problem will simply go away on its own. Pitchers are not about to forget that a hitter has trouble with the inside pitch; batters are not likely to ignore a pitcher's predictable patterns.

The ability to make adjustments begins with attitude, and the first attitude is accepting that failure is an education, then learning from the experience rather than becoming engulfed in frustration, which might have a snowball effect. Yastrzemski understood that when pitchers found a way to get him out, he had to learn to plug the hole. This is failure as an education put into practice. Baseball is a crazy world: just when you think you have it all figured out, someone comes along to knock you back to humility. The mentally tough find a way to make the adjustments that allow them to prosper.

The ability to take instruction is the key to improvement. Players must develop their ability to learn or they are doomed to repeat their mistakes again and again. It is easy to assume that learning is a cinch, since we have all spent years in classrooms listening to lectures and writing assignments. The problem is that many folks think they already have the answers, or they are embarrassed to ask for help. Learning is really an attitude— "I want to learn"; "I want to be better than I am"; "I want to know more than I do." Once players take the attitude that they will become learners, they make a major step forward in their ability to make adjustments.

Here are a few key attitudes in the learning process:

1. **I can learn from anyone**. Good ideas can come from unexpected places. When Karl Kuehl played in the minor leagues, a woman he met in a dry cleaner's shop told him that he looked nervous, as if he lacked confidence, when he came to the plate. The next day he adjusted his body language and attitude, and broke out of a slump. College coaches without big-league resumés sometimes have trouble convincing their players that they know the game. A good learner must recognize that an

important tip may come from anywhere: from a veteran big-league coach to a fan in the stands. Tony Gwynn once said, "Naturally, I talk hitting with guys who can hit. But I also like to talk hitting with the guys who are hitting .240 because I never know when I might hear something that will help me." Some of the best coaches and managers lacked the physical gifts to become stars or major leaguers, so they compensated by becoming learners, then teachers.

2. **I am a student of the game**. It is important to recognize that there is always more to learn, and the learning process is never finite. Learn your own and your opponents' strengths, weaknesses, and tendencies. Study the strategies and intricacies of the game.

3. **Even if I have mastered a skill, I can still improve**. After dominant seasons of seventy-three homers in 2001 and a batting title in 2002, Barry Bonds kept searching for ways to improve. During an off-season trip to Japan, he began working with David Eckstein's brother and batting coach, Rickey, because he saw elements in Eckstein's swing that might benefit him. "I really liked his approach," Bonds said of Eckstein. "So I asked him how he does it. I'd never seen anything like it." Bonds worked on adding his new adjustments to his swing during 2003 spring training, when he hit a remarkable ten home runs. "I never stop looking for things to try to make myself better," Bonds said. "I can never stop thinking about being quick, and what Eckstein does could help me at my age. Right now, I beg pitchers to throw as hard as they can." This attitude of continued improvement becomes a mandate for players who are consistently successful. Omar Vizquel, perhaps the most masterful defensive shortstop of the 1990s, still found ways to improve his glovework or footwork nearly every year. Alex Rodriguez spends extra hours on his own every year practicing defensive plays, tinkering with his skills, looking for ways to be smoother and

better. Taking the attitude that improvement is possible makes
that improvement more likely to happen.

4. **It is not embarrassing when the coach singles me
out**. Many players cringe when a coach singles them out individually in order to explain a situation. Players must learn to
avoid resenting being singled out and see it for what it is: a
chance to learn. Joe Torre has said that one of the reasons the
young second baseman Alfonso Soriano improved so quickly
during his time with the Yankees was that he did not become
timid when a coach corrected him. Instead Soriano recognized
that even what might seem like criticism was intended for his
benefit, and he put it to his advantage. A player takes the advantage when he adopts the attitude, "I will not feel embarrassed or angry when a coach singles me out, because I know he
is trying to teach me something that will make me better."

5. **I believe in myself, I know I can find a way to improve**. More than anything, making adjustments demands self-
confidence. A player must believe in himself in order to believe
he is good enough to find a better method. After Juan Marichal
signed with the Giants in 1958, he put up staggering numbers in
the minor leagues, going 21-8 with a 1.89 ERA at Michigan City,
then 20-10 at Springfield in the Eastern League. The native of
the Dominican Republic dominated minor league hitters with a
sidearm delivery. Toward the end of that second year, his manager, Buddy Gilbert, told him, "Juan, if you're going to be effective against left-handed major league hitters, you have to have
more angle on your pitches and get them down." Marichal went
home to the Caribbean island and considered the advice. Even
though he had been pitching sidearm his entire life, he saw the
wisdom in the suggestion, and he was confident he could make
the change. He committed to the change and spent the winter
learning to come over the top. He added another change, developing his famous high leg kick, and pitched his way to the

Hall of Fame. This is what confidence is all about—even after winning forty-one games in two minor league seasons, Marichal had an open mind and the supreme confidence to make a critical change that could advance his career.

6. **I will take responsibility for everything I do, or for everything I fail to do.** As players advance, they learn that to ignore, deny, or shift blame only halts the learning process. Making excuses or hiding from a problem only serves to extend the problem. Spiezio needed a few not-so-gentle reminders from his manager that he had to make adjustments, then he accepted the challenge with dedication.

Learning to learn is all about attitude. It is about learning not to beat yourself up for mistakes, but rather considering failure an education and finding ways to improve. It is about being open to change and recognizing that improvement is a result of change. Everyone has the ability to improve by making the right adjustments and by learning to learn.

BE YOUR OWN MAN

What players—and some coaches—must understand is that there is no perfect way for everyone to do everything in baseball. We are all different people, mentally and physically. We are wired differently. Our thinking, builds, agility, coordination, quickness, speed, and the way we move are as individual as our fingerprints. Consequently the thinking patterns, mechanics, and techniques that provide the best results for one player may not work for others. What might be the best stance, stride, and swing for Bret Boone will not work for Ichiro Suzuki. Jim Edmonds's style would make a mess of Albert Pujols.

Ultimately a player must take responsibility for his own decisions and his career. A player must decide to be his own man.

This means that the player must make the decision to accept adjustments that he thinks will help his performance and decline those that he thinks will be a detriment. A coach's job is to help a player see how he can improve, then give ideas about adjustments that will make the improvements happen. Neither players nor coaches are perfect. Some coaches can be rigid in insisting that players follow a set style; some players will refuse suggestions that could improve their performance. Ultimately it is the player's decision and responsibility to find the right path. That can mean doing exactly what the coach suggests, tweaking what the coach says to fit his own situation, or taking a little from each of a few sources in order to find what works for him. There are no panaceas, no perfect solutions that will solve every problem for every player. It is a matter of experimentation, trial and error. Good players learn quickly that they are responsible for making their own adjustments and controlling their own destiny.

This can be a difficult process for some players. Some fear receiving too many ideas and complain that they are confused by having too many thoughts bouncing around in their head. This is where the sifting process comes in. And, frankly, this is often what separates a successful major leaguer from the many players who flash superior talent but never quite develop the consistency to hold a job. Onetime Oakland A's first-round pick Lee Tinsley had such a problem. Intelligent, gifted, and extremely coachable, Tinsley took every suggestion from his coaches, but he failed to sift them out and did not try anything on his own. He gave the responsibility for what he was doing, for his success, to his coaches. He was their man, not his own. He wrongly believed that his best chance for success was to do exactly what the coaches told him, nothing more and nothing less.

Tinsley's approach led to still another problem. Because he was not succeeding as the coaches knew he could, every couple of days he was instructed to make another adjustment. He would change stances or swings seemingly every other day, constantly trying to find the right formula. The result was that he never grew confident, comfortable, or committed to any particular adjustment. As Tinsley matured, he became his own man: he listened and used his coaches, but he took responsibility for figuring out his own adjustments. He went on to play briefly in the majors for the Red Sox and the Mariners.

Ted Williams, perhaps the greatest pure hitter in the game's history, constantly searched for ways to improve. "If a hitter came into the league and did something at the plate that looked real good, I would try it on, I would see if it fit me," Williams said. "Most of the time I was better the way I was doing things. But every now and then I would find something that fit and was better. When that happened, I changed." Players benefit from being open to suggestion, as was Karl Kuehl with the woman he met at the dry cleaner. It takes only a moment to consider an idea and to determine whether it might have value. Any suggestion can be discarded quickly or held for future evaluation. The player is in charge of the decision process, and it is for him to accept or reject the ideas presented to him.

Before a player can effectively become his own man, he must know himself. He must know his strengths, weaknesses, capabilities, limitations, tendencies, and how consistent he is in every phase of his game. He needs to know and understand his mechanics and mental game. He must be aware of his emotions during competition, knowing how they affect his game. Getting to know oneself takes time, thought, open-mindedness, and honesty. Without self-knowledge, a player is not well equipped to be his own man.

Players who know themselves must continue to learn from their instructors. Being your own man does not mean obstinately rejecting every suggestion: it means taking responsibility for your own decisions. Taking responsibility while remaining coachable is no easy task, and it is an ability that often separates stars from average players, major leaguers from minor leaguers. As difficult as it may sound, big leaguers for decades have been finding a way to make it work.

MAKING EXCUSES VERSUS MAKING ADJUSTMENTS

During the last dozen years or so, it has become almost a ritual: a pitcher comes off the field with an oozing blister and insists that it had no impact on his poor performance. A hitter strikes out three times, then assures the media that his swollen hand did not bother his swing. Often players will sound almost haughty as they say, "I'm not making any excuses, I just didn't get the job done." It has reached a point of seeming silly to fans and sportswriters who can see that the injury obviously impaired the performance.

Players do not wish to be accused by their teammates of making excuses. Mentally tough players do not want to make excuses to themselves. There is good reason for this: making excuses or offering explanations for gaffes gets in the way of achieving. A player tends to focus on finding a way to avert the blame rather than concentrating on learning how to improve. Making excuses can become a barrier to making adjustments. Players often come up with a reason why they do not need to make an adjustment, but it's nothing more than a rationalization for their problem.

There are always reasons that limit performance. Some are absolutely legitimate, some are outrageous. The challenge for a mentally tough player is to overcome all obstacles and give a solid performance. A player can focus on the problem, or he can focus on the solution. He cannot do both at the same time. If a pitcher admits to himself, "I'm lousy because my blister won't let me get any pressure on my fastball," he is beaten. If the same pitcher thinks, "I'm not going to let this bother me. I'm going to adjust and find a way to make my pitches work," at least he has a chance of putting together a decent performance.

No matter how valid the obstacle, a mentally tough player must approach the situation with the attitude, "I will get the job done. I will find a way." This will not always happen, and even the strongest and toughest will falter at times when injuries or personal problems surround them. Just about every player goes through a traumatic experience that divides his concentration, whether it is an unexpected romantic breakup or the serious illness of a family member. At times it may seem impossible to focus on the task at hand. Injuries and sickness may make it extremely difficult to pull out a decent performance. These are all legitimate reasons for failure. Mental toughness comes from not giving in to even the most legitimate reasons for failure. These are the times when a player must dig deep into his soul and pull out the resolve of a warrior to find a way to get the job done. Barry Bonds went through a difficult public divorce during the season, and he told reporters that he used baseball to escape from his off-field problems, so he could focus all his attention on what occurred on the field. As his personal problems mounted, he forged a hot streak. Tim Hudson made two starts for the A's during the 2002 American League division series despite a hip problem that severely limited his ability to pivot. He did not mention it during the playoffs and never brought it up. It only became public during spring training of 2003 when teammate Mark Mulder told a reporter. Hudson responded by saying, "That's no excuse. You win or you lose, and we lost." Hudson refused to give in to the injury at the time, and he would not use it as an excuse later.

Excuses do their worst damage when they are made before a game. When a player admits to himself, "I feel sick today.

Everyone will understand if I have a bad day, and nothing will be expected of me, even by myself," he is simply giving himself an easy out for failure. He is accepting failure and letting his teammates down rather than making the mental and physical adjustments that could lead to a successful performance. Obstacles are part of the game. Overcoming obstacles is cause for satisfaction and teaches a player that he can achieve when faced with similar circumstances in the future. Injuries, illness, and personal problems will inevitably force players out of the lineup, but once the player makes the decision to play, he must reach within himself to give his strongest possible performance rather than simply go through the motions.

Some people, in and out of baseball, rely on excuses to avoid the challenge of overcoming obstacles. They choose *flight* over *fight*. They lack the discipline of a *grind-it-out* personality to find a way to meet challenges. Some players, amateur and professional, will fabricate injuries to avoid a tough pitcher who might damage their average, or come up with lame excuses for skipping stretching or fielding drills. Everyone has had school acquaintances who presented absurd excuses for not completing homework assignments, or skipped class to escape a test. The George Costanza character on TV's "Seinfeld" was a parody of a compulsive excuse-maker whose imaginary reasons led to terminal mediocrity. These are the excuses of the weak; those who shrink from obstacles rather than even making the effort to overcome them.

Most players who make even a minimal effort toward mental toughness are not plagued by Costanza-ism. The more difficult hurdle is to not let outside forces become a cause for failure. It will happen, on occasion, but the supreme challenge is to make the critical adjustments that lead to overcoming the obstacle. It is the same toughness that led Stephen Hawking to write important books from his wheelchair, Stevie Wonder to pursue an inspiring musical career despite his blindness, and Jim Abbott to pitch in the majors although he had only one hand. So when a major leaguer claims that an injury or personal problem has not hampered his performance, he is refusing to give in to the problem in his own mind, whether it is a valid reason or not. Rather than dwelling on the injury, he is attempting to find a solution.

HOW SUCCESS CAN LEAD TO FAILURE

When a young player goes on a hot streak, he sometimes boasts, "I've got it now." Merv Rettenmund, a former major league player and hitting coach, responds to those comments by saying, "I cringe when I hear that, because I am afraid the hitter will get locked in and stop making the little adjustments that are needed from pitch to pitch. You've never got it. Each pitch is a new experience, a new challenge, and you have to keep making little adjustments to keep succeeding. That's what makes this a great game."

Strange as it sounds, success can send a player into a slump. Keith Lieppman, the Oakland A's director of minor league operations, had just that experience during his playing days in 1979. Lieppman was a high-ball hitter, hitting off his front foot. While playing in an exhibition against the Oakland A's, he faced sinkerballer Jim Todd. The first time up, Lieppman swung over every pitch, striking out quickly. Teammate Tim Hosley came over and told Lieppman how bad he looked, then showed him how to stay back and turn on a pitch down in the strike zone. Hosley then instructed Lieppman to swing easily. "The next pitch was down and inside, and I turned on it, just like Tim had said," Lieppman recalled. "I couldn't believe the way the ball jumped off of my bat. It was the longest home run I had ever hit, and it was so easy. It was like, wow. It was magic. I was excited. And it was so easy I knew I could do it again. I tried to repeat the swing, looking for the same pitch day after day, but it didn't happen, and I went into a slump."

Those magical home runs can turn into bad mojo, and it happens with great regularity. Success causes the hitter to change his thinking. These changes can come fast and furious, starting with a new self-image. The hitter believes that he has more power than he had in the past. Everyone is talking about the shot, and he can't put it out of his mind even if he wanted to, adding a new element to his thinking routine. His expectations and goals change—he begins believing he can repeat the action at will. Visualizations change as he keeps replaying the event time after time. Approaches change: he keeps looking for the same pitch. Lieppman did just that: "I got away from looking for what the pitcher was going to throw, and I looked for the same pitch again and again." It sent him spiraling into a slump.

Lieppman learned a difficult lesson: there are times *not* to make adjustments. Sometimes an instant adjustment will lead to a home run or a great pitch, and the player will attempt to repeat the method exactly, only to learn that it does not work. Almost every hitter will experience this at some point in his career. After that magical moment, the hitter begins looking for the same pitch and trying to repeat the result. Of course, this was not how the magic happened the first time around. When thoughts of repeating results are substituted or added to the thought process, they create a major change of approach. They are adjustments that should not be made. Those monster home runs just happen sometimes, and a mentally tough hitter must learn not to be affected by the success: enjoy the moment and maintain the mental and mechanical routines that have been working and lead to consistency.

The best advice comes from Yankee manager Joe Torre: "To repeat success, repeat preparation." This means repeating the preparation as if the home run never happened, and guarding against changes in the thought process. The player must learn to celebrate, then drive it from his mind. Players who frequently accomplish feats that maximize their abilities are players who do not become overly impressed with themselves. They have the mental toughness to control their emotions, reactions, and thought processes. Mark McGwire spent years insisting to himself and to others that he was not a home-run hitter, he was a line-drive hitter who sometimes hit the ball out of the park. He never tried to hit tape-measure home runs.

When a player goes on a hot streak and takes that "I've got it now" attitude, he often begins taking things for granted— cutting back routines, losing discipline, and not paying as much attention to the little things. Hitters often get hot when they are swinging only at strikes, and with their stronger confidence they believe they can hit anything they swing at. They then expand their strike zone and continue to hit for a short period of time before they come crashing down by swinging at balls they cannot reach.

Success can also lead to failure after a player has a good month or even a good season. He may believe he has everything figured out and knows what it takes to succeed. He may even grow giddy and believe that his success will not go away because he has mastered the game. With all the congratulations and adulation coming his way, it's easy for him to grow comfortable— before it all comes crashing down. Players must learn to guard against complacency and recognize that there is never a time when the game becomes easy.

This is a challenge for the mentally tough—to know when to make adjustments and when to avoid them. That magical home run can be called upon to build confidence or ignite passions, but players must guard against using one blast to adjust their mind-set and mechanics. Some adjustments should not be made.

Players should study and learn from their approaches when they are successful, but they must keep in mind that the approach and adjustments are only good as long as they work. Yesterday's approach may become outmoded against a different team or a different pitcher. It is effective to carry an approach into the next game, but it becomes detrimental to cling to it when it is no longer effective. A certain approach might work for a day, a week, a month, or even a season. But at some point the magic will disappear, and it will be time to make adjustments.

Young players often make mechanical changes during a practice even though everything is going right in games. The player should make adjustments based on game performance, not because he is having a bad practice. When his execution in practice is not up to his normal standards, he should push himself but not change mechanics. The game tells players when adjustments are needed.

THE MANY KINDS OF ADJUSTMENTS

Adjustments come in so many ways, shapes, and forms. They can range from changing pre-game eating habits to making a full-scale alteration in mechanics. Everyone must understand that nothing stays the same—the competition changes, the body changes, experience adds to knowledge. Because of all the changes, it becomes essential to adjust again and again.

Adjustments fall into three general categories: mental, physical, and structural. All adjustments have a mental aspect, but some are specifically mental and refer to changes in thinking. Physical adjustments include mechanics, footwork, fielding, delivery, and the many physical details that go into playing the game. Structural adjustments deal with issues that form the structure that surrounds the player. What a player does with his free time and his diet are areas for structural adjustment.

SPECIFIC MENTAL ADJUSTMENTS

Many players overlook mental adjustments because they cannot be seen or are simply taken for granted. Instead they look for a physical correction to solve their problem. In fact, mental adjustments should be the first check on the list. For example, when a hitter finds himself struggling through a slump and recognizes he is pressing to perform, he needs to make the mental adjustment to calm his mind and relax, adjusting his effort and tension to productive levels. When the game becomes tough and stressful, players at every level remind themselves that baseball is fun, and adding tension only gets in the way of performance. When the Philadelphia Phillies struggled during the 2003 season, manager Larry Bowa told radio broadcaster Ray Fosse, "If you get frustrated in this game, it's not going to happen. In this game, if you go up there and start squeezing sawdust out of that bat, it's not going to happen."

Major league veteran Marquis Grissom owned starting jobs and made two All-Star teams early in his career before landing with the Los Angeles Dodgers and becoming a backup outfielder in 2001 and 2002. He struggled to make the mental adjustment to his role until he finally recognized the necessity. "It's tough to go out there feeling so angry at yourself or feeling indifferent," Grissom told Josh Suchon of the *San Mateo Times*. "When you get that one opportunity, you have to produce. That's what they pay us for. If you don't, you have nobody to blame but yourself." In 2002 he learned to make the mental adjustment to being a spot starter, and he learned not to let frustration get the better of him. "Last year [2002] was one of my best years because of that. I stayed focused and didn't worry about when I was going to play. That's my mind-set from now on."

Mental adjustments are also the first step in making physical adjustments. For instance, many hitters come to the plate with the attitude "Make sure it's a strike before I swing." This approach attitude inevitably causes a longer, harder swing because the hitter is going to be late on the pitch if he begins his movement when the pitch is already halfway to the plate. A natural reaction to being late on a pitch is to muscle up on the swing to catch up to the speed of the ball. When a hitter makes the mental adjustment to "I'm swinging until I recognize the pitch is out of the zone, at which point I will check my swing," his swing is more likely to take an unforced approach to the ball with a shorter bat path. Too much muscular tension in the swing will make it almost impossible to have a short, quick path to any pitch. This simple mental adjustment can make a critical difference between having a long, unwieldy swing and taking a short, quick path to the ball.

Numerous aspects of a player's mental game need continual adjusting, some as often as game to game, some as infrequently as season to season. Areas that fall under mental adjustments include:

• **Attitudes**. If an attitude is not working, or working only part of the time, that attitude must be adjusted. Attitudes should be kept positive, and conflicting attitudes should be eliminated.

• **Goals**. Destination goals will need adjusting as a player progresses in his career. Journey goals may need to be tweaked daily.

• **Perception of job**. Having a role as a starting pitcher or a cleanup hitter does not totally define a player's job. Situations and strategies define a player's job. When a No. 4 hitter is leading off the eighth inning with his team trailing by three runs, his job is that of a leadoff hitter. His thoughts should center on getting on base. He should make the pitcher pitch deep into the count, possibly pitching himself into trouble. When a pitcher gets into a jam, his job may change from not allowing any runs to making sure of damage control—getting out of the inning with only one or two runs allowed. But his precise job is to throw quality strikes with each pitch. Every player must reevaluate his job in every situation and readjust his game plan to get the job done.

Priorities. Values, needs, desires, and job identification are factors in establishing priorities. Priorities are constantly changing. If a person has not eaten in ten hours, food will be a high priority. With the tying run on second base with two outs, the infielders have a high priority to keep the ball in the infield so the run cannot score. With Rafael Furcal threatening to steal second base, a pitcher's priority is to hold him close and not let him get a good jump. Throwing a quality strike should have an even higher priority, because if the pitcher retires the hitter, Furcal cannot score the run whether he steals second or not. Reevaluating priorities and readjusting the game plan in each situation provides an edge.

• **Strategy and plan.** These must be adjusted when they are no longer effective, as situations change or when the opponent changes his strategy or his plan of attack. For example, the book on some hitters is to pitch them away with off-speed stuff, because they try to pull everything. If the hitter begins to wait back and hit effectively to the opposite field, the pitcher must also adjust his plan, perhaps going hard inside. If the hitter then reverts to pulling the pitch, the pitcher may again need to readjust. Game plans and strategies must be prepared before a game, but there is a constant need to adjust to the opposition's adjustments.

• **Level of commitment, dedication, and determination.** These should not be taken for granted when it comes to attitude, quality of work, effort, goals, and approach. They need to be constantly revitalized. Many great players reaffirm their dedication and hustle every day with one simple thought: "Play today's game as if it will by my final game."

• **Concentration**. When the level of concentration is unsatisfactory, a player should stop and start over, thinking slowly and adjusting mental routines. If that does not work, another alternative is for a player to talk aloud to himself, blocking out distracting thoughts until his level of concentration is satisfactory.

• **Emotions**. Players must manage their emotions. Some situations demand more emotion, some less emotion. Certain emotions may be right for one situation and wrong for another. Anger helped Bob Geren overcome his fear of facing Nolan Ryan, but it was an exploding time bomb for Carl Everett when he head-butted an umpire.

• **Level of relaxation and tension**. Players may learn to control their state of relaxation and tension levels through breathing and stretching. Attitudes also can control tension. If a player takes the attitude "I'm going to kill the ball," his tension level will be higher than by taking the attitude "Let it happen, nice and easy."

• **Effort level**. Many competitors want to play at maximum effort—throw the ball harder, swing the bat quicker, run into walls—but some players learn that their highest efficiency comes at a reduced level of effort. If the current level is not getting the job done, a player needs to change. A hitter may have days when his bat feels sluggish, so he needs to turn it up a notch on good fastballs. On other days the same hitter may need to tune down a notch because he is swinging too hard and missing good pitches.

• **Response to success, failure, and frustrations**. A player can adjust his body language and self-talk to make quick recoveries after emotional plays, whether negative or positive. He must always be ready to prepare for the next pitch.

• **Self-evaluation**. When a player changes his evaluation criteria, it will alter his focus, plan, and motivation. For example, if a pitcher evaluates himself on whether or not he is pitching ahead in the count and making first-pitch strikes, his game plan and focus will reflect that when he is pitching.

• **Mental routines, preparation, and self-coaching**. This includes pre-game, during the game when the player is waiting to become involved, and when he is directly involved in the action.

Hitters will face numerous specific mental adjustments. Here are a few possible adjustments for hitters:

• **Look at the ball**. When a hitter is not getting his best look at the ball, he must figure out where he can see it better and adjust his focus.

• **Adjust timing**. Being a good hitter has more to do with timing than with strength or quickness. A hitter must have his "A look" at the ball in order to have good timing. Anything less than the best view of the ball is not acceptable and will result in poor timing. A hitter does not have to be strong to hit a ninety-five-mile-per-hour fastball, he must time it correctly. When a hitter is late on the fastball, the suggested adjustment is to move the desired point of contact closer to the pitcher. For example, instead of trying to make contact at the front edge of home plate, try to make contact six to ten inches in front of the plate. When a hitter is too early on the fastball, he should move his point of contact back toward the catcher.

• **Swing easily against a hard-throwing pitcher**. The flame thrower provides the power. It is a normal reaction for hitters to try to swing harder when facing a mid-nineties fastball, but that tends to disrupt hand-eye coordination. Anticipating the speed and taking an easy swing often result in good timing and solid contact.

• **Adjust where you are trying to hit the ball**. Ted Williams said, "If I was trying to hit a line drive between the second baseman and the bag, but instead was hitting two hoppers to the second baseman, I wouldn't try to adjust my swing. I would adjust my target and try to hit it up the middle." If a hitter is not hitting a certain pitch the way he wants to hit it, he can try adjusting where he is trying to hit the ball.

• **Visualizations**. When a hitter misses a pitch because of a glitch in his approach or swing, such as swinging at a change-up, the quick adjustment is to take mental batting practice before the next pitch. Hall of Famer Billy Williams said, "If I missed a pitch I should hit, I would step out of the batter's box and take the time to visualize hitting that pitch a number of times. Then I would challenge the pitcher to throw it again." The physical adjustments Williams made were in those visualizations.

• **Adjusting your sights**. Ted Williams had a slightly different plan: "First of all, if you just miss a pitch, you are talking about a small fraction from hitting the sweet spot, so I don't want to change my swing. The second thing was, I trusted my swing, so I wasn't going to change my swing. If I fouled a pitch back one time, I would forget about it. If I fouled the same pitch back again, though, I would adjust my sights. By that I mean, instead of trying to center the ball, I would try and hit the top of the ball, and that should put me right on it." Great hitters often make very simple adjustments because they know that changing their swing in the middle of an at-bat or game can create an even greater need to adjust timing.

• **Improving plate coverage**. Poor plate coverage means that the hitter is not hitting pitches on both sides of the plate. He may be hitting inside pitches well but not having success with those outside. The hitter must examine all his attitudes that could be a factor, both positive and negative. The attitude "I'm a pull hitter. I'm going to get a pitch on the inside part of the plate and get in front of it," will leave the pitcher with a big hole to throw into. Conflicting attitudes are a common issue with plate-coverage problems. "I am going to get a pitch on the outside part of the plate and drive it past the second baseman" will give the hitter good coverage on the outside part of the plate. But if in the back of a hitter's mind, he thinks, "If he tries to surprise me and throws it inside, I am going to turn on it," that conflicting attitude can lead to hesitation toward any pitch over the plate because the brain is receiving mixed messages. There can be many possible problems and potential solutions for hitters with poor plate coverage. All effective solutions will require a change of attitude.

• **Improving strike-zone discipline.** Swinging at bad pitches results from inadequate preparation. Hitters who have a tendency to chase pitches out of the strike zone will continue to do so until they change their thinking. The late Willie Stargell had nearly reached his fortieth birthday when he said, "Even now, at the end of my career, if I don't anticipate the big curve in the dirt, I am a sucker for it. I will chase it like I did when I was eighteen years old." Recognizing and staying off bad pitches is a matter of anticipation. A hitter must adjust his mental game—adding the visualization of bad pitches that he has a tendency to chase, recognizing them, and seeing himself taking them. A hitter steps into the box with the intent to "see ball, hit ball." Therefore, taking a pitch is a decision he makes after recognizing that this is not a pitch he wants to hit. By previously visualizing himself taking those unhittable pitches, the hitter becomes less likely to chase them. He should always follow the mental images of taking with strong visualizations of hitting good pitches, thus emphasizing the dominant thought of hitting and not taking.

Hitters who begin their swings with extreme effort rarely have good strike-zone discipline because once they begin their swing, they cannot stop. Great hitters have an effortless beginning. They start their swing smoothly and without effort, consequently they can check their swing. This allows them to see the ball longer before they totally commit themselves. Changing effort level at the start of a swing is part of preparation, and it is a mental adjustment.

• **Becoming a better breaking-ball hitter**. Hitters usually swing and miss curves either because they are swinging over the top or because they are too early. Even hitters who recognize the curve early often swing too soon. One suggested adjustment is for the hitter to move his intended point of contact closer to the catcher. Old-timers talked about hitting the curve out of the catcher's mitt, which means making contact near the back of the plate. If the curve is breaking away or is on the outside part of the plate, the hitter should hit to the opposite field. Only when the breaking ball is coming to the hitter's hands should he try to pull it. Hitters have a tendency to spend their preparation time visualizing hitting only fastballs. It is important to visualize hitting off-speed pitches as well. Knowing how the pitcher's ball will break, and visualizing driving it, gives the hitter an advantage before he steps to the plate.

• **Four ways for a hitter to change his swing without dealing with mechanics**. 1) Loosen or tighten the grip. 2) Change the effort level—how hard the hitter swings. 3) Change the point of contact. Making contact with a pitch as it crosses the middle of the plate may jam some bats that are trying to get extended for power. Contacting the same pitch a few inches in front of the plate will give the hitter an entirely different bat angle at contact and extend the follow-through. 4) Adjusting where the hitter is trying to hit the ball can also change his swing. Hitters who are trying to hit the ball into the outfield may start trying to lift the ball, swinging up. Adjusting their target, trying to hit a solid one-hopper through the infield, can change the angle of their bat path. Mike Schmidt tried to hit a one-hopper toward the shortstop when he was attempting to get better backspin on balls, or when he tried to correct a swing gone bad without thinking about mechanics.

Pitchers, too, face specific mental adjustments. Here are a few areas:

• **Attitudes**. So much of pitching is mental that virtually every adjustment becomes more mental than physical. Pitching begins with attitude. When a pitcher is dissatisfied with the way he is throwing the ball, the first check must be attitude. Attitude issues can result in many problems, including overthrowing, being too careful, poor pitch selection, poor concentration, poor mechanics, to name only a few. Learning to make quick attitude adjustments is vital to pitching success. For example, if a pitcher begins with the attitude, "I'm going to blow this hitter away," he is likely to try to overthrow and will lose the smoothness of his delivery. Or if he thinks, "If I can get out of this inning, I will have a good day," he is likely to lose his focus on one pitch at a time. A pitcher must constantly be aware of his attitude in order to find the thought process that works best for him.

• **Goals**. When a pitcher grows sloppy with his goals, he tends to lose direction. Getting a hitter out and winning the game are fine goals, but they are too broad and do not provide specific direction. When a pitcher finds himself thinking, "I don't want to walk this hitter," or "I am going to get this hitter out," or "I am not going to let them score," he is not giving himself enough guidance. He has become unfocused. A better approach is to use more focused goals such as "I am going to hit the target, knee high on the corner of the plate," or "Just me and the glove. I am going to put the ball right in the glove," or "My goal is to concentrate on making one pitch at a time, not letting the count, situation, or score affect how I throw." Hall of Fame pitcher Steve Carlton said his challenge was to throw the ball how and where he wanted. He believed if he did that, good results would follow.

• **Concentration**. For a pitcher's delivery to be consistent, his thinking must be consistent. This means that concentration levels need to remain high. When a pitcher begins thinking too fast or too much, it will have a negative effect on his delivery. Rushed thinking always results in a rushed delivery. When a pitcher gets out of the groove, he can adjust his concentration with self-talk, controlled breathing, and visualization.

• **Pace of the game**. More than anyone else, pitchers control the pace of the game. Working at a brisk pace normally makes it easier for a pitcher to get his rhythm and also gives him less time to think about things he should not be considering. When he is pitching well he should maintain his tempo, but if he gets off his game, taking more or less time between pitches may help.

• **Adjusting the target**. When a pitcher is consistently just missing his target, his easiest change is to adjust his target. For example, if he is trying to throw a low strike in the middle of the plate and his pitches are at the hitter's waist, the pitcher should move his target below the knees. If the pitcher is trying to throw to the outside corner and nailing the middle of the plate, adjust the target farther outside, possibly at the knee of the catcher's shinguard.

• **Visualizations**. Pitchers often must adjust their release point. While this may seem like a mechanical change, the roots are mental. One of the easiest ways to adjust the release point is to visualize the entire flight of the ball from the hand to the catcher's mitt. Visualizing from the release point sets the release in the pitcher's mind. Many pitchers visualize the flight of the ball only during its final few yards, which does not help provide a release point. Some pitchers speak of visualizing a laser beam from their hand to the catcher's mitt, and they throw the ball on a line with the laser beam.

Major leaguers learn quickly that mental adjustments are critical to survival. Pat Burrell endured a miserable 2003 season for the Phillies, hitting .209 with 21 homers and 64 RBIs, a year after he hit .282 with 37 homers and 116 RBIs. He began the 2004 season sizzling hot, and he attributed the difference to his mental approach. "The physical stuff is a result of the mental stuff," Burrell told *USA Today Sports Weekly*'s Lisa Winston. "Most of the trouble we get into as hitters is between our ears, I think, and that's the hardest part to eliminate."

SPECIFIC PHYSICAL ADJUSTMENTS

When it comes to making changes and trying to improve, most players focus on physical adjustments—the mechanics of playing the game. When a player needs to work on something because he is performing poorly, mechanics are usually the first element examined. But it is not that simple. All physical adjustments require a change in a player's mind-set. If a player is to change stride or adjust a stance or grip, he must consider it first. Minor physical adjustments are made constantly, such as a hitter raising his hands a half-inch in his stance in order to get on top of a ball, or a pitcher making a slight change in his grip in order to achieve a different movement on the ball. Minor adjustments need only a quick thought to make them work, and they are often so subtle that they go unnoticed by others. More extreme physical adjustments, such as a pitcher using a slightly different arm angle or a hitter making over his swing, require significant changes in a player's thought process and take patience and time before they are done unconsciously in a game.

During the course of any player's career, he will face the need to make adjustments in various mechanical elements of his game. Here is a sampling of specific physical adjustments for hitters:

• **Stance**. Adjustments may be made to gain better plate coverage, see the ball better, get into a stronger launch position, and so forth.

• **Grip**. Hold the bat in the hand at the bottom joint of the fingers, where the fingers meet the palm of the hand. Players who wrap the thumb around the bat will force the bat into the palm of the hand and have a tendency to tighten the grip. Begin by holding the bat loosely, since the grip will naturally grow more firm during the swing. A tight grip at the outset will slow the hands and impair hand-eye coordination. Longtime major league manager Bill Rigney would try to grab the bat from his hitters' hands during batting practice to make sure they were not holding it too tightly while in their stance. "Hold the bat firm," said Ted Williams, but "if you hold the bat tight before you get to the hitting zone, you will never get there on time." The amount of tension in the grip and the position of the bat can alter bat speed.

• **Stride**. This is very individualized. Some hitters, like Barry Bonds, prefer to load weight on their rear leg and move forward only a few inches with their swing. Others, like Carlos Delgado, are successful with a pronounced leg kick. The direction of the stride and how the foot lands also vary. Despite many differences in strides, great hitters have two elements in common: they are balanced when their stride foot lands, and their foot lands softly before their swing starts. The stride and the swing are separate actions. The stride is part of the cocking action—often called the load—getting the hitter into a strong hitting position. Changing a stride has the potential to change everything that follows.

• **Head position**. This is one of the most important and least-coached fundamentals of hitting. Every hitter knows that he must have his head down, in the direction of the point of contact when the ball is in the hitting zone, in order to see the ball. Poor head position will affect the mechanics of a swing. When the head is up or back, it can result in the hitter pulling out his front shoulder prematurely, dropping his back shoulder, and/or creating a long swing.

• **Swing**. This should be the final adjustment a hitter attempts, rather than the first. The swing is a result of goals, preparation, reaction, and hand-eye coordination. If an experienced hitter loses his swing, he must ask why. There are three basic reasons why hitters lose their swing: 1) They are not properly prepared. 2) They swing too hard. 3) They do not see the ball well. Adjustments to the swing can change the hitter's timing. The most common adjustments to a hitter's swing are: starting the stride earlier and being slow and soft with it; changing the launch position; changing the angle or path of the swing; changing the follow-through; or changing the head position at contact.

• **Follow-through**. You will see a variety of swings and follow-throughs at the major league level. A hitter's bat path to the ball and how he uses his hands will determine his follow-through. Some hitters make swing adjustments by focusing on changing their follow-through. Adjusting the finish forces a change elsewhere in the swing, whether at the start, in the middle, or both.

Physical adjustments for pitchers:

• **Grip**. Changing the grip can change the spin, movement, and speed of a pitch. Finding the best grip for every pitch requires some experimentation. Hand size, arm angle, arm speed, grip firmness, and specific finger pressure will all affect how a specific grip will make a pitch perform for each individual pitcher.

• **Speed of delivery**. Changing the tempo of a delivery can affect a pitcher's stuff and control. A pitcher who winds up slowly and then cranks his arm at release will usually have more control problems than a pitcher who flows into his release. Also, speeding up or slowing down a delivery from pitch to pitch will usually make it difficult to repeat effective release points.

• **Leg lift**. The speed, height, and line between the knee and the foot can affect balance and control of the body. Poor balance and body control results in inconsistent release points and command.

• **Hands separation and backswing**. Adjustments may be necessary to get the arm and hand in position to start forward at the right time and to reduce stress.

• **Staying back**. When the hips start forward too soon, the arm will be late, disturbing the path of the arm and control.

• **Head position**. A pitcher's head position can affect his balance and arm action. Pitchers who fall off the mound during their follow-through may be able to correct themselves by keeping their head lined up to home plate.

• **Stride**. The length and direction of the stride will affect control and ball movement in the strike zone.

• **Release point**. When a pitcher has control problems, he needs to adjust his release point. Elements of the delivery that occur before a pitcher gets to a release point can cause inconsistency. Release point can also alter movement and deception.

• **Follow-through**. Adjusting the follow-through with a different arm angle, more extension, or a looser finish will affect arm action through the release area.

SPECIFIC STRUCTURAL ADJUSTMENTS

Aside from what occurs on the playing field, players must also adjust to what goes on in their life off the field. The structure that surrounds a player's life will have an impact on how he feels, the strength and energy he possesses, and the attitudes he brings to the ballpark. Amateur players attending school have class schedules, homework, and tests that can present challenges to a player's physical and mental well-being at practices or games. Student athletes must effectively manage their time away from the field in order to give academics and baseball their proper focus and the necessary energy to excel in both. For professional ballplayers, too much free time can present different challenges, such as barhopping and staying out all night, continually eating at fast-food restaurants on a minor league budget, or losing interest in practice because of the monotony of repetition that occurs during a long pro season. Making adjustments to the structure surrounding a player's life will have an impact on his baseball performance.

Those areas where structural adjustments can be made include:

• **Diet**. How a player eats will affect how he plays, and this becomes more important as the player ages. When and what a player eats can affect energy levels and performance. Players must recognize this and realize that everyone has a different body and different nutritional needs. Players must be aware of getting a proper balance of proteins, fruits, and vegetables. Derek Jeter adjusted his diet after the 2002 season and reduced his body fat to only 10 percent. He once ate desserts daily. "Cookies, ice cream. I used to go to the Cheesecake Factory for lunch and have cheesecake, then go play," he told the *New York Daily News*. At the age of twenty-eight he decided to make a change. "I'm getting old, man," Jeter said. "I don't have much of a choice but to do something. When you're young, you can eat anything up to about twenty minutes before game time. Now if I did that, it'd be heavy in my stomach." This need also becomes apparent with the move from high school to college and from college to professional levels. The longer the season, the more important diet becomes to sustaining performance.

• **Rest**. Players must understand how much rest they need in order to prepare for competition, then make the adjustments to be sure they get it. Many professional players who enjoy the nightlife find themselves sleeping until noon or later. This routine can actually make them feel more fatigued because they are skipping meals and not getting adequate nutrition.

• **Mental breaks**. Finding the right time to take mental breaks—mental rest during a game—can stave off mental fatigue. The mind can take a rest when teams are changing sides or between hitters. A fielder must remember to lock in before the pitcher steps on the rubber so his mind does not have to rush through pre-play routines.

• **Schedule**. If players are so involved in extracurricular affairs that they do not have time to properly prepare for the game, they must adjust, whether this means passing up fishing trips or golf games. Former major league catcher Joel Skinner recalls a 1990 game when his Indians battery mate Eric King was completely out of synch and getting battered. It turned out that King had spent the day shopping for a new Porsche and came to the park with his mind on his sports car, not his game plan. Then he failed to make the adjustment. Sometimes, too, a player is so focused on the game that he becomes overly tense and may need to schedule a diversion to relax and clear his mind.

• **Time management**. Learning how to set priorities and making a to-do list helps a player learn to take care of what is most important and helps alleviate stress when he runs out of time to accomplish everything.

• **Weather and field conditions**. Players must learn to adjust to rain, wind, cold or heat, poor fields, poor lights, fence height, warning-track depth, lack of padding on a fence, and other obstacles that are part of the game.

• **Practice**. What is practiced and how time is divided need to be reevaluated and adjusted on a regular basis. Goals for what is to be accomplished at practice should be reevaluated almost daily.

• **Off-the-field influences**. At times a player may find himself spending much time in situations that distract from or diminish his playing abilities, such as hanging out with a barhopping crowd or drug-using friends. It takes mental toughness to make the choice to say no to friends and avoid such influences.

The longer a player plays, and the further he advances, the better he understands the importance of adjustments. Being open-minded to change and seeking areas for improvement can lead to dramatic changes in performance. A player who is unwilling to change is unlikely to improve.

UNDERSTANDING THE PROCESS

A player must first understand that adjustments are more about mental concepts than physical. The adjustment itself may be physical—fixing a mechanical flaw or changing a stance—but what makes it happen is mental. Making adjustments demands that a player call upon elements of mental toughness. In order to make the adjustment work, he must combine attitude, confidence, focus, and concentration, and maintain the ability to keep his cool during the transition period in order for the adjustments to take effect.

Most adjustments are mental: changes of what, when, and how the player is thinking. Players are always adjusting, but too often without a process or plan. Without those, they are usually lost and grasping for some elusive solution. The process of adjusting falls into two categories: quick-check adjustments for changes that can be made almost immediately, and major mechanical adjustments for changes that will take contemplation and extensive work hours.

Quick check adjustments. Pitchers, hitters, and defenders may have a preparation process between pitches that has been working for them, but suddenly the magic in the preparation is gone, and so is the execution. Even the greatest players get off track. Longtime observers of Mark McGwire could tell by his body language when he was forcing and rushing his preparation. When major leaguers do not execute the way they know they can, they try to find a solution before the next pitch is thrown. They evaluate how they can prepare differently to get back on track and find the minor adjustment that will make that happen. With years of experience, they already have an idea of what to check in every situation. Their quick-check plan takes only a few seconds because they have a routine and keep it simple. They do not rush their thinking while looking for a quick fix, instead they think slowly and methodically. The process is called "self-coaching."

Hitters must step out of the batter's box because of the self-imposed rule, "No thinking allowed in the box." They will then evaluate two points:

1. **Mechanical.** Willie Stargell said, "I check my stride after every pitch, because if that wasn't right, everything that followed would be off. When my stride was right, there was a good chance everything would fall in place." Other mechanical checks include: the start, the bat path, and balance. If the hitter takes the pitch, was he in a good position to hit the ball had he decided to swing? More than one or two checks are too many during an at-bat, so hitters must develop a quick and simple routine.

2. **Mental.** The hitter will ask himself, "Was I ready mentally and physically?" "Could I have seen the ball better?" "Am I trying too hard, or do I need to become more aggressive?"

Pitchers should step off the rubber when they are dissatisfied with their execution, and do a quick check. They do not necessarily have to leave the mound.

1. **Mechanical**. The pitcher can ask himself any of the following questions: "Was my release point right?" "Did I stay back long enough?" "Were my rhythm and stride right?" "Were my balance and leverage right?"

2. **Mental**. The pitcher should ask himself, "Was I prepared, confident, and determined to execute the pitch?" "Were my mental timing and rhythm right?" "Was my effort level correct?"

For mechanical adjustments to work, players must remain positive with their thoughts while working on the adjustment. Should a hitter have a problem in lunging at the ball, his instruction to himself should be, "Stay back and let the ball come to me," rather than barking to himself: "Stop lunging at the ball." Negative commands usually have bad results because they present mixed messages—the brain must consider what the body is doing wrong, then how to correct it. A mental command framed in a positive manner forces the mind to consider only the correction and not relive the error.

Another key to making mechanical adjustments is to pre-play how the action should feel with the adjustment in place. A hitter may do this between pitches of an at-bat by stepping out of the box and taking a couple of practice swings with the adjustment in place. A pitcher who is visualizing behind the mound should include in his visualization how his delivery and release feel in order to get the greatest value from his self-coaching.

Poor execution results from poor preparation. When a player's mechanics fall apart during a game after being good for a period of time, he should review what he was thinking, his preparation, his self-talk, his visualizations, his mind-set, and his approach. When a player begins to encounter execution problems during a game, he should not immediately begin tinkering with mechanics. More times than not, a mental key has been forgotten or rushed, and preparation was not complete. A player should examine the elements of his mental game that need tweaking, then visualize succeeding with those adjustments on the next pitch. If more work is demanded, it may take more time. Juan Marichal said, "When I started having problems, I would go onto the grass behind the mound and have a meeting with myself. I would even talk out loud. When I got it straightened out, I would go back to work."

When the quick check does not work, and a player cannot get himself righted between pitches, between at-bats, or between innings, he should look at all aspects of his mental game. Initially he may want to use a personal checklist of all possible areas for adjustment. As he gains experience and grows to know himself better, the process becomes streamlined and easier.

Even quick-check adjustments may require changing more than one thought. For example, if Willie Stargell did not like his stride because he landed too heavily, his thinking might have been: Mechanical check: "Landed too hard." Mental check: "Too aggressive. Wanted to hit it too hard." He would respond with the adjustment: "Slow it up. Nice and easy. Nice and soft. Just let it happen." While still standing out of the batter's box, he would pre-play the next pitch, then practice his stride the way he intended to do it on the next swing. He would then clear his mind and prepare for the pitch.

The same procedure works on the mound. A pitcher who is attempting to hit a target at the knees on the outside corner, but instead is throwing up and in, will think: Mechanical check: "My arm was late and too low." Mental check: "I'm rushing my thinking and my delivery." He will then adjust his thinking to: "Slowly, one thing at a time. Stay back and get my arm up and release in front." While still off the rubber, the pitcher visualizes throwing the next pitch perfectly a couple of times. He then returns to the rubber and goes through his pre-pitch routine.

Significant mechanical adjustments. Sometimes players must make big-time changes in their mechanics in order to adjust to the competition around them. When this happens, it will demand a combination of mental work, patience, tenacity, and the mental toughness to carry it through. Following a pre-set process simplifies what otherwise seems an enormous challenge. A process that has worked for many professionals is:

1. **Recognize the possibility for improvement.** There is always a way to improve, and a player must be watching for ways to make himself better. This can become apparent when his current method is not working. Or he may receive some good advice. Scott Spiezio did not recognize the need for change until Mike Scioscia let him know that he needed to adjust or become a platoon player. Some players are always searching for a better way—an edge, as Ted Williams described it when he talked about "trying it on" and testing approaches that might help him. Ozzie Smith's attitude, "Keep reaching," should become part of all game plans.

2. **Evaluate the possible improvements or solutions to problems.** The player considers what result he is looking for and the changes that might work. First he evaluates the smallest, easiest change, then progresses to the next easiest, and so on.

3. **Test the adjustments in practice.** A player must experience how the choices feel, how easy they are to execute. Most important, he must discover which adjustment choices give him the desired result when performed properly. This is the experimentation part of the process, where he tests the new ideas.

4. **Select the appropriate adjustment.** A player chooses among the different ideas tested and finds the adjustment that provides the best results.

5. **Visualize the adjustment being successful**. Before making the adjustment on the field, the player must make it in his mind. He stops to visualize the adjustment step by step, then puts it all together.

6. **Dedicate to the adjustment**. Once the player has seen the results and recognized that this adjustment is most likely to work for him, he must take an attitude of dedication and belief in the adjustment, then convince himself that he will make it work. Players rarely make successful adjustments if they are burdened by conflicting attitudes and the thought that something may or may not work. This is the point where the player must fully believe in the adjustment.

7. **Practice for consistency and until the adjustment seems natural**. At first the player must focus on the mechanical changes. They may be uncomfortable, and he will be conscious of every movement, but with practice they will become more comfortable and unconscious. When he becomes consistent, returning his focus to the ball and to competing, he is ready to take the adjustment into a game.

8. **Take it into a game and make game adjustments**. Taking mechanical adjustments into a game will almost always require fine-tuning the mental approach, attitudes, emotions, effort level, timing, and targets. When the player takes adjustments into a game, the process becomes slightly different for pitchers and hitters. A pitcher may focus on an adjustment during his delivery, but he still must be completely comfortable with it before he takes it into the game. Hitters must focus on the ball, consequently it may take them longer to work out the adjustments.

9. **Stick with it**. It is unrealistic to expect that the first time a player tries an important mechanical adjustment in a game, it will work. When a player first attempts a change, his focus will likely be on correctly performing the adjustment, which is initially a distraction. As the player becomes comfortable with the

adjustment, it becomes almost unconscious. Too often players will invest great time and effort in making an adjustment, only to give it up when it does not show immediate results. It is vital to give the adjustment a fair chance to work in order for all the mental and physical elements to come together.

10. **Evaluate the progress.** After a few games, a player needs to determine whether the adjustment is successful, or at least showing a glimpse of the desired results so he can determine whether he is heading in the right direction. If the evaluation is negative, he may decide to try a different adjustment or start over with the process.

Oakland A's prospect first baseman Dan Johnson needed a major adjustment during the 2002 season. Johnson owned a long swing that worked just fine when he was using an aluminum bat against college pitchers: he hit 46 home runs in two years for the University of Nebraska. But when he came to the A's, coaches advised him that his swing was too long to be successful against professional pitchers who possessed more weapons. During the 2001 Instructional League and 2002 spring training, coaches worked to shorten the swing, and Johnson passed through an adjustment period during the first two months of 2002 when he hit .215 with 4 home runs for Modesto of the California League. Coaches regularly came to him and told him not to worry about the numbers, to stick with it, because they knew he was making an adjustment. As Johnson grew comfortable with his revamped swing, the results became apparent. During the last three months he batted .313 with 17 homers. He followed that in 2003 by leading the Double A Texas League in homers (27) and RBIs (114) while batting .290 for Midland as the adjustments further took hold. In 2004 he advanced to Triple A where he batted .299 with 29 homers, and was named the Pacific Coast League's Most Valuable Player.

Pitchers and coaches must remember that any time a pitcher makes an adjustment that changes arm swing, arm action, arm slot, or release point, the pitcher may have to recondition his arm. Even changes that are made to reduce stress and the possibility for injury can stress muscles and joints differently and put the pitcher in jeopardy.

Understanding this adjustment process decomplicates what seems like a very complex issue. Understanding and experience build confidence. As players learn that they have the ability to make successful adjustments, they will become confident that they can make the next adjustment that is needed. In baseball, the next adjustment is always on the horizon.

WORKING FROM THE POSITIVE

When young George Brett joined the Royals in the 1973 season, he was a less-than-willing pupil for hitting coach Charley Lau.

"When I came up I really lost it if I had a bad at-bat or sometimes just because I made a hard out. I would throw things, hit the water cooler or the trash can," Brett said. "After I had a bad at-bat he [Lau] would come to me and ask me, 'George, what did you like about that at-bat?' I would go off on him and tell him to leave me alone and walk away from him. The next inning he would come down the bench to where I was, sit down, and while he was looking out to the field he would quietly tell me two, three, or four things that he liked and then suggest something minor that might help. Like, 'Your stride was good, you stayed off the high fastball and got a good pitch to hit, you had a good swing at it. I think if you would hit that pitch up the middle instead of in the hole, you would hit it the way you want to.'

"That teed me off, too," Brett continued. "I'd walk away and tell Charlie to leave me alone. But Charlie wouldn't leave me alone. Then after about two weeks, I struck out and on the way back to the dugout, I caught myself thinking about what I had done well. That was the turning point for me—I learned to work from the positive. Adjustments started coming a lot easier, and I didn't fight myself as much."

Working from the positive is sort of a self-preservation method to make adjustments come more easily. By recognizing that much of the process is already in place, a player can focus on the exact elements that need adjusting rather than scrapping everything and working in confusion. This approach also offers a mental solace that the situation may not be as desperate as it seems.

The players at Regis University in Denver learned this during the 2003 season, much to their surprise. The team started the season with a 15-18 record and lost five of its first eight Rocky Mountain Athletic Conference games. After being swept in a doubleheader by Southern Colorado, Regis coach Dan Mc-Dermott went out to an Italian dinner in Pueblo, Colorado, with an old friend, A's area scout John Kuehl. McDermott was mystified by his team's performance, since he knew the club had far greater ability than it was showing on the field. Kuehl responded by telling the story that Brett had confided to Karl Kuehl a few years earlier: how Lau had taught his prize hitter to work from the positive.

The concept immediately intrigued McDermott. The next day he turned the idea into action. When his players failed to execute, he would concentrate on the positive, pointing out what the players did well and slipping in a corrective. This proved a contrast to his previous style of teaching by emphasizing what they had done improperly. McDermott later recalled that the first few games the players thought he was crazy. "I could hear them in the dugout saying, 'What's up with coach?' or 'Why is he acting differently?'"

With the positive approach, Regis suddenly surged, going 13-6 and 10-5 in conference the rest of the season to earn a berth in the playoffs. McDermott was named RMAC coach of the year, which added another positive for the season. "When I get new players, they expect someone to yell at them when they do something wrong," McDermott said. "When I started working from the positive, it was a big, unexpected surprise, the effects of which carried over into this year." Regis finished 32-18 overall and 16-8 in the conference in 2004.

McDermott coached his players to think about the positives and correct only what needed correcting. This may sound easy, but in many ways it goes against human nature. Players tend to think first about their failure to get the job done; they consider the larger issues rather than evaluating only what needs to be fixed. The natural immediate reaction is to get mad and think about all that went wrong. This makes the task of adjusting seem enormous. When a player learns to work from the positive, he becomes almost like a pilot with a checklist—crossing off everything that is satisfactory, then concentrating on tweaking what needs fixing.

While working from the positive can be an effective tool for making adjustments, it often must be handled with care. A player may focus so heavily on the positive elements that he forgets the negatives. This can be especially difficult for coaches who must avoid mixed messages to their players. Working from the positive becomes a valuable asset for players who learn to use it effectively, as did George Brett. It helps preserve confidence and positive attitudes while allowing players to ease into adjustments.

WHY PLAYERS RESIST ADJUSTMENTS

Just about every player who makes it to a high school varsity team hears his coaches preach about the importance of adjustments. Rationally, everyone knows adjustments must be made. But even established, intelligent major leaguers still resist, victims of emotional responses they often cannot pinpoint. As players advance, they must learn to conquer these emotions in order to make successful adjustments and become better players. Here are a few reasons players resist adjustments:

• **Lack of confidence**. Deep inside, many players fear they do not have the ability to make a significant change; that if they toy with their swing or delivery, they will lose that magic that led them to success in the first place. They fear that if they experiment with a new pitch, they will lose the feel for the ones they already have. Players must develop confidence in order to make changes. Juan Marichal had supreme confidence that he could discard his sidearm delivery and develop a new repertoire, and that confidence led him ultimately to the Hall of Fame. Lack of confidence may also apply to a player's perception of his coach. If a player lacks confidence in his coach, he will not trust his coach's advice to be effective.

• **Discomfort**. Nobody wants to be uncomfortable. Players often experience an initial sense of discomfort when they experiment with changes, particularly if the adjustment is not their own idea. Tension results from being conscious of trying to do something differently or trying to perfect a new alteration, and tension leads to discomfort. This is natural, and a player must develop the confidence to believe he can succeed at making the adjustment. When someone learns to ride a bicycle, he is at first conscious of everything from holding the handlebars to remembering to pedal while attempting to balance. In a very short time, all this seems a completely natural action that requires no thought process. Adjustments occur the same way—they require conscious thinking while being sampled, then they become a natural process.

• **Ego**. Many players believe their way is the right way, come what may. Hitters may think they are exclusively pull hitters and need never go the other way; pitchers may think their fastball is so dominant they have no need for a change-up. Many extremely talented players with this mind-set linger in the lower minor leagues or get stuck in Triple A, and never know what kept them down. Some players have such overwhelming egos that they believe their way will work, even when it clearly does not. Juan Marichal, because of his tremendous success in his first two years, could have been full of himself and been insulted that anyone with his numbers could be asked to change, but he was a learner with an open mind. Players must learn to develop a balance between ego and confidence, where they can recognize the value of adjustments while still having the confidence to reject an adjustment that does not work for them.

• **Mistaken beliefs**. Some players are certain they are executing in a particular way and will insist they are doing it just right. This is where videotape becomes important, because it gives them the opportunity to watch and evaluate their own mechanics.

• **Failure to recognize the need for change**. Players sometimes simply do not believe they need to make adjustments. This is often a product of poor self-evaluation. Even if a hitter is consistently being retired on pitches inside, he will wait for the ball over the plate until it becomes painfully obvious to him and the world that the adjustment is overdue. As Carl Yastrzemski said, if pitchers found a hole, he had to plug it right away or word would quickly get around the league.

• **Failure to take responsibility**. Some players believe that problems are not their fault, or are some conspiracy of light and air to make them fail. A player must determine whether there really is a problem, then take responsibility for resolving it. Conversely, if the problems are just bad luck—such as a hitter's average taking a plunge while he is hitting line drives—the player must decide that no adjustment is needed and be patient enough to ride out his unlucky streak.

• **Fear of failure**. Many players are afraid, deep inside, that a failed adjustment will lead to embarrassment and only make their situation worse. This is where a player needs the confidence and determination to overcome that fear of failure and find a better way. Failure is an education, and baseball is a game filled with failure. Players achieve by making adjustments to overcome failure. Players can relax and improve almost immediately once they recognize that a poor performance provides information that will help them succeed in the future. True failure occurs only when someone continues to repeat the same mistakes in the same manner over and over again.

• **Just not the right time**. If a player is attempting to make a team or earn a promotion to a higher minor league level, or if his team is heavily involved in a pennant race, the timing may not be right for an adjustment. In these situations tweaking may help, but it is not the time for a major change unless the coach tells the player he will allow the time for the adjustment to take effect.

It is easy and almost natural to resist change, just hoping the planets will somehow align to resolve every little problem. Neither baseball nor life really works that way. Players must learn to accept the need for adjustments, then develop the ability to recognize adjustments that will benefit them while discarding those that will not.

ADJUSTING TO UNMET EXPECTATIONS

During the winter of 2001, the Oakland Athletics traded four quality prospects to the Texas Rangers for Carlos Peña, a first baseman with a history of hitting well in the minors, to fill the vacancy left by former MVP Jason Giambi. The A's quickly benefited from the trade as Peña started the major league season with a hot bat and was named the American League's Rookie Player of the Month for April. Three weeks later Peña was back in Triple A after struggling mightily with the bat. Hot one minute, cold the next. A baseball player may ride a roller coaster of emotion if he lets his confidence and morale ride up and down with his play. Veteran big-league ballplayers talk of keeping an even keel with their emotions during a long baseball season: not feeling too happy when things are going well, and not feeling too depressed when struggling. That can be easier said than done, especially when a player feels highly emotional after a terrible game.

The best and most effective way of dealing with unmet expectations is to view failure as an education: learn from poor performances, and make any necessary adjustments in order to be prepared for the next game. Too often players will let a bad game fester in their mind and let doubt and frustration enter their thoughts. Negative feelings are a prime ingredient of failure. Learning and adjusting bring positive expectations and excitement for future rewards.

Knowing what does not work for a player is just as important as knowing what will bring success. Players need to avoid bad habits and focus on the positive aspects of playing the game. For most professional baseball players, one or two bad habits usually cause mechanical breakdown. For example, a pitcher tends to rush forward in his delivery and leave his arm dragging behind him, which leads to erratic control and pitching up in the zone. The pitcher who learns this about himself may establish a mental key that he uses on the mound, reminding himself to hit his balance point before moving forward. This will allow his arm to get up in time and permit his delivery to flow. There are other keys a pitcher may use to fix a rushing problem. It is just a matter of learning—usually from failure—what works and what does not. There can be more than one way to fix a pitcher's

problem. Should the problem surface in the middle of an out-
ing, the pitcher may need a few pitches in the bullpen or during
the game, to find the key that will work in that moment. But the
adjustments all stem from failing experiences, and the answers
for each individual come from a trial-and-error learning model.

In learning and making adjustments, a player's first step is to
evaluate his performance. In order for him to have unmet expectations and experience failure, he must first define success.
Destination goals, journey goals, and game plans are all a part of
a player's definition of success, because they outline what the
player is trying to accomplish. In surviving the emotional down-
fall of unmet expectations, the proper perspective is required.
Destination goals, which detail a player's long-term and seasonal
goals, should not be a subject for concern during the first week
of the season or after a bad game. Because a player is hitting
.195 after six games, or a pitcher sees his ERA climb to 8.75 after enduring one terrible inning, there is no need for a player to
put pressure on himself to have a spectacular game or two in order to get back on track for his destination goals. It's a long season. Great games do help statistics, but it is the consistency of
good performances that keeps averages and ERAs steadily in
range of goals.

A player must learn to define and evaluate his success by
what he can control about his game. No hitter can control
whether the opposing outfielder leaps over the wall to steal a
homer; no pitcher can expect a perfect pitch to turn into a bloop
single. This is just part of baseball. As difficult as it may be to
avoid being tormented by statistics, a mentally tough player defines his success by accomplishing journey goals. Succeeding at
the journey goals will almost always make the destination goals
attainable in the long run.

If a hitter's game plan is to stay back on off-speed pitches and
hit them up the middle, his post-game evaluation should consider

whether he did just that, not whether he got a hit on an off-speed pitch. Eric Karros said that Mike Piazza taught him to evaluate his hitting by judging how many balls he hit hard out of every ten mistake pitches he saw. Mistake pitches can be defined as the pitches a hitter should hit hard—a fastball down the middle or a hanging breaking ball. Of the three mistake pitches he does not hit hard, Karros is realistically allowing that he may foul off a couple of those pitches or may be surprised and not swing at one. Of the seven balls he does hit hard, he expects major league fielders to make the play on four of them, leaving him with three hits for every ten mistake pitches he receives over a course of consecutive games. That is how Eric Karros attempts to hit .300, a destination goal. He uses a journey goal of hitting seven of ten mistake pitches hard, and he can evaluate his daily game plans by reflecting on how many good pitches he actually saw versus how many of them he hit hard. His expectations are within his control and achievable. He can tell whether he is getting himself out on pitcher's pitches and needs to make an adjustment concerning his plate discipline. He can see if a mechanical or mental adjustment is needed if he is getting good pitches to hit and making poor contact or missing them altogether.

Successfully surviving unmet expectations requires mental toughness to deal with the lows a player may feel after a poor game. Beating up water coolers, yelling obscenities, or feeling depressed will not correct what went wrong. By using failure to learn and improve, a player can refocus his sights on productive actions and work toward fulfilling goals and plans instead of obsessing on what he failed to accomplish.

FIND YOURSELF

Through the minor leagues, Eric Gagne seemed to have the perfect tools for a starting pitcher, mixing a ninety-seven-mile-per-hour fastball with a brilliant curve, plus a slider, a dominating splitter, and a change-up. Five solid pitches and effective control. But when Gagne arrived with the Los Angeles Dodgers, starting just did not work out. He fought his own emotions for three years as a starting pitcher, bobbing from the Dodgers to the minors, and putting together an 11-14 record. Finally in 2002 he moved to the bullpen and quickly claimed the job of closer, where he could use his emotional bursts to his advantage. Gagne found himself and saved fifty-two games during a remarkable 2002 season when he went from the pitching scrap heap to become a legitimate star by making the adjustment to becoming a reliever. He followed with an even better 2003, winning the National League Cy Young Award, then saved forty-five games in 2004.

Making adjustments are about a player finding himself, finding his optimal performance level. That will change continually throughout a player's carrer, so adjustments will be an ongoing process that he must repeat and review with every twist and turn down the paths of his life.

Learning to make adjustments may appear to be a maze of contradictions: learn from everyone yet be able to ignore advice; be open to adjustments yet be stubborn enough to refuse what does not fit. But that is how baseball works. There are no panaceas, no magic coaches who can bestow the perfect gem of wisdom for every situation. A player must have the confidence, courage, acumen, and mental toughness to find his own way. He must learn to accept failure as an education, then try to learn from his failures. It should be some consolation that every successful major leaguer since the game began has faced the same challenge—from Ty Cobb to Jim Thome. A mentally tough player will take the attitude, "If they can do it, so can I."

And so they shall. The next generation of major leaguers, allstars, and Hall of Famers will be made up of those players who best develop their abilities to make adjustments.

8

TOUGHNESS WITH DETERMINATION

Mike Scioscia spent his first two years as a major
league manager telling his Angels players how much he believed in them, even as they missed the post-season and struggled to mediocre records. Scioscia kept the faith. Then
everything seemed to collapse around him. Depleted by injuries, the 2002 Angels got off to the worst start in franchise
history, losing fourteen of their first twenty games and facing
being out of the race by the end of April. Scioscia never pan-
icked. He called his team together—a rarity for a manager who
almost never called team meetings—and told them again how
much he believed in them.

"We think you are a great team, and we think you guys are
great players. We're not making changes. We just want you to
believe in yourselves," was how first baseman Scott Spiezio recalled his skipper's speech.

"This meeting was, 'Hey we're going to be fine,'" recalled
pitching coach Bud Black. "He said, 'We haven't been at full
strength. You guys are a good club and I believe in you. You guys

Mike Scioscia kept telling his team that he
believed in them.

are championship caliber. If you keep going out there and playing hard, things will turn around.'"

After the disastrous beginning, the Angels embarked on almost a magical journey, winning the American League wild card,
then knocking out the Yankees and the Twins to reach the World
Series. This was not a team of superstars who regularly convene
at the All-Star Game. There was talent, no question, but more
than anything the 2002 Angels played hard and played right. It
was a team that hustled, made few mental mistakes, and executed extremely well. This band of Angels was the type of team

that made even grizzled old baseball cynics rejoice with the old-fashioned style of intensity and team play. And, most of all, the Angels played with confidence, individually and in each other.

"I think it's simple. We've got good players," said reliever Dennis Cook. "There's no secret to it. We've got good guys and good players. They play as a team, they move people over, they give up an at-bat to move a guy ninety feet, they run the bases well, they do everything good. We've got good players."

The Angels did have *good* players, though perhaps not *great* players. They put together a team built around execution and intensity; doing the little things well to achieve big results. They showed how baseball is an individual sport in a team framework. A player can reach remarkable heights while the team fizzles. The Angels learned to believe in themselves *and* their teammates— that they could do the individual job at hand, whether it was advancing a runner or driving a key hit in the clutch.

"The more success we had, the more confidence we developed, in ourselves and in each other," Spiezio said. "The wins kept piling up, and with all the comeback wins we were having, we started believing that even if we were down five or six runs, we're coming back; we've got a good chance to win this game. We've got this thing called the rally monkey in Anaheim, and that's our rallying cry. A lot of us feel that we're going to show the fans, we're going to show ourselves, that we're going to come back, no matter what. As a team, we never give up until the last out's made."

This may sound a little trite to jaded cynics, but the Angels backed it up all the way to the World Series, playing aggressive, up-tempo, team baseball. Those 2002 Angels embodied the concepts of mental toughness.

The Angels were not the most talented team in baseball, brimming with recognized superstars and leaders in all the statistical categories. They had legitimate stars in Garret Anderson, Troy Glaus, Darin Erstad, and Jarrod Washburn, but no more stars than most teams. What they did have was an intense drive to achieve, work ethic, attitude, team character, focus, and confidence. They played as a team with a common goal of team success, rather than putting individual statistics ahead of victories. They had mental toughness, and it proved to be their winning edge.

"I think more and more, teams realize it's not just the five-tool players and 'can't-miss prospects' with no work ethic that they want," says Sean Casey of the Cincinnati Reds. "I think teams are starting to realize that if we put a team of good-character people together in the clubhouse, winning will take care of itself."

This is not a magic formula now being discovered. Baseball people have known it for generations. It is the difference between Strat-O-Matic or Fantasy Leagues and real life. "You can get twenty-five of the best players in the league, and you'd think you'd win everything, but it doesn't happen that way. To me, the bottom line is we've got good players who are unselfish players," reliever Cook said.

The Angels of 2002 were virtually an embodiment of the pillars of mental toughness: *attitude, character and values, confidence, the concepts of cool, focus, and concentration*, and *the ability to make adjustments*. This was a team that fought to the end, worked hard, and got the most out of their God-given talent.

The attitudes started early. The team was built with the concept of acquiring players of character who would play hard, and Scioscia spent his first two years as manager imbuing the attitudes of success. By the beginning of the 2002 season, most of the Angels players combined proper attitudes with solid on-field character, and these mental strengths flourished under Scioscia's leadership.

Bud Black: "These guys have a passion to play. It's their main priority in life."

"I think it's just the collection of our players; the character of our entire group," said pitching coach Black. "As a group, these guys have a passion to play. They like to play. It's their main priority in life. I don't want to discount their feelings for their families or anything like that, but these guys place a high priority on their careers. I think that explains in part not ever thinking the game's over. They continue playing until the game's over. That's just the group that's been assembled. A lot stems from the veteran players—[Tim] Salmon, Erstad, Anderson—about the way guys go about their business. We have a lot of younger guys, but the young guys do it too—[David] Eckstein, [Adam] Kennedy, [Bengie] Molina, Glaus—these guys love to play. It's an unselfish group, there's no big egos on this team. They recognize and respect each other's ability.

"I think it comes down to the individual makeup of the players. In clubhouses on good teams, there's always a check-and-balance system of each other. Being an ex-player, you know that if guys start getting out of hand or getting away from the team concept, other guys step in and straighten them out. I think that happens on our club. I think these guys police themselves very well."

With the 2002 Angels, attitudes and character came together in the clubhouse and on the field. Attitudes grow from character, and character is built upon values and priorities. The individual Angels players placed an enormous priority upon their passion to play, and to play the game right. They were willing to suppress their own egos for the good of the team, for the good of teamsmanship, and it carried them to a championship.

If ever a team, as a whole, played with confidence, it was the Angels. As Spiezio said, the more success the team had, the more confidence it developed, among the players individually and in their teammates. Success breeds confidence, and confidence leads to greater success. Scioscia understood that from the beginning.

"I think the seed was planted a couple of years ago when Mike came on board as our manager and told the players up front that he believed in them and thought they were championship caliber," Black said. Scioscia took over the Angels in 2000 and put together seasons of 82-80 and 75-87 before the championship run. "Granted, our first year we were just slightly above .500, and last year we had a tough year. But I think Mike really believed in our players, as we did as coaches," Black continued. "I think it finally set into the players this year, once we finally started winning games. Once we got through April, got into May, the players saw the talent that Mike saw, and it just really gave them a whole new level of self confidence.

"If there's a feeling among the team that you can accomplish something, the level of confidence in your play will rise. With our guys, we're a tough group because there's an inner confidence among all our guys about their abilities. We didn't have a Barry Bonds–type player, or a Jason Giambi, or an Alex Rodriguez–type player, but there was a sense of every day, every pitch by our pitchers, every at-bat by our hitters, a sense of confidence that lifted our team. Our guys really felt they could get it done. I think we as coaches, and Mike especially, just constantly telling these guys, 'Hey, you are good'—it finally settled in and gave them not only confidence but made them a tougher group. Then when we went against the Yankees and Twins, and we played the A's, and we played the Mariners during the season and the Bostons and all the good clubs, we felt we were on a level playing field. We felt we could play right with them all the time."

This is *team confidence*; it is confidence raised to a higher level. Not only do players believe individually in themselves, they believe in their teammates. It is the combination of confidence and teamsmanship that is inspired by great team leaders, such as a Derek Jeter. Mike Scioscia instilled team confidence in the Angels, and it reached fruition as the team built on its success.

With confidence, the Angels played clutch. They consistently displayed the concepts of cool and thrived in crucial situations. Confidence built cool. Confident players learn to play clutch baseball. And Scioscia created an atmosphere where cool thrives.

"Something Mike has related to the team—and this goes deep into spring training and to the minor leaguers who come to big-league camp, and to our players at the big-league level— is to treat every game the same, whether it's a spring training game, a game in April, or a World Series game in October," Black said. "The game still has to be played under control. You still have to win. You're competing. I think that in itself went a long way with our players. I think our players understand that concept. If you didn't play a spring training game hard, Mike got pissed. Obviously, guys are going to play a World Series game hard because it's the World Series. But if you play every game at a high level, you will have the right approach to the game. Our guys did that. Our guys didn't turn it up when the bell rang April 1st, they didn't turn it up when the A's took off and won twenty games, we didn't turn it up another level in the playoffs. We played the same way the whole year, and I think that lent a level of comfort to our club because we knew how to play. Our guys didn't need to try to do too much because they played every game at a high level. We didn't want guys to try to do more because they were playing the post-season. We said, 'Play your game. Play the way we've been playing the whole year. Play the way the Angels play. Worry about ourselves. Play the game hard, play it the right way.'"

With confidence and success, focus and concentration improved further. These Angels players, as individuals and as a team, already excelled at focus and concentration before their championship season. The excitement of the season only enhanced their concentration levels. After the season-opening falter, the mood around the Angels changed. "After the first twenty, twenty-five games, you could see the attitude and the professionalism and the everyday preparation by the players. Everybody prepares his own way, but you could see that each guy was preparing to play. Ultimately, with that focus on preparing to play and playing hard, and with talent, you win games," Black said.

As mentally tough players, the Angels were good at adjustments. It was a collection of players with the aptitude to adjust.

Spiezio's slight adjustment in spring training turned around his career, and the team as a whole understood the need to adjust. "First of all, you've got to have the open-mindedness to be able to adapt and not be so stubborn that you're not open to suggestion, not open to constructive criticism, not open to advice," Black said. "If you have that ability to listen, you have the aptitude and ability to put it to work. Here again, our guys have that. Overall we don't have a group of guys who think they know it all. We don't have a group of guys who say, 'I'm going to do it my way because I've been successful.' I think you look at all great players, all great leaders, all the people at the top of any profession—they're all good listeners. They take constructive criticism, they take advice, and they put it to work in their own way.

"From a pitching standpoint, I find that my guys are very open, very receptive to my teaching. But, then again, I'm realistic enough to know they're not going to use everything that I say to them. As long as there's dialogue, that's where the learning comes in. And I think that's what's happened to our club. It finally sunk in this year. Offensively, we talked about a number of things in spring training that would help. Last year [2001], offensively, we were statistically toward the bottom of the league. This year we're the exact opposite. Mike and [hitting coach] Mickey Hatcher put some things in front of these players in spring training, and they grasped them and took them to heart and made them work. That carried over through the season."

The elements of mental toughness interrelate. Character and values mold attitudes; attitudes provide the basis for achievement. A player, or a person, must establish and understand his priorities in both his life and career, then develop the attitudes that will lead him to achieve. There is no single best attitude for everyone; each individual must find and develop the attitudes that work best for him, in his particular situation.

Situations change, and attitudes must change with them. Character and attitudes help develop confidence, and confidence provides players with the belief they can succeed, which is essential for achievement. A player must first come to learn himself and his abilities, then get the most from them. Had David Eckstein decided he wanted to be Mark McGwire, all the confidence and the best attitude in the world would not have carried him far. He learned what he could do and made the most of his abilities.

With confidence, character, and attitude comes the concept of cool: the self-control to thrive in tension-packed situations and the inner strength to battle through hard times to an ultimate achievement. In this process a player must develop his abilities of focus and concentration to bring that to fruition. And, after all that, a player must learn flexibility and be ready to make adjustments to meet whatever challenge comes his way.

There are many steps to the process. A player must understand the difference between journey goals and destination goals, and use both to full advantage. He must recognize that effective visualization demands incorporating all the elements of action rather than just the final outcome. He must comprehend that he is his own man, that he is responsible for his future and must take control of his destiny.

Mental toughness is hard. It means working when you are tired, taking extra practice when you would rather be hanging at the mall watching girls, eating parsnips instead of pizza, and making sacrifice after sacrifice in order to attain an ultimate goal.

Mental toughness demands determination. It demands conviction. It demands the old-fashioned concept of grit. Players must be dedicated to the belief that they will find a way to be mentally stronger than their opposition or their situation. For an attitude to be effective, a player must be dedicated to that attitude. For an adjustment to work, a player must dedicate himself to it. Halfway efforts will be little more than token gestures and self-delusions of mental toughness. For a player to thrive mentally, he must view mental toughness with the determination to get the job done.

Mental toughness demands that a player take responsibility for his own life and career. At some point a player must determine that he will be his own man and meet these challenges. Not every suggestion in this or any other book will work for every player. Each player must find his own way, taking the information he acquires, processing it, and finding his own path. Everyone must determine his own priorities and values, because everyone faces a different set of circumstances in life. One standard of adulthood is when a person takes responsibility for who he is, and who he wants to become, then strives to succeed by determining his own set of values and priorities.

Boys mature into men in different ways, at different times. In many ways it is a lifelong process. Scott Spiezio moved through the minor leagues with an excellent work ethic, then grew a little too comfortable once he established himself as a major leaguer with the A's. His conditioning and drive lapsed, and he lost his job. Once he caught on with the Angels, his work ethic and drive for excellence were rekindled. He won a starting job and a World Series ring. Everyone will experience lapses, ebbs and flows, times when the world seems to fall apart around him. The mentally tough fight through to find the right attitude, make the adjustment, and find a way to persevere.

Mental toughness is the drive for each player to get the most from his own set of skills and abilities. It will not make David Eckstein into Mark McGwire, or Tim Wakefield into Roger Clemens. What it will do is allow you to become the best baseball player, and the best person, you can be. In the end, that is a huge reward.

PLAYING THE GAME RIGHT

College and professional coaches speak of "playing the game right," though they rarely explain exactly what that means. Here is a point-by-point checklist of the qualities of "playing the game right":

1. Be prepared. Be ready to give your best at all times.

2. Hustle as hard as possible for as long as it takes. Grind it out.

3. Be alert, always looking for an edge. Anticipate what may happen around you. Be into every pitch.

4. Sacrifice yourself for the team. Play to win rather than for personal numbers. Help teammates whenever possible.

5. Know the game. Know yourself. Know the opposition and strategies.

6. Do what is supposed to be done. Take the time and make the effort to do it properly.

7. Focus only on what you can control.

8. Play tough, focused defense. Make the opposition earn every baserunner and every run.

9. Win the game on the bases by being aggressive and making good decisions.

10. Play tough. Intimidate with your effort and focus.

11. Be poised at all times. Have self-control, emotional control, and physical control.

9

MENTAL TOUGHNESS OFF THE FIELD

"You've got to have luck in this life. And if you don't have luck, you've got to make your own."—*the late Dan Geller, former co-owner of the San Francisco Giants and successful San Francisco businessman*

"Luck is the residue of design."—*Branch Rickey, former general manager, Brooklyn Dodgers*

The same skills of mental toughness that lead to achievement on the diamond carry over onto the playing fields of life. Very few high school or college athletes will have the talent necessary to play professional sports, no matter their level of mental toughness. Yet each and every player, and person, will have the ability to achieve in some arena. The skills of mental toughness they carry with them will be crucial ingredients in their success. Whether in business, the newsroom, the military, or some other career, the combination of attitudes and approaches that creates mental toughness will lead to achievement.

The crux of mental toughness is responsibility: taking responsibility for one's own actions and asserting control over destiny. Rather than withering and hoping for a lucky break, a person who prepares and places himself in the right position is far more likely to have that element of good fortune find him. Life will inevitably throw up roadblocks and pitch a few curveballs, but those who place themselves in a position to achieve are far more likely to find success and a degree of satisfaction than those who spend their lives yearning to win the lottery or catch the whims of fortune.

A person who continually makes excuses, slacks, and works at diminished capacity is not likely to be successful in his endeavors. The same mental skills learned in athletics so often lead to achievements in real life. Sean Casey had goals both on the field and off, and his meticulous dedication to his goals carried him to the major leagues as well as to satisfaction off the field. The ability to overcome obstacles will lead to further achievement. Life is about learning to use the tools you have, whether mental or physical, and making the most of them.

TOUGHNESS IN ACTION

Dan Geller grew up the son of a New York City grocer, then went to war to become a pilot, flying from England on missions over Germany during World War II. Only 6 percent of his bomber group survived, and he spent the rest of his years cherishing his life. He built a real estate empire and devoted himself to family and to the San Francisco Giants. He never blinked at hurdles and found a way to make his own luck when luck did not turn his way. Life is a combination of choices, fortune, and opportunity.

The pillars of mental toughness apply to just about every facet of life, and the lessons learned through mental toughness in baseball become part of an effective strategy for living. Virtually everything in life begins with *attitude*. Achieving in almost any arena starts with the right attitude. For example, a student who takes the attitude that his classes are a challenge to learn new skills and an opportunity to improve his mind will have an immediate advantage over a student who views school as simply an ordeal on the path to getting a job. A carpenter who takes the attitude that every job is a chance to display his quality craftsmanship and build his clientele will command more respect than a hack with a hammer. In any business, attitudes for success will make success more likely. Consciously or unconsciously, everyone chooses his own attitudes. The mentally tough understand that they are in control of this decision and attempt to find the best attitude for the situation.

Those Americans born in the final three decades of the twentieth century have enjoyed a relatively comfortable life, unmarred by global warfare. The events of September 11, 2001, shocked many into a recognition that evil still lives in the hearts of men, and that even the most advanced societies can be attacked. During the 1940s a generation of American farmboys put down their baseballs and bats and went off to the South Pacific and Europe to fight a war against aggressors intent on global conquest. In combat, and in survival, attitudes made an enormous difference. Viktor E. Frankl spent most of World War II in a Nazi concentration camp, knowing death could come any day. He recalled, "We who lived in concentration camps can remember the men who walked through the huts comforting others, giving away their last piece of bread. They may have been few in number, but they offer sufficient proof that everything can be taken from a man but one thing: the last of the human freedoms—to choose one's attitude in any given set of circumstances, to choose one's own way. . . . And there were always choices to make. Every day, every hour, offered the opportunity to make a decision, a decision which determined whether you would or would not submit to those powers which threatened to rob you of your very self, your inner freedom; which determined whether or not you would become the plaything of circumstance."

Not just success but survival itself can be built on attitude. The boys who went to war to save the world, and the victims of Nazism who endured life in the death camps, found their attitudes of survival. Attitudes determine how a person faces the challenges that surround him, wherever he is.

Attitudes are built on *character*, and character is made from what a person *values*. Every person has the conscious ability to determine what principles and values he will choose to follow. If a person subscribes to the biblical Golden Rule of "Do unto others as you would have them do unto you," that person is much more likely to be treated with respect. If a person treats others as crap, the crap usually comes back at him. Character demands taking responsibility for one's own actions, and taking responsibility means that a person takes a level of control in his life. It also involves understanding that one's actions have consequences. A school bully who picks on his classmates puts himself in a position where his victims will eventually defend themselves and turn the bully into a laughingstock. A student caught cheating on a test is likely to be punished. Someone who cheats on his spouse risks ending his marriage. An athlete who acts irresponsibly with women could wind up in court and lose a college scholarship, or millions in endorsements as a professional. Or he might suffer the worst indignity of all and become the subject of a Lifetime Channel movie.

The mentally tough establish their priorities, in life, sports, and business. They also weigh immediate gratification against long-term satisfaction. If family is a high priority, is it really worth the risk of engaging in an extramarital affair that could ruin that family? If a sterling public image is a priority, is it worth taking the risk of being caught carrying pot through the airport? If staying out of jail is a priority, engaging in illegal activities is foolhardy. Character and values involve thinking before acting—weighing gain against risk—rather than doing something stupid and trying to pass it off as a spur-of-the-moment decision. The mentally tough minimize their mistakes by understanding that actions have consequences, and by deciding whether the consequence is worth the risk.

Confidence, real confidence, is what makes great deeds possible. A person must truly believe in his ability to achieve in order to take on great challenges. It takes confidence to leave a comfortable job and start a business, or to write a book and subject your work to public criticism. Edison needed confidence to change the world with his inventions; Jefferson needed confidence to change the world with his ideas. It is a tough and often cruel world, and confidence makes it possible to survive the many pitfalls that enter every life. Confidence is also elusive. Many people try to substitute bravado for confidence, or cloak their insecurities in cockiness. Confidence in the real world is built on those same concepts of destination goals and journey goals—succeeding in the individual journey goals builds the confidence that make the destination goals appear possible. Learning to inspire personal confidence builds success. A student who approaches a test gains confidence from preparing well, and from self-talk and self-inspiration. Studying begins the process, then a Ted Williams–like chant—"I can master this. I will ace this exam"—will often carry over into the study hall. Overconfidence and false confidence become burdens in the outside world, as they do on the playing field. Believing there is no need to study before a test can damage even the best student. Believing it will be a cinch to fake it through a business report can derail a career. No matter what a person's level of confidence may be, he can find a way to build upon it and channel it to his advantage. Confidence, when it is well placed and properly directed, becomes one of life's greatest assets.

Careers, friendships, and relationships can be shattered by runaway emotion. The concept of *cool* is an asset in every arena, whether it is home, school, office, or on some distant battlefield. Everyone will face the need for clutch performances at some points in their lives, and the techniques that help players become clutch on the diamond also help in every facet of life. Simple as it sounds, learning to control emotions through breathing is a trick that can make the difference between failing a tough test or getting an A, stumbling through a sales call or delivering impact in a presentation. Anger is an emotion that happens. The key is to learn to control anger and use it to advantage rather than becoming a victim of one's own rage. Cool in the clutch becomes a way of life when a person has the confidence to believe he can succeed.

Focus and concentration seem almost a lost art in our modern world of massive distractions. So many people find themselves at loose ends because of an inability to concentrate on their tasks, or to think out the problems in their personal lives. The same concepts that made Dave Stewart and Ted Williams masters of focus will work equally well in the classroom or in writing reports and legal briefs. Learning to focus on a task can make the difference between being effective in business or being just another workplace drone.

In every career, in every life, there is a need to make *adjustments*. Many people have a panacea concept of existence—that if only one goal can be achieved, or some material object acquired, ultimate happiness will result. Children often think in terms of the "if onlys"—if only they had a certain doll or midget race car or tennis shoe, it would bring them happiness. But then they see something newer and cooler on TV a week later. Experience teaches that the "if onlys" are unrealistic, and that life is a constant series of adjustments as situations change around us. The flexibility to deal with an ever-changing world brings greater satisfaction in the long run. Understanding that failure is an education rather than an end in itself creates a confidence that the experience will help us get it right the next time. Everyone makes mistakes. Some learn from their mistakes, some blame others or pretend the mistakes never occurred. The learners are more likely to get it right the next time.

The qualities of mental toughness that a player carries with him off the field can serve to enrich his life in so many different ways. The drive to achieve enables him to take satisfaction and pleasure in the achievements. He knows there is always room to improve while he enjoys the success already attained.

DEALING WITH SELF-DECEPTION

Oakland outfielder Terrence Long saw his playing time diminish during the 2003 season, and he struck out at manager Ken Macha for leaving him out of the lineup. "For some reason, [Macha] doesn't think I'm good enough to play here. I'm pretty sure some team out there thinks I am. I think it's personal, but I don't know what it is."

Long hit .245 with 14 homers and a .293 on-base percentage for the 2003 season, not the type of performance that is likely to earn playing time for a corner outfielder. Just about every observer in baseball knew why Long was not playing, but Long did not understand. General Manager Billy Beane made the situation clear: "Obviously, Terrence is personally frustrated with a disappointing season," Beane said. "Terrence is accountable for his own performance. Maybe what's needed here is a mirror. I think his comments are way off base."

In the spring of 1991, rumors began circulating in the A's camp when Jose Canseco reported bigger and bulkier than in past seasons. The whispers were that he was using steroids to build huge chest and arm muscles. Karl Kuehl, then a special adviser to the A's, noticed the former MVP's swing was tighter and not as free as it had been in the past.

"Do you feel like your swing is as good as it was in Huntsville?" Kuehl said, referring to Canseco's minor league days when he was blasting the ball.

"No, not really," the slugger answered.

"What's the difference?"

With a knowing grin, Canseco ran his finger across his chest as he replied, "Because of my size across here."

Kuehl avoided the steroid issue and dealt only with the bulking up. "Then why do you do it?"

"It gives me confidence," Canseco replied.

A decade later, Canseco acknowledged that he had used steroids. During that period he had gone from one of the best all-around players in the game to a one-dimensional power hitter whose off-field antics had greatly diminished his reputation and probably cost him a plaque in the Hall of Fame.

Baseball players are always teetering on a fine line between confidence and self-deception. They must believe in themselves even when others do not. Yet it becomes very easy to elevate confidence into self-deception. The cases of Long and Canseco illustrate the ludicrous ends of self-deception. Even the most casual observer could see that Long's lack of production cost him his starting job, but Long assumed there must be some personal animosity involved. In baseball it should be easier to see this self-deception than it is in life. Baseball has lines of statistics and results to demonstrate achievement and flops; the real world can be harder to evaluate.

In life, as on the field, it is vital to be able to take a critical eye to one's performance without losing confidence. That line between effective self-evaluation and hyper-perfectionism will lead to greater achievement. If a person learns to analyze his own performance critically and honestly, he can build upon his performance and improve. The key is to learn to take satisfaction in achievement and build on that achievement to still greater ends. It is not easy to be honest in self-evaluation, but it is a valuable ability. Self-justification is a roadblock to self-evaluation. So many people are so busy covering their rear ends that they are unable to properly evaluate their actions. Justifying oneself may be necessary at times to survive in business, but it can only get in the way of proper self-evaluation that leads to personal improvement.

Just as Terrence Long deceived himself to believe he was succeeding with a .245 average, and as Jose Canseco deceived himself into believing that his steroid-enhanced body made him a better player, professionals in all areas deceive themselves. Lawyers may deceive themselves into thinking they can get away with less than full preparation for their cases; students may deceive themselves into believing they can wing a test. Mental toughness is about building confidence while retaining effective self-evaluation.

THE CONCEPT OF SELFLESSNESS

The New York media could scarcely believe it. At the age of thirty-five, Scott Brosius was telling them he planned to scrap his major league career, return to rural Oregon, and concentrate on raising his three children. It made no sense to many people—giving up the spotlight of New York baseball and stardom just to hang out with his kids.

Scott Brosius walked away from his major
league career to return to his family.

"Every situation is different, for every family it's different,"
Brosius said during the summer of 2004, as he reflected on his
decision after the 2001 season. "For me, what it boiled down to
was that my wife [Jennifer] and I had made a commitment when
we first started having kids that when our kids were junior high
age, we would be settled into a home base. We felt it was unfair
to pull the kids out of their activities.

"After 2001, it came down to three choices: 1) Move the
family to whatever city I'd be playing in. I was a free agent, so I
didn't know if I'd be going back to New York. 2) Leave Jennifer
and the kids home in Oregon, then have them come out during
the summer. Or 3) have me stay at home.

"Option three was our best option. I knew our family. If I
continued to play and spend time away, it would hurt our family. I just chose the family first."

Brosius put the welfare of his family ahead of his own personal desires. His decisions were based not on what he wanted but on what he believed to be best for his family. "We home-schooled for part of the year," Brosius said. "Our kids would stay in school until April, then Jennifer and I would home-school. We got to the point where the oldest [Allison] was getting tough to home-school; she was advancing faster than the teacher. There's only so much algebra I can teach."

Brosius prematurely ended a solid career. He was part of three World Series championships with the Yankees and was named MVP of the 1998 Series. The decision he made would not be right for every person or every family. In contrast, relief pitcher Chris Hammond returned to baseball *because* of his family. A combination of injuries seemed to end his career after the 1998 season, at the age of thirty-two. He sat out 1999 and 2000, then his wife, Lynne, had a suggestion. "My wife was disappointed that my kids didn't have a chance to see me on the field," Hammond said. "So we went down to spring training and figured that even if things didn't work out, my kids would have a chance to see me there on the field."

Everything did work out, though, and Hammond returned to pitch 2001 in the minors before putting together a dream season with the Braves in 2002—a 7-2 record and a 0.95 ERA. He continued his career from there, with his three young children watching him play. "I want to keep playing until the kids are in school and need to be settled down," he said during the 2004 season.

Mental toughness in life demands facing difficult decisions and being able to analyze what is best in the larger picture rather than just looking to fulfill individual desires. With responsibility comes a need at times for an individual to make his own desires secondary to the needs of others. In the case of Brosius, it was to family. At other times it may be to a team or a job. When someone takes on the responsibility of parenthood, he accepts that his children's welfare will become a priority. Or assisting an ailing or aging parent may become a priority, taking precedence over recreation time or even career moves. Many of those who entered the military to defend the United States from terrorism placed the welfare of their country ahead of their personal needs. Pat Tillman, an NFL player, selflessly gave up his career to serve in the military and paid the ultimate price for his service.

The concept of selflessness has grown rare in a society that has passed through what was called the "Me Generation," when it became a societal norm for individuals to place their personal needs ahead of those around them. Those who choose to be mentally tough in life will recognize the need to balance what is best for the individual with what is best for the greater good of those around him.

Three years after his retirement from professional baseball, Brosius said he was completely satisfied with his decision. He now spends his time coaching college and youth league baseball in McMinnville, Oregon, and loves being with his children. He says that whenever he questions his choice, he does not look back on the highlights or the excitement of his career. Quite the opposite: "I remember sitting alone in my hotel room in Toronto, wondering what my wife and kids were doing and wishing I was with them," Brosius says.

Life entails tough decisions, and the mentally tough learn how to make those decisions for the benefit of all around them.

TOUGHNESS AND LIFE

Most players will eventually be forced to put down their gloves and pick up a briefcase, a hammer, or a stethoscope. The lessons a player takes from the field will stay with him for the rest of his life, even if he never again turns a double play or throws a curveball.

Baseball is a mass of contradictions waiting to be resolved— play with intensity but stay loose; take the game seriously but have fun; follow your coaches' advice but make your own decisions. Life is that way too, and navigating through those contradictions is one of the most difficult aspects of the road to achievement.

The mentally tough learn to take satisfaction and pleasure from their accomplishments while still striving for higher goals. They learn that attitudes carry over into every aspect of life. Abraham Lincoln said, "People are just about as happy as they make up their minds to be." Lincoln's message is that happiness itself is really an attitude.

It is the ultimate challenge to take control of your destiny and ride your abilities to their fullest potential. The skills of mental toughness are the elements that lead to lives of greater achievement and satisfaction, both on and off the playing field. These are the skills that will teach you how to make your own luck, and how to make the most of the life you have. Mental toughness is a champion's state of mind.

Afterword

The champagne hardly had time to dry in the streets of Boston when scandal broke out after the 2004 season. The Red Sox won the World Series for the first time since 1918, an accomplishment that electrified baseball. But within a month, the issue of steroids took over the headlines. The *San Francisco Chronicle* published a leaked grand jury report indicating that New York Yankees slugger Jason Giambi had admitted to taking steroids, and that San Francisco Giants outfielder Barry Bonds had used an illegal steroid, though he claimed he did not know it was a steroid when he took it.

In the aftermath of these revelations, major league baseball finally moved toward instituting more severe penalties for steroid use by its players. In the early years of the new millennium, the minor leagues had gradually been increasing testing and penalties for steroid use, and more and more players were being found to use the drugs, and quietly counseled or punished.

Steroid use is a blot against baseball that must and will be controlled and abolished. Not only does it damage the level of competition in the major leagues, it also has a trickle-down effect. When major leaguers use steroids, college and high school players believe they too must use them in order to compete.

"This is crazy," said Karl Kuehl, co-author of this book and a former minor league director for two major league organizations.

"Young players should not make themselves a guinea pig for mad scientists. That's just stupid. Kids are putting things into their body that could lead to long-term damage and destroy their lives. It's a big mistake."

Much of this book has been about how players can make personal sacrifices to become better at their sport, or whatever their life's passion may be. It would be easy for some players to assume that "paying the extra price" means taking the risk of using steroids or other dangerous compounds. It does not.

The risks include medical problems, public humiliation, and suspension from baseball. With more intense testing programs, players are far more likely to be caught in the minor leagues and weeded out. This makes steroids a big risk with little chance of reward for the prep and college players who expect steroids to be their shortcut to success.

Teams will be far less likely to take a chance on a player who they fear may face suspension every time the cups are handed out, and that player's marketability will diminish. In addition, he will face chants and derision every time he steps into an opposing ballpark.

The short-term results of steroids will not help achieve long-term destination goals. In fact, steroids will become counterproductive as baseball works to eliminate drug-enhanced players from the game. Mental toughness is a discipline: the strong learn to refuse temptation while those around them are submitting. There are no easy substitutes for the dedication that leads to success, and consequences of steroid use are too dangerous. Mentally tough players will recognize that such a risky practice, with little chance of long-term reward, is simply foolish. Rather than buying into some dangerous magic potion, the champion's path to success is through the process and routines of mental toughness.

Suggested Reading

Gary Carter with Ken Abraham. *The Gamer.* Dallas: Word Publishing, 1993.

Elwood Chapman. *Life Is an Attitude.* Menlo Park, Calif.: Crisp Publications, 1992.

Bob Costas. *Fair Ball.* New York: Broadway Books, 2000.

Stephen Crane. *The Red Badge of Courage.* New York: Appleton, 1895.

H. A. Dorfman. *The Mental ABC's of Pitching.* South Bend, Ind.: Diamond Communications, 2000.

H. A. Dorfman. *The Mental Keys of Hitting.* South Bend, Ind.: Diamond Communications, 2001.

H. A. Dorfman and Karl Kuehl. *The Mental Game of Baseball.* South Bend, Ind.: Diamond Communications, 1989.

Howard Ferguson. *The Edge.* Cleveland: Howard E. Ferguson, 1983.

Daniel Goleman. *Emotional Intelligence.* New York: Bantam Books, 1995.

Keith Harrell. *Attitude Is Everything.* New York: Cliff Street Books–HarperCollins, 1999.

Orel Hershiser with Robert Wogemuth. *Between the Lines: Nine Principles to Live By.* New York: Warner Books, 1989.

Orel Hershiser with Jerry Jenkins. *Out of the Blue.* Brentwood, Tenn.: Holgemuth & Hyatt, 1989.

Whitey Herzog and Kevin Horrigan. *White Rat: A Life in Baseball.* New York: Harper & Row, 1986.

Derek Jeter. *The Life You Imagined.* New York: Random House, 2000.

James E. Loehr. *The Mental Toughness Training for Sports.* New York: Stephen Green Press, 1986.

Vince Lombardi Jr. *What It Takes to Be #1*. New York: McGraw-Hill, 2001.

Gary Mack with David Casstevens. *Mind Gym*. Chicago: Contemporary Books, 2001.

David Maraniss. *When Pride Still Mattered*. New York: Touchstone Books, 2000.

Norman Vincent Peale. *The Power of Positive Thinking*. New York: Simon & Schuster, 1952.

Danny Peary. *We Played the Game: Memories of Baseball's Greatest Era*. New York: Black Dog and Leventhal, 2002.

Arnold Rampersad and Rachel Robinson. *Jackie Robinson: A Biography*. New York: Ballantine Books, 1997.

Jackie Robinson and Alfred Duckett. *I Never Had It Made*. New York: G. P. Putnam's Sons, 1972.

Mike Schmidt with Barbara Walder. *Always on the Offense*. New York: Atheneum, 1982.

Joe Torre. *Ground Rules for Winners*. New York: Hyperion, 1999.

Jules Tygiel. *Baseball's Great Experiment: Jackie Robinson and His Legacy*. New York: Oxford University Press, 1983.

John Wooden with Steve Jamison. *Wooden: A Lifetime of Observations and Reflections On and Off the Court*. Chicago: Contemporary Books, 1997.

Index

Abbott, Jim, 207

ABC's of Pitching, The, (Dorfman), 97

Adjustments: for attitudes, 197–201, 212; how they begin, 198, 212; breathing, 214, 220; coaches' job, 202; commitment, 213, 232; concentration, 214, 220; determination, 213–214; discomfort, 237; effort level, 214; emotions, 214; how excuses hurt, 204; unmet expectations, 239–242; during game, 186, 213, 228–232; goals, 212, 219; hitters, 215–219, 222–223; too many ideas, 202–203; perception of job, 212–213; shouldn't be made, 208–210; significant mechanical, 231–233; mental, 211–221; overcoming obstacles, 206–207; pitchers, 219–220, 223–224; plan, 186, 213; working from the positive, 234–236; in practice, 210; preparation, 215; priorities, 213; understanding the process, 227–234; quick-check, 228–231; relaxation level, 214; resistance, 236–239; responses to success and failure, 214; routines, 215; self-coaching, 215; self-evaluations, 215, 230, 241; strategy, 213; structural, 224–227; tension level, 212, 214; visualizations, 216–218, 220. *See also* Hitters; Pitchers; Process.

Affirmations, 16

Anderson, Garret, 247–248

Andujar, Joaquin, 148

Antonen, Mel, 96

Approach: baserunners, 32–34; defense, 35–36; definition, 26; dictate who we are, 13–14; hitters, 26–32; pitchers, 37–40; receiving signs, 34–35; success can change, 207–209

Associated Press, 115

Attitudes: that help adjusting, 197–201; what they affect, 20–21; affirmations, 16; approach, 26–40; awareness, 19; built on, 259–260; combination, 21, 29, 39; commit to, 16; competitor, 23; conflicting, 40–50, 216–217; attitude of the day, 25–26; definition for baseball, 13–14; developing, 19–20, 50–53, 74; emotional, 41–42; experiment

A NOTE ON THE AUTHORS

KARL KUEHL is special adviser for baseball operations for the Cleveland Indians. Formerly manager of the Montreal Expos, he has also been a minor league manager; a coach for the Minnesota Twins; a scout for Houston, Seattle, and Milwaukee; and director of player development for the Oakland A's and the Toronto Blue Jays. He has also written *The Mental Game of Baseball* with Harvey Dorfman.

JOHN KUEHL played in the minor league organizations of the Oakland A's and the San Diego Padres, and was named to three all-star teams before injuries abbreviated his baseball career. He has been a regional scout for the A's and has managed in the minor leagues for their organization.

CASEY TEFERTILLER wrote on baseball for the *San Francisco Examiner* and is now a staff correspondent for *Baseball America*. His earlier book, *Wyatt Earp: The Life Behind the Legend*, was a New York Times Notable Book of 1997.